NHibernate 4.x Cookbook

Second Edition

Over 90 incredible and powerful recipes to help you efficiently use NHibernate in your application

Gunnar Liljas

Alexander Zaytsev

Jason Dentler

BIRMINGHAM - MUMBAI

NHibernate 4.x Cookbook
Second Edition

First published: October 2010

Second edition: January 2017

Production reference: 1200117

Published by Packt Publishing Ltd.
Livery Place
35 Livery Street
Birmingham B3 2PB, UK.

ISBN 978-1-78439-642-8

www.packtpub.com

Credits

Authors

Gunnar Liljas

Alexander Zaytsev

Jason Dentler

Reviewer

Amro El-Fakharany

Commissioning Editor

Dipika Gaonkar

Acquisition Editor

Prachi Bisht

Content Development Editor

Trusha Shriyan

Technical Editor

Varsha Shivhare

Copy Editor

Sneha Singh

Project Coordinator

Kinjal Bari

Proofreader

Safis Editing

Indexer

Rekha Nair

Graphics

Kirk D'Penha

Production Coordinator

Arvindkumar Gupta

Cover Work

Arvindkumar Gupta

About the Authors

Gunnar Liljas is a software architect with more than 20 years' experience in developing and designing web-based solutions. His focus has been on data-driven content publishing, not only for the Web, but also for automated and on-demand print publishing. Currently, he spends most of his waking hours at the Swedish CRM supplier Revide, where he uses tools such as NHibernate and Redis to create targeted emails, text messages, and campaign web sites based on massive data sources.

He's also one of the lead contributors to the NHibernate open source project.

In his spare time, Gunnar sings in two classical choirs and often performs with the renowned Norrköping Symphony Orchestra.

Alexander Zaytsev discovered his passion for IT when he was a small kid, and since then he has dedicated his life to becoming an excellent software developer. Alexander has many years' experience in the IT field, analyzing, designing, and developing .NET-based enterprise applications, using cutting-edge technologies. He works as an independent consultant in the .NET space, providing technical expertise to all kinds of software development companies. He is an active member of open source and local development communities, and writes a blog at `http://alexzaytsev.me`. He is one of the main contributors to the NHibernate project, and one of the few people who really know the NHibernate internals.

He is adept in Agile software development, and he believes that Agile practices such as test-driven development, pair programming, automated testing, continuous integration, and deployment are the keys to quality software.

He lives in Auckland with his wife, Olga, and son, Stepan. In his spare time, he loves spending time with his family, cycling, and doing coding just for fun.

Jason Dentler grew up in the small Texas town of Mission Valley. He started tinkering with computers as a kid in the late 1980s, and all these years later, he hasn't stopped. He's worked in a few different industries. Currently, he builds really awesome software in higher education. He's an Eagle Scout and a graduate of the University of Houston – Victoria.

I'd like to thank my family and friends for all their support, and especially my parents, who encouraged and tolerated my computer obsession all those years. Thanks, Mom & Dad. I love you.

About the Reviewer

Amro El-Fakharany has more than 15 years' experience as a software developer. Coming from an electrical engineering background, he has a passion for solving industrial problems, and maintaining and extending those solutions. In 2002, he established an engineering consultancy helping and providing solutions in the bulk-material-handling sector. He has been working with NHibernate since its early days and is also a contributor to the project.

www.PacktPub.com

eBooks, discount offers, and more

Did you know that Packt offers eBook versions of every book published, with PDF and ePub files available? You can upgrade to the eBook version at www.PacktPub.com and as a print book customer, you are entitled to a discount on the eBook copy. Get in touch with us at customercare@packtpub.com for more details.

At www.PacktPub.com, you can also read a collection of free technical articles, sign up for a range of free newsletters and receive exclusive discounts and offers on Packt books and eBooks.

https://www.packtpub.com/mapt

Get the most in-demand software skills with Mapt. Mapt gives you full access to all Packt books and video courses, as well as industry-leading tools to help you plan your personal development and advance your career.

Why Subscribe?

- ▸ Fully searchable across every book published by Packt
- ▸ Copy and paste, print, and bookmark content
- ▸ On demand and accessible via a web browser

Customer Feedback

Thank you for purchasing this Packt book. We take our commitment to improving our content and products to meet your needs seriously—that's why your feedback is so valuable. Whatever your feelings about your purchase, please consider leaving a review on this book's Amazon page. Not only will this help us, more importantly it will also help others in the community to make an informed decision about the resources that they invest in to learn.

You can also review for us on a regular basis by joining our reviewers' club. If you're interested in joining, or would like to learn more about the benefits we offer, please contact us: customerreviews@packtpub.com.

Table of Contents

Preface   **v**

Chapter 1: The Configuration and Schema   **1**

Introduction   1

Installing NHibernate   2

Configuring NHibernate with hibernate.cfg.xml   4

Configuring NHibernate with App.config or Web.config   10

Configuring NHibernate with code   12

Configuring NHibernate with Fluent NHibernate   14

Configuring NHibernate logging   15

Generating the database   19

Scripting the database   21

Updating the database   22

Using NHibernate schema tool   24

Chapter 2: Models and Mappings   **27**

Mapping a class with XML   28

Creating class hierarchy mappings   36

Creating class components   43

Mapping a one-to-many relationship   46

Mapping a many-to-many relationship   56

Mapping collections of elements and components   59

Setting up a base entity class   63

Handling versioning and concurrency   66

Mapping by code   70

Mapping by convention   76

Creating mappings fluently   82

Bidirectional one-to-many class relationships   86

Mapping enumerations   92

Immutable entities   95

Mapping relations to non-primary keys	98
Using lazy properties	102
Mapping joins	104
Using calculated properties	107
Using serializable values	110
Dynamic components	114
Mapping <subselect>	119
Chapter 3: Sessions and Transactions	**123**
Introduction	123
Setting up session-per-web request	124
Setting up session-per-presenter	127
Creating a session ASP.NET MVC action filter	135
Creating a transaction ASP.NET MVC action filter	140
Save entities to the database	143
Using session.Merge	149
Using session.Refresh	152
Handle concurrency using session.Lock	155
Using dictionaries as entities	160
Using NHibernate with transaction scope	164
Chapter 4: Queries	**173**
Introduction	174
Query entities by ID	175
Using LINQ to NHibernate	177
Using CriteriaQueries	184
Using QueryOver	189
Using QueryOver projections and aggregates	193
Using the Hibernate Query Language	197
Using native SQL	204
Eager loading with LINQ	207
Eager loading with Criteria	211
Eager loading with QueryOver	212
Eager loading with HQL	214
Eager loading with SQL	216
Using named queries	218
Using detached queries	221
Using HQL for bulk data changes	223
Filtering collections	226
Using result transformers	229
Extra lazy collections	233

Chapter 5: Improving Performance — 237

Reducing application startup time — 237
Using MultiCriteria — 241
Using MultiQuery — 244
Using Futures — 248
Eager loading child collections — 251
Using stateless sessions — 259
Using read-only entities — 262
Use the second-level cache — 265
Configuring the second-level cache with code — 271
Sharding databases for performance — 275

Chapter 6: Testing — 283

Introduction — 283
Using NHibernate Profiler — 283
Profiling NHibernate with Glimpse — 290
Fast testing with the SQLite in-memory database — 292
Preloading data with SQLite — 300
Using Fluent NHibernate persistence testing — 304
Using the Ghostbusters test — 306

Chapter 7: Data Access Layer — 313

Introduction — 313
Transaction auto-wrapping for the data access layer — 314
Setting up an NHibernate repository — 316
Using named queries in the data access layer — 320
Using ICriteria in the data access layer — 328
Using paged queries in the data access layer — 332
Using LINQ specifications in the data access layer — 336

Chapter 8: Extending NHibernate — 339

Introduction — 339
Creating an encrypted string type — 340
Creating a money type — 348
Using well-known instance types — 353
Using dependency injection with entities — 358
Creating an audit-event listener — 363
Creation and change stamping of entities — 367
Generating trigger-based auditing — 372
Implementing a soft-delete pattern — 375
Setting Microsoft SQL's Context_Info — 378
Using dynamic connection strings — 385
Using custom dialect functions — 387

Using custom functions in LINQ   388

Extending the LINQ provider   390

Chapter 9: NHibernate Contribution Projects   **393**

Introduction   393

Property validation with attributes   393

Creating validator classes   399

Setting up full-text searches   403

Auditing data with Envers   410

Using NHibernate Spatial   414

Index   **423**

Preface

This book explains many features of NHibernate 4 in detail through example recipes that you can quickly apply to your applications. These recipes will take you from the absolute basics of NHibernate through its most advanced features and beyond, showing you how to take full advantage of each concept to quickly create amazing database applications.

What this book covers

Chapter 1, The Configuration and Schema, explains various methods for configuring NHibernate and generating your database.

Chapter 2, Models and Mappings, introduces mappings in both XML and code, and includes more advanced topics such as versioning and concurrency.

Chapter 3, Sessions and Transactions, covers several techniques for proper session and transaction management in your application, including distributed transactions.

Chapter 4, Queries, demonstrates a number of rich query APIs, including the LINQ provider and the QueryOver API.

Chapter 5, Improving Performance, lets you know how to reduce application startup time by using serialized configuration. We also dig deep into how caching and advanced querying techniques can improve the performance of your application.

Chapter 6, Testing, introduces some techniques you can apply to quickly test your NHibernate applications and includes an introduction to NHibernate Profiler.

Chapter 7, Data Access Layer, shows how to build a flexible, extensible data access layer based on NHibernate and its many query APIs.

Chapter 8, Extending NHibernate, shows a number of ways to customize and extend NHibernate to provide additional services such as audit logging and data encryption.

Chapter 9, NHibernate Contribution Projects, introduces several NHibernate Contribution projects, adding features such as caching, data validation, full text search, geospatial data, and horizontal partitioning of databases.

What you need for this book

To complete the recipes in this book, you'll need the following tools:

- Windows 7 or later versions
- Visual Studio 2015 or later versions
- Microsoft SQL Server 2008 Express edition or later versions

Who this book is for

This book is written for .NET developers who want to use NHibernate and those who want to deepen their knowledge of the platform. Examples are written in C# and XML. Some basic knowledge of SQL is assumed. If you build .NET applications that use relational databases, this book is for you.

Sections

In this book, you will find several headings that appear frequently (Getting ready, How to do it, How it work, There's more, and See also).

To give clear instructions on how to complete a recipe, we use these sections as follows:

Getting ready

This section tells you what to expect in the recipe, and describes how to set up any software or any preliminary settings required for the recipe.

How to do it...

This section contains the steps required to follow the recipe.

How it works...

This section usually consists of a detailed explanation of what happened in the previous section.

There's more...

This section consists of additional information about the recipe in order to make the reader more knowledgeable about the recipe.

See also

This section provides helpful links to other useful information for the recipe.

Conventions

In this book, you will find a number of text styles that distinguish between different kinds of information. Here are some examples of these styles and an explanation of their meaning.

Code words in text, database table names, folder names, filenames, file extensions, pathnames, dummy URLs, user input, and Twitter handles are shown as follows: "Add a new folder named `NamedQueries` to the project."

A block of code is set as follows:

```
var sessionFactory = ProductModel
  .CreateExampleSessionFactory(true);
var kernel = new StandardKernel();
kernel.Load(new NinjectBindings());
kernel.Bind<ISessionFactory>()
```

When we wish to draw your attention to a particular part of a code block, the relevant lines or items are set in bold:

```
public class BooksController : Controller
{
  [NHibernateSession]
  public ActionResult Index()
  {
    var books = DataAccessLayer.GetBooks()
```

Any command-line input or output is written as follows:

```
Install-Package NHibernate -project SessionRecipes
```

New terms and **important words** are shown in bold. Words that you see on the screen, for example, in menus or dialog boxes, appear in the text like this: "Don't forget to set the **Build action** to **Embedded Resource**."

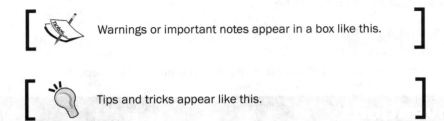

Warnings or important notes appear in a box like this.

Tips and tricks appear like this.

Reader feedback

Feedback from our readers is always welcome. Let us know what you think about this book—what you liked or disliked. Reader feedback is important for us as it helps us develop titles that you will really get the most out of.

To send us general feedback, simply e-mail feedback@packtpub.com, and mention the book's title in the subject of your message.

If there is a topic that you have expertise in and you are interested in either writing or contributing to a book, see our author guide at www.packtpub.com/authors.

Customer support

Now that you are the proud owner of a Packt book, we have a number of things to help you to get the most from your purchase.

Downloading the example code

You can download the example code files for this book from your account at http://www.packtpub.com. If you purchased this book elsewhere, you can visit http://www.packtpub.com/support and register to have the files e-mailed directly to you.

You can download the code files by following these steps:

1. Log in or register to our website using your e-mail address and password.
2. Hover the mouse pointer on the **SUPPORT** tab at the top.
3. Click on **Code Downloads & Errata**.
4. Enter the name of the book in the **Search** box.

5. Select the book for which you're looking to download the code files.

6. Choose from the drop-down menu where you purchased this book from.

7. Click on **Code Download**.

Once the file is downloaded, please make sure that you unzip or extract the folder using the latest version of:

- ▸ WinRAR / 7-Zip for Windows
- ▸ Zipeg / iZip / UnRarX for Mac
- ▸ 7-Zip / PeaZip for Linux

Downloading the color images of this book

We also provide you with a PDF file that has color images of the screenshots/diagrams used in this book. The color images will help you better understand the changes in the output. You can download this file from `https://www.packtpub.com/sites/default/files/downloads/NHibernate4_0Cookbook_ColorImages.pdf`.

Errata

Although we have taken every care to ensure the accuracy of our content, mistakes do happen. If you find a mistake in one of our books—maybe a mistake in the text or the code—we would be grateful if you could report this to us. By doing so, you can save other readers from frustration and help us improve subsequent versions of this book. If you find any errata, please report them by visiting `http://www.packtpub.com/submit-errata`, selecting your book, clicking on the **Errata Submission Form** link, and entering the details of your errata. Once your errata are verified, your submission will be accepted and the errata will be uploaded to our website or added to any list of existing errata under the Errata section of that title.

To view the previously submitted errata, go to `https://www.packtpub.com/books/content/support` and enter the name of the book in the search field. The required information will appear under the **Errata** section.

Piracy

Piracy of copyrighted material on the Internet is an ongoing problem across all media. At Packt, we take the protection of our copyright and licenses very seriously. If you come across any illegal copies of our works in any form on the Internet, please provide us with the location address or website name immediately so that we can pursue a remedy.

Please contact us at copyright@packtpub.com with a link to the suspected pirated material.

We appreciate your help in protecting our authors and our ability to bring you valuable content.

Questions

If you have a problem with any aspect of this book, you can contact us at questions@packtpub.com, and we will do our best to address the problem.

1
The Configuration and Schema

In this chapter, we will cover the following recipes:

- ▶ Installing NHibernate
- ▶ Configuring NHibernate with hibernate.cfg.xml
- ▶ Configuring NHibernate with App.config or Web.config
- ▶ Configuring NHibernate with code
- ▶ Configuring NHibernate with Fluent NHibernate
- ▶ Configuring NHibernate logging
- ▶ Generating the database
- ▶ Scripting the database
- ▶ Updating the database
- ▶ Using NHibernate schema tool

Introduction

NHibernate is a popular, mature, open source **Object-Relational Mapper** (**ORM**) based on Java's Hibernate project. ORMs, such as LINQ to SQL, Entity Framework, and NHibernate, translate between the database's relational model of tables, columns, and keys to the application's object model of classes and properties.

The NHibernate homepage, `http://nhibernate.info`, contains blog posts, the complete reference documentation, and a bug tracker. Support is available through the very active `nhusers` Google group at `http://groups.google.com/group/nhusers`. The NHibernate source code is hosted on GitHub at `http://github.com/nhibernate/nhibernate-core`. Precompiled binaries of NHibernate releases are also available on SourceForge and through NuGet at `http://nuget.org/packages/NHibernate`.

NHibernate provides an incredible number of configuration options and settings. The recipes in this chapter demonstrate several methods for configuring NHibernate and generating the necessary database schema.

Installing NHibernate

Before we begin, let's get our Visual Studio solution and database set up. The following information will get you up and started with NHibernate.

Getting ready

1. Install Microsoft SQL Server 2012 Express (or a newer version) on your PC, using the default settings.

2. Create a blank database named `NHCookbook`.

How to do it...

1. In Visual Studio, create a new C# class library project named `Eg.Core` with a directory for the solution named `Cookbook`.

2. Delete the `Class1.cs` file.

3. In the **Solution Explorer**, right click the **References** node in the `Eg.Core` project and select **Manage NuGet Packages**. In the top navigation of the now-opened NuGet Package Manager, make sure **Browse** is selected. Enter the word `NHibernate` in the search box and wait for the results to show up:

4. Select the **NHibernate** package in the search results and click **Install**. This will install NHibernate and all required dependencies.

5. Add a new class named `TestClass`, to the `Eg.Core` project:

```
public class TestClass
{
  public virtual int Id { get; set; }
  public virtual string Name { get; set; }
}
```

There's more...

Instead of using the graphical package manager, you can use the **Package Manager Console**. It provides a faster way to install or update NuGet packages. To open the **Package Manager Console** simply click **Tools** | **NuGet Package Manager** | **Package Manager Console**. In the opened window you can simply write the following:

```
Install-Package NHibernate -Project Eg.Core
```

This will produce the same effect as the main recipe.

Configuring NHibernate with hibernate.cfg. xml

NHibernate offers several methods for configuration and a number of configuration settings.

In this recipe, we will show you how to configure NHibernate using the `hibernate.cfg.xml` configuration file, with a minimal number of settings to get your application up and running quickly. The recipe also forms the base for several other recipes in this chapter.

Getting ready

1. Complete the steps from the *Installing NHibernate* recipe in this chapter.
2. Add a console application project to your solution called `ConfigByXml`.
3. Set it as the **Startup** project for your solution.
4. Install NHibernate to `ConfigByXml` project using the NuGet Package Manager Console.
5. In `ConfigByXml`, add a reference to the `Eg.Core` project.

How to do it...

1. Add an XML file named `hibernate.cfg.xml` with the following contents:

```xml
<?xml version="1.0" encoding="utf-8"?>
<hibernate-configuration xmlns="urn:nhibernate-configuration-2.2">
  <session-factory>
    <property name="dialect">
      NHibernate.Dialect.MsSql2012Dialect, NHibernate
    </property>
    <property name="connection.connection_string">
      Server=.\SQLEXPRESS; Database=NHCookbook;
      Trusted_Connection=SSPI
    </property>
    <property name="adonet.batch_size">
      100
    </property>
  </session-factory>
</hibernate-configuration>
```

2. On the **Solution Explorer** tab, right-click on `hibernate.cfg.xml` and select **Properties**.
3. Change **Copy to Output Directory** property from **Do not copy** to **Copy if newer**.

4. Open `Program.cs` and add `using NHibernate.Cfg;` to the beginning of the file

5. Add the following code to the `Main` method:

```
var nhConfig = new Configuration().Configure();
var sessionFactory = nhConfig.BuildSessionFactory();
Console.WriteLine("NHibernate Configured!");
Console.ReadKey();
```

6. Build and run your application. You will see the text **NHibernate Configured!**

How it works...

The connection string we've defined points to the NHCookbook database running under the local Microsoft SQL Server.

Next, we define a few properties that tell NHibernate how to behave.

The `dialect` property specifies a `dialect` class that NHibernate uses to build SQL syntax specific to a **Relational Database Management System** (**RDBMS**). We're using the Microsoft SQL 2012 dialect. Additionally, most dialects set intelligent defaults for other NHibernate properties, such as `connection.driver_class`.

The `connection.connection_string_name` property references our connection string by name.

By default, NHibernate will send a single SQL statement and wait for a response from the database. When we set the `adonet.batch_size` property to 100, NHibernate will group up to 100 SQL INSERT, UPDATE, and DELETE statements in a single ADO.NET command and send the whole batch at once. In effect, the work of 100 round trips to the database is combined in one. Because a roundtrip to the database is, at best, an out-of-process call, and at worst, a trip through the network or even the Internet, this can improve performance significantly. Batching is currently supported when targeting Microsoft SQL Server, Oracle, or MySQL.

We change `Copy to Output` directory to ensure that our `hibernate.cfg.xml` file is copied to the `build` output directory.

There's more...

By default, NHibernate looks for its configuration in the `hibernate.cfg.xml` file. However, the `Configure` method has three extra overloads, which can be used to provide configuration data from other sources, such as:

▶ From a different file:

```
var cfgFile = "cookbook.cfg.xml";
var nhConfig = new Configuration().Configure(cfgFile);
```

> ▸ From a file embedded into an assembly file:

```
var assembly = GetType().Assembly;
var path = "MyApp.cookbook.cfg.xml";
var nhConfig = new Configuration().Configure(assembly, path);
```

> ▸ From an XmlReader:

```
var doc = GetXmlDocumentWithConfig();
var reader = new XmlNodeReader (doc);
var nhConfig = new Configuration().Configure(reader);
```

NHibernate architecture

There are several key components to an NHibernate application, as shown in this diagram:

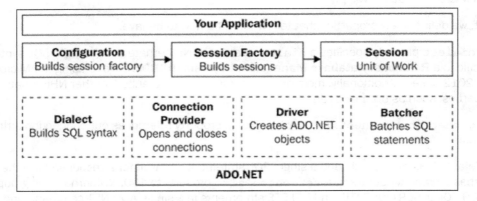

On startup, an NHibernate application builds a `Configuration` object. In this recipe, we build the configuration from settings in the `hibernate.cfg.xml` file. The `Configuration` object is responsible for loading mappings, investigating the object model for additional information, building the mapping metadata, and finally building a session factory. Building the session factory is a rather resource intensive operation, and is normally only done once, when the application starts up.

A **session** represents a **Unit of Work** in the application. *Martin Fowler* defines a Unit of Work as something that "maintains a list of objects affected by a business transaction and coordinates the writing out of changes and the resolution of concurrency problems". An NHibernate session tracks changes to entities and writes those changes back to the database all at once. In NHibernate, this process of waiting to write to the database is called **transactional write-behind**. In addition, the session is the entry point to much of the NHibernate API. More information about the Unit of Work pattern is available at `http://martinfowler.com/eaaCatalog/unitOfWork.html` and in Fowler's book, *Patterns of Enterprise Application Architecture*. A session factory is responsible for creating sessions.

The session acts as an intermediary between our application and several key NHibernate components. A typical application will not interact with these components directly, but understanding them is critical to understanding NHibernate. Unlike a session factory, building a session is very cheap.

A **dialect** is used to build correct SQL syntax for a specific RDBMS. For example, in some versions of Microsoft SQL Server, we begin a select statement with SELECT TOP 20 to specify a maximum result set size. Only 20 rows will be returned. Similarly, to perform this operation in SQLite, we append LIMIT 20 to the end of the select statement. Each dialect provides the necessary SQL syntax string fragments and other information to build correct SQL strings for the chosen RDBMS.

A **driver** is responsible for building a **Batcher**, creating IDbConnection and IDbCommand objects, and preparing those commands.

A **connection provider** is simply responsible for opening and closing database connections.

A **batcher** manages the batch of commands to be sent to the database and the resulting data readers. Currently, only the SqlClientDriver, OracleDataDriver, and MySqlDataDriver support batching. The drivers that don't support batching provide a NonBatchingBatcher to manage IDbCommands and IDataReaders and simulate the existence of a single logical batch of commands.

NHibernate properties

Here are some of the commonly used NHibernate properties:

Property name	Description
connection.provider	This property is a provider class to open and close database connections.
connection.driver_class	This property is specific to the RDBMS used, and is typically set by the dialect.
connection.connection_string	This property is a database connection string.
connection.connection_string_name	This property is the name of connection string in <connectionStrings> element.
connection.isolation	This property is at the transaction isolation level.
dialect	This property is required. A class to build RDBMS-specific SQL strings. Typically, this is one of the many dialects from the NHibernate.Dialect namespace.
show_sql	This is property is a Boolean value. It is set to true to log all SQL statements to Console.Out. Alternatively, log4net may be used to log to other locations.
current_session_context_class	This property is a class to manage contextual sessions. This is covered in depth in *Chapter 3, Sessions and Transactions*.

Property name	Description
`query.substitutions`	This property is a comma-separated list of translations to perform on query strings. For example, True=1, Yes=1, False=0, No=0.
`sql_exception_converter`	This property is a class to convert RDBMS-specific ADO.NET Exceptions to custom exceptions.
`prepare_sql`	This property is a Boolean value. Prepares SQL statements and caches the execution plan for the duration of the database connection.
`command_timeout`	This property is the number of seconds to wait for a SQL command to complete before timing out.
`adonet.batch_size`	This property is the number of SQL commands to send at once before waiting for a response from the database.
`generate_statistics`	This property enables tracking of some statistical information, such as the number of queries executed and entities loaded.
`format_sql`	This property adds line endings for easier-to-read SQL statements.

Additional information about each of these settings is available in the reference documentation at `http://nhibernate.info/doc/nhibernate-reference/index.html`.

Dialects and drivers

Many dialects set other NHibernate properties to sensible default values, including, in most cases, the `connection.driver_class`. NHibernate includes the following dialects in the `NHibernate.Dialect` namespace and drivers in the `NHibernate.Driver` namespace:

RDBMS	Dialect(s)	Driver(s)
Microsoft SQL Server	`MsSql2012Dialect`	`SqlClientDriver`
	`MsSql2008Dialect`	`SqlServerCEDriver`
	`MsSqlAzure2008Dialect`	
	`MsSql2005Dialect`	
	`MsSql2000Dialect`	
	`MsSql7Dialect`	
	`MsSqlCE40Dialect`	
	`MsSqlCEDialect`	

RDBMS	Dialect(s)	Driver(s)
Oracle	Oracle12cDialect Oracle10gDialect Oracle9iDialect Oracle8iDialect OracleLiteDialect	OracleClientDriver OracleDataClientDriver OracleLiteDataDriver OracleManagedDataClientDriver
MySql	MySQL55Dialect MySQL5Dialect MySQL55InnoDBDialect MySQL5InnoDBDialect MySQLDialect	MySqlDataDriver DotConnectMySqlDriver
PostgreSQL	PostgreSQLDialect PostgreSQL81Dialect PostgreSQL82Dialect	NpgsqlDriver
DB2	DB2Dialect Db2400Dialect	DB2Driver DB2400Driver
Informix	InformixDialect InformixDialect0940 InformixDialect1000	IfxDriver
Sybase	SybaseASA9Dialect SybaseASE15Dialect SybaseSQLAnywhere10Dialect SybaseSQLAnywhere11Dialect SybaseSQLAnywhere12Dialect	SybaseAsaClientDriver SybaseAseClientDriver SybaseSQLAnywhereDotNet4Driver SybaseSQLAnywhereDriver
Firebird	FirebirdDialect	FirebirdClientDriver
SQLite	SQLiteDialect	SQLite20Driver
Ingres	IngresDialect Ingres9Dialect	IngresDriver

See also

- ▶ Configuring NHibernate with hibernate.cfg.xml
- ▶ Configuring NHibernate with code
- ▶ Configuring NHibernate with Fluent NHibernate

Configuring NHibernate with App.config or Web.config

Another common method for configuring NHibernate uses a .NET configuration file. In this recipe, we will show you how to configure NHibernate using `App.config` or `Web.config` files, to provide an identical configuration to the previous recipe.

Getting ready

1. Complete the steps in the *Installing NHibernate* recipe.
2. Add a console application project named `ConfigByAppConfig` to your solution.
3. Set it as the **Startup** project for your solution.
4. Install NHibernate to the `ConfigByAppConfig` project using the NuGet Package Manager Console.
5. In `ConfigByAppConfig`, add a reference to the `Eg.Core` project.
6. Add an `App.config` file to your project.

How to do it...

1. Open the `App.config` file.
2. Declare a section for the NHibernate configuration, as shown here:

```
<configSections>
  <section name="hibernate-configuration" type="NHibernate.Cfg.
ConfigurationSectionHandler,
NHibernate" />
</configSections>
```

3. Add a `connectionStrings` section with a connection string:

```
<connectionStrings>
  <add name="db" connectionString="Server=.\SQLEXPRESS;
Database=NHCookbook; Trusted_Connection=SSPI"/>
</connectionStrings>
```

4. Add your hibernate-configuration section:

```
<hibernate-configuration xmlns="urn:nhibernate-configuration-2.2">
  <session-factory>
    <property name="dialect">
      NHibernate.Dialect.MsSql2008Dialect, NHibernate
    </property>
```

```xml
      <property name="connection.connection_string_name">
        db
      </property>
      <property name="adonet.batch_size">
        100
      </property>
    </session-factory>
</hibernate-configuration>
```

5. Your completed `App.config` file should look similar to this:

```xml
<?xml version="1.0" encoding="utf-8"?>
<configuration>
  <configSections>
    <section name="hibernate-configuration" type="NHibernate.Cfg.
ConfigurationSectionHandler,
      NHibernate" />
  </configSections>
  <connectionStrings>
    <add name="db" connectionString="Server=.\SQLEXPRESS;
Database=NHCookbook; Trusted_Connection=SSPI" />
  </connectionStrings>
<hibernate-configuration xmlns="urn:nhibernate-configuration-2.2">
    <session-factory>
      <property name="dialect">
        NHibernate.Dialect.MsSql2008Dialect, NHibernate
      </property>
      <property name="connection.connection_string_name">
        db
      </property>
      <property name="adonet.batch_size">
        100
      </property>
    </session-factory>
</hibernate-configuration>
</configuration>
```

6. Open `Program.cs` and add `using NHibernate.Cfg;` to the beginning of the file.

7. In the `Main` method, add the following code to configure NHibernate:

```csharp
var nhConfig = new Configuration().Configure();
var sessionFactory = nhConfig.BuildSessionFactory();
Console.WriteLine("NHibernate Configured!");
Console.ReadKey();
```

8. Build and run your application. You will see the text **NHibernate Configured**!

How it works...

This recipe works in the same way as the previous recipe. However, in this recipe, we have moved the `hibernate-configuration` element from the `hibernate.cfg.xml` file to `App.config`. The `connection.connection_string_name` property references our connection string named `db`. We can name the connection string anything we like, as long as this property matches the connection string's name.

There's more...

An ASP.NET application's `Web.config` uses the common .NET framework configuration platform and has the same structure as `App.config`. You can therefore use the same technique to configure NHibernate in a web application.

See also

- ▸ Configuring NHibernate with hibernate.cfg.xml
- ▸ Configuring NHibernate with code
- ▸ Configuring NHibernate with Fluent NHibernate

Configuring NHibernate with code

You can also configure NHibernate entirely in code. In this recipe, we'll show you how to do just that.

Getting ready

1. Complete the steps in the *Installing NHibernate* recipe.
2. Add a console application project to your solution called `ConfigByCode`.
3. Set it as the Startup project for your solution.
4. Install NHibernate to `ConfigByCode` project using NuGet Package Manager Console.
5. In `ConfigByCode`, add a reference to the `Eg.Core` project.

How to do it...

1. Add an `App.config` file with this configuration:

```xml
<?xml version="1.0" encoding="utf-8"?>
<configuration>
  <connectionStrings>
```

```
    <add name="db" connectionString="Server=.\SQLEXPRESS;
Database=NHCookbook; Trusted_Connection=SSPI" />
  </connectionStrings>
</configuration>
```

2. In `Program.cs`, add the following `using` statements:

```
using NHibernate.Cfg;
using NHibernate.Dialect;
```

3. In your `Main` function, add the following code to configure NHibernate:

```
var nhConfig = new Configuration().DataBaseIntegration(db =>
{
  db.Dialect<MsSql2012Dialect>();
  db.ConnectionStringName = "db";
  db.BatchSize = 100;
});
var sessionFactory = nhConfig.BuildSessionFactory();
Console.WriteLine("NHibernate Configured!");
Console.ReadKey();
```

4. Build and run your application. You should see the text **NHibernate Configured**!

How it works...

In this recipe, we create an NHibernate configuration using methods in the `NHibernate.Cfg` namespace. These methods offer full type safety and improved discoverability over code configurations in the previous version of NHibernate.

We specify `dialect`, `connection.connection_string_name`, and `adonet.batch_size` with the `DatabaseIntegration` method. Finally, we build a session factory using the `BuildSessionFactory` method.

There's more...

Notice that we are still referencing the `db` connection string defined in our `App.config` file. If we wanted to eliminate the `App.config` file entirely, we could hardcode the connection string with this code:

```
db.ConnectionString = @"Connection string here...";
```

This, however, is completely inflexible, and will require a full recompile and redeployment for even a minor configuration change.

See also

- ▶ Configuring NHibernate with App.config or Web.config
- ▶ Configuring NHibernate with XML
- ▶ Configuring NHibernate with Fluent NHibernate

Configuring NHibernate with Fluent NHibernate

The third-party **Fluent NHibernate** library has its own syntax to configure NHibernate. In this recipe, we'll show you how to configure NHibernate using this syntax.

Getting ready

1. Complete the steps in *Installing NHibernate* recipe.
2. Add a console application project to your solution called `ConfigByFNH`.
3. Set it as the Startup project for your solution.
4. Install NHibernate to the `ConfigByFNH` project using NuGet Package Manager Console.
5. Install the package `FluentNHibernate` to `ConfigByFNH` project using NuGet Package Manager Console.
6. In `ConfigByFNH`, add a reference to the `Eg.Core` project.

How to do it...

1. Add an `App.config` file with this configuration:

```xml
<?xml version="1.0" encoding="utf-8"?>
<configuration>
  <connectionStrings>
    <add name="db" connectionString="Server=.\SQLEXPRESS;
Database=NHCookbook; Trusted_Connection=SSPI" />
  </connectionStrings>
</configuration>
```

2. In `Program.cs`, add the following `using` statements:

```csharp
using FluentNHibernate.Cfg;
using FluentNHibernate.Cfg.Db;
```

3. In the `Main` method, add this code:

```
var config = MsSqlConfiguration.MsSql2012
  .ConnectionString(connstr => connstr.FromConnectionStringWithKey
("db"))
  .AdoNetBatchSize(100);
var nhConfig = Fluently.Configure()
  .Database(config)
  .BuildConfiguration();
var sessionFactory = nhConfig.BuildSessionFactory();
Console.WriteLine("NHibernate configured fluently!");
Console.ReadKey();
```

4. Build and run your application. You should see the text **NHibernate configured fluently!**

How it works...

Our fluent configuration can be broken down into three parts. First, we configure these properties:

1. We set the `dialect` property to `MsSql2012Dialect` when we use the `MsSql2012` static property of `MsSqlConfiguration`.

2. The `connection.connection_string_name` object is set to `db` with a call to `FromConnectionStringWithKey`.

3. We set `adonet.batch_size` to 100 with a call to `AdoNetBatchSize`.

Next, from the fluent configuration, we build a standard NHibernate configuration. Finally, we build a session factory using the `BuildSessionFactory` method.

See also

► Configuring NHibernate with App.config or Web.config

► Configuring NHibernate with XML

► Configuring NHibernate with code

Configuring NHibernate logging

NHibernate has a very extensible logging mechanism, and provides a `log4net` log provider out of the box. The log4net library is a highly customizable, open source logging framework. In this recipe, we'll show you a simple log4net configuration to log important NHibernate events to the Visual Studio **debug** output window.

Getting ready

Complete the earlier *Configuring NHibernate with App.config or Web.config* recipe.

How to do it...

1. Install `log4net` using NuGet Package Manager.

2. Open your application configuration file.

3. Inside the `configSections` element, declare a section for the log4net configuration:

```
<section name="log4net"
type="log4net.Config.Log4NetConfigurationSectionHandler,
log4net"/>
```

4. After the hibernate configuration element, add this log4net configuration:

```
<log4net>
<appender name="trace"
      type="log4net.Appender.TraceAppender, log4net">
  <layout type="log4net.Layout.PatternLayout, log4net">
  <param name="ConversionPattern"
      value=" %date %level %message%newline" />
  </layout>
</appender>
<root>
  <level value="ALL" />
  <appender-ref ref="trace" />
</root>
<logger name="NHibernate">
  <level value="INFO" />
</logger>
</log4net>
```

5. At the beginning of your `Main` function, insert the following code to configure log4net:

```
log4net.Config.XmlConfigurator.Configure();
```

6. Run your application.

7. Watch Visual Studio's **debug** output window.

How it works...

The log4net framework uses appenders, layouts, and loggers to format and control log messages from our application, including log messages from NHibernate.

Appenders define the destination for log messages. In this recipe, we've defined a trace appender, which writes our log messages to `System.Diagnostics.Trace`. When we debug our application, Visual Studio listens to the trace and copies each message to the debug output window.

Loggers are the source of log messages. The root element defines values for all loggers, which can be overridden using the logger element. In our configuration, we've declared that all messages should be written to the appender named `trace`.

In `log4net`, the log messages have priorities. In ascending order, they are DEBUG, INFO, WARN, ERROR, and FATAL. In our configuration, we can define a log level with one of these priorities, or with ALL or OFF. A level includes its priority and all the priorities above it. For example, a level of WARN will also log ERROR and FATAL messages. ALL is equivalent to DEBUG: all messages will be logged, and OFF suppresses all messages.

With our configuration, `log4net` will write messages from NHibernate with a priority of INFO, WARN, ERROR, and FATAL, and ALL messages from other sources.

There's more...

We can use `log4net` in our own application. Here's a simple example of what some code might look like with `log4net` logging:

```
using System.IO;
using log4net;
namespace MyApp.Project.SomeNamespace
{

    public class Foo
    {
        private static ILog log = LogManager.GetLogger(typeof(Foo));

        public string DoSomething()
        {
            log.Debug("We're doing something.");
            try
            {
                return File.ReadAllText("cheese.txt");
            }
```

```
                    catch (FileNotFoundException)
                    {
                        log.Error("Somebody moved my cheese.txt");
                        throw;
                    }
                }
            }
        }
```

We've defined a simple class named `Foo`. In the `DoSomething()` method, we write the log message, "We're doing something.", with a priority of `DEBUG`. Then we return the contents of the file `cheese.txt`. If the file doesn't exist, we log an error and throw the exception.

Because we passed in `typeof(Foo)` when getting the logger, the `Foo` logger is named `MyApp.Project.SomeNamespace.Foo`, similar to the type. This is the typical naming convention when using `log4net`.

Suppose we were no longer concerned with debug level messages from `Foo`, but we still wanted to know about warnings and errors. We can then redefine the log level with this simple addition to our configuration, as shown in the following code:

```
<logger name="MyApp.Project.SomeNamespace.Foo">
  <level value="WARN" />
</logger>
```

Alternatively, we can set the log level for the entire namespace or even the entire project with this configuration, as follows:

```
<logger name="MyApp.Project">
  <level value="WARN" />
</logger>
```

Using logger to troubleshoot NHibernate

When we set NHibernate's `show_sql` configuration property to true, NHibernate will write all SQL statements to `Console.Out`. This is handy in some cases, but many applications don't use console output. With a properly configured logger, we can write the SQL statements to the trace output instead.

NHibernate also writes every SQL statement to a logger named `NHibernate.SQL`. These log messages have `DEBUG` priority. When we add the following snippet to our configuration, we can redefine the log level for this specific logger. We will get every SQL statement in the trace output, as follows:

```
<logger name="NHibernate.SQL">
  <level name="DEBUG" />
</logger>
```

Using other log providers

NHibernate also provides the `IInternalLogger` interface which facilitates logger abstraction. If you want to use other log providers you can provide an implementation for your favorite logger. There is also an `NHibernate.Logging` project which provides implementation for the `Common.Logging` logging abstraction framework. `Common.Logging` supports `log4net`, `NLog`, and `Enterprise Library logging` frameworks, so you can use any of them with NHibernate via this abstraction. Download `NHibernate.Logging` from `https://github.com/mgernand/NHibernate.Logging` or install it from NuGet.

To enable the log provider you have to add the following lines to your `App.config` or `Web. config`:

```
<appSettings>
  <add key="nhibernate-logger"
      value =
"NHibernate.Logging.CommonLogging.CommonLoggingLoggerFactory,
NHibernate.Logging.CommonLogging"/>
</appSettings>
```

See also

▶ Configuring NHibernate with App.config or Web.config

▶ Using NHibernate Profiler

Generating the database

In this recipe, we'll show you how to generate all the necessary tables, columns, keys and relationships in your database - with two lines of code.

Getting ready

Complete the *Configuring NHibernate with App.config* recipe at the beginning of this chapter.

 This recipe works for any RDBMS supported by NHibernate. To use a different system, switch to the dialect for your RDBMS, and use a connection string appropriate for your system.

How to do it...

1. Open `Program.cs`.

2. Add these using statements to the beginning of the file:

```
using Eg.Core;
using NHibernate.Mapping.ByCode;
using NHibernate.Tool.hbm2ddl;
```

3. Modify the `Main` method to look like this:

```
var nhConfig = new Configuration().Configure();
var mapper=new ConventionModelMapper();
nhConfig.AddMapping(mapper.CompileMappingFor(new[] {typeof
(TestClass)}));

var schemaExport = new SchemaExport(nhConfig);
schemaExport.Create(false, true);

Console.WriteLine("The tables have been created"));
Console.ReadKey();
```

4. Build and run your application.

5. Open your database and examine the tables. If everything worked, a table representing `TestClass` should have been created.

How it works...

The **hbm2ddl (hibernate mapping to data definition language)** tool uses the mapping metadata in the configuration object to build a SQL script of our database objects. It then connects to our database and runs this script. In order to demonstrate the functionality, we added a mapping for `TestClass`. How mappings are created and used will be further discussed in *Chapter 2, Models and Mapping*.

There's more...

Alternatively, we can use the `hbm2ddl.auto` configuration property to build our database schema automatically whenever our application calls `BuildSessionFactory`. We can set the property to the following values:

▶ `update`: The `SchemaUpdate` class updates our database schema, avoiding destructive changes. This only works for dialects that implement the IDataBaseSchema interface, such as the SQL Server, Oracle, MySQL, PostgreSQL, SQLite, and Firebird dialects.

- ▸ create: The SchemaExport class creates our database schema from scratch for a fresh database.
- ▸ create-drop: SchemaExport recreates the database schema by first dropping and then creating each table.
- ▸ validate: The SchemaValidate class compares the existing database schema to the schema NHibernate expects, based on your mappings. Similar to update, this requires a dialect that implements IDataBaseSchema.

While create-drop is immensely helpful during development, only validate is suggested for production environments, as the tiniest mistake can have huge consequences. Rather, you should script the database, as shown in the next recipe, and run the script explicitly to set up your production database.

See also

- ▸ Configuring NHibernate with App.config or Web.config
- ▸ Scripting the database

Scripting the database

It's usually not appropriate for your application to recreate database tables each time it runs. In this recipe, we'll generate a SQL script to create your database objects.

Getting ready

Complete the *Configuring NHibernate with App.config or Web.config* recipe at the beginning of this chapter.

 This recipe works for any RDBMS supported by NHibernate. To use a different system, adjust your connection string and dialect accordingly.

How to do it...

1. Open Program.cs.
2. Add these using statements to the beginning of the file:

```
using Eg.Core;
using NHibernate.Mapping.ByCode;
using NHibernate.Tool.hbm2ddl;
```

3. Modify the `Main` method to look similar to this:

```
var nhConfig = new Configuration().Configure();
var mapper = new ConventionModelMapper();
nhConfig.AddMapping(mapper.CompileMappingFor(new[] {
typeof(TestClass) }));

var schemaExport = new SchemaExport(nhConfig);
schemaExport
    .SetOutputFile(@"db.sql")
    .Execute(false, false, false);

Console.WriteLine("An sql file has been generated at {0}",
                 Path.GetFullPath("db.sql"));
Console.ReadKey();
```

4. Build and run your application.

5. Inspect the newly created `db.sql` file.

How it works...

Using the mapping metadata from the configuration object and the current dialect, `hbm2ddl` builds a SQL script for your entities.

See also

▸ Configuring NHibernate with App.config

▸ Configuring NHibernate with hibernate.cfg.xml

▸ Configuring NHibernate with code

▸ Configuring NHibernate with Fluent NHibernate

▸ Generating the database

▸ Updating the database

Updating the database

It's usually required to update your database if mappings for your application have changed. In this recipe, we'll generate a SQL script to update your database objects.

Getting ready

Complete the *Configuring NHibernate with App.config or Web.config* recipe at the beginning of this chapter.

 This recipe works for any RDBMS supported by NHibernate. To use a different system, adjust your connection string and dialect accordingly.

How to do it...

1. Open `Program.cs`.

2. Add these `using` statements to the beginning of the file:
   ```
   using Eg.Core;
   using NHibernate.Mapping.ByCode;
   using NHibernate.Tool.hbm2ddl;
   ```

3. Modify the `Main` method to look similar to this:
   ```
   var nhConfig = new Configuration().Configure();
   var mapper = new ConventionModelMapper();
   nhConfig.AddMapping(mapper.CompileMappingFor(new[] {
   typeof(TestClass) }));
   var update = new SchemaUpdate(nhConfig);
   update.Execute(false, true);
   Console.WriteLine("The tables have been updated");
   Console.ReadKey();
   ```

4. Build and run your application. Inspect the table(s) in the database.

5. Modify `TestClass` to include an additional property:
   ```
   public virtual string Description { get; set; }
   ```

6. Build and run the application again. The `TestClass` table should now have a new column corresponding to the `Description` property.

How it works...

Using the mapping metadata from the configuration object and the current dialect, `hbm2ddl` analyzes the existing structure of your database and generates a script to fulfill the differences. The `SchemaUpdate` only adds missing objects, and does not try to remove anything.

See also

- ▸ Configuring NHibernate with App.config
- ▸ Configuring NHibernate with hibernate.cfg.xml
- ▸ Configuring NHibernate with code
- ▸ Configuring NHibernate with Fluent NHibernate
- ▸ Generating the database
- ▸ Scripting the database

Using NHibernate schema tool

In many cases, you'll want to include building or updating your database in some larger process, such as a build script or installation process. In this recipe, we'll show you how to use this command-line tool to run our `hbm2ddl` tasks.

Getting ready

Download the latest release of NHibernate Schema Tool from `http://nst.codeplex.com/`.

To install NHibernate Schema Tool, follow these steps:

1. Create a new folder in `C:\Program Files` named `NHibernateSchemaTool`.
2. Copy `nst.exe` to the newly created folder.
3. Add `C:\Program Files\NHibernateSchemaTool` to your `PATH` environment variable.
4. Complete the *Configuring NHibernate with hibernate.cfg.xml* recipe from the beginning of this chapter.

 This recipe works for any RDBMS supported by NHibernate. To use a different system, adjust your connection string and dialect accordingly.

How to do it...

1. Build your solution.
2. Open a command prompt window, and switch to the directory containing your compiled mapping assembly and `hibernate.cfg.xml`.

To open the command prompt window quickly, in Visual Studio, right-click on your project, and choose **Open Folder in Windows Explorer**. Open the `bin` folder. While holding down *Shift*, right-click on the **Debug** folder. Choose **Open Command Window Here**.

3. Run the following command:

   `nst /c:hibernate.cfg.xml /a:Eg.Core.dll /o:Create.`

We haven't added any HBM mapping files to the `Eg.Core` project yet, so no tables will be created. In the next chapter, however, we will go into some depth on how these mappings are created.

How it works...

NHibernate Schema Tool is a command-line wrapper for the `hbm2ddl` tool. This makes NST ideal for use in build scripts and continuous integration servers.

The `/c` argument specifies the configuration file. The `/a` argument specifies the assembly with our classes and mapping embedded resource files. The `/o:Create` option tells NHibernate to create our database objects. It also supports `Update` and `Delete`.

There's more...

NST has several options, enabling a number of creative uses. NST supports these command-line options:

Command-line option	Description
`/c:<path-to-hibernate-config>`	Specifies NHibernate `config` file to use.
`/a:<assembly[;assembly2]>`	Path to assembly or semicolon-separated list of assemblies containing embedded `.hbm.xml` files. These assemblies may also contain persistent classes.
`/m:<assembly[;assembly2]>`	Path to assembly or semicolon-separated list of assemblies containing persistent classes.
`/d:<path[;path2]>`	Directory or directories containing `.hbm.xml` mapping files.
`/s`	Generate script, but don't execute. Script is written to the console.
`/v`	Generate script and execute. Script is written to the console.

Command-line option	Description
`/o:<Create|Update|Delete>`	Specifies the `Create`, `Update`, or `Delete` operation.

See also

▶ Configuring NHibernate with App.confiig or Web.config

▶ Configuring NHibernate with hibernate.cfg.xml

▶ Configuring NHibernate with code

▶ Configuring NHibernate with Fluent NHibernate

▶ Generating the database

▶ Scripting the database

2

Models and Mappings

In this chapter, we will cover the following topics:

- ► Mapping a class with XML
- ► Creating class hierarchy mappings
- ► Creating class components
- ► Mapping a one-to-many relationship
- ► Mapping a many-to-many relationship
- ► Mapping collections of elements and components
- ► Setting up a base entity class
- ► Handling versioning and concurrency
- ► Mapping by code
- ► Mapping by convention
- ► Creating mappings fluently
- ► Bidirectional one-to-many class relationships
- ► Mappings enumerations
- ► Immutable entities
- ► Mapping relations to non-primary keys
- ► Using lazy properties
- ► Mapping joins
- ► Using calculated properties
- ► Using serializable values
- ► Dynamic components
- ► Mapping <subselect>

Mapping a class with XML

The suggested first step in any new NHibernate application is mapping the model. The mapping describes how objects O should be retrieved and stored as relational data R in the database. In the simplest scenarios, this is merely a straightforward mapping between classes in the code and tables in the database. Still, the structure of the code or of the database will usually require careful mapping in order to get correct behavior and optimal performance.

Most of the recipes in this chapter utilize a custom library called NH4CookbookHelpers, which makes it possible to visualize the results and behaviors of the mappings described. For convenience, we use NuGet to reference this library, but feel free to download the source code from https://github.com/gliljas/NH4CookbookHelpers if you want to modify its functionality or just see how it works.

Getting ready

Before we begin mapping, let's get our Visual Studio solution set up. Follow these steps to set up your solution with NHibernate binaries and schemas:

1. Complete the steps from the *Installing NHibernate* recipe.

2. Add a Windows forms application project to your solution called MappingRecipes and set it as the startup project.

3. Install NH4CookbookHelpers to the MappingRecipes project using the NuGet package manager console:

   Install-Package NH4CookbookHelpers -Project MappingRecipes

4. Add a reference to for Eg.Core (from *Installing NHibernate*) in the MappingRecipes project.

5. Remove the class Form1.cs from the project.

6. Add using NH4CookbookHelpers; to the top of Program.cs.

7. Edit Program.cs so that the last line in Main reads, Application.Run(new WindowsFormsRunner());:

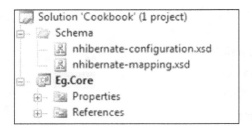

The original technique for NHibernate mapping is the use of XML files.

In this first example, we'll show you how to map a simple `Product` class.

How to do it...

Now, let's start by creating our `Product` class with the following steps:

1. In `Eg.Core`, create a new C# class named `Entity` with the following code:

    ```csharp
    using System;

    namespace Eg.Core
    {
      public abstract class Entity
      {

        public virtual Guid Id { get; protected set; }

      }

    }
    ```

2. Create a new class named `Product` with the following code:

    ```csharp
    using System;

    namespace Eg.Core
    {
      public class Product : Entity
      {

        public virtual string Name { get; set; }
        public virtual string Description { get; set; }
        public virtual decimal UnitPrice { get; set; }

      }
    }
    ```

3. Build your application and correct any compilation errors.

4. Next, let's create an NHibernate mapping for our `Product` class by following these steps:

    1. In the **Solution Explorer** window, right-click on the `Eg.Core` project and choose **Add | New Item**.

    2. Choose the **Data** category on the left pane.

3. Choose `XML file` on the right pane.

4. Name the file `Product.hbm.xml`.

5. In the **Solution Explorer**, right-click on `Product.hbm.xml` and choose **Properties**.

6. Change **Build Action** from **Content** to **Embedded Resource**.

7. In the editor, enter the following XML in `Product.hbm.xml`:

```xml
<?xml version="1.0" encoding="utf-8" ?>
<hibernate-mapping xmlns="urn:nhibernate-mapping-2.2"
    assembly="Eg.Core"
    namespace="Eg.Core">
  <class name="Product">
    <id name="Id">
      <generator class="guid.comb" />
    </id>
    <property name="Name" not-null="true" />
    <property name="Description" />
    <property name="UnitPrice" not-null="true"
      type="Currency" />
  </class>
</hibernate-mapping>
```

5. Finally, we will make use of the mapping by reading from the embedded resources and adding the parsed result to NHibernate's configuration.

6. Add a new folder `MappingWithXml` to the `MappingRecipes` project.

7. Add a new class `Recipe` to the newly created folder:

```csharp
using Eg.Core;
using NH4CookbookHelpers;
using NHibernate;
using NHibernate.Cfg;

namespace MappingRecipes.MappingWithXml
{
    public class Recipe : BaseMappingRecipe
    {
        protected override void Configure(Configuration cfg)
        {
            cfg.AddAssembly(typeof(Product).Assembly);
        }

        public override void AddInitialData(ISession session)
        {
            session.Save(new Product
```

```
                        {
                            Name = "Car",
                            Description = "A nice red car",
                            UnitPrice = 300
                        });
                    }
                }
            }
```

8. Run the `MappingRecipes` application and start the `MappingWithXml` recipe.

9. Investigate the query log and the created tables.

How it works...

In this recipe, we begin by creating our own model. The `model` is a collection of classes that will be persisted or stored in the database. A persistent class is any class that will be persisted. An `entity` class is a `persistent` class with an Id. An instance of an entity class is called an `entity`. So far, our model only contains the `Product` entity class. We will expand on this model over the next few recipes.

Note that our `Product` class looks just like any other **Plain Old CLR Object** (**POCO**) class. One of the strongly held design decisions in NHibernate is that all entity classes should be persistence ignorant, that is, they should not know about or be dependent on NHibernate.

Let's examine the Id property a little closer. The `Id` property of each `Product` instance will contain the primary key value from the database. In NHibernate, this is named the **Persistent Object Identifier** (**POID**). Just as the primary key value uniquely identifies a row in a database table, the POID will uniquely identify an entity in memory.

If you are new to NHibernate, this protected setter may look strange to you:

```
        public virtual Guid Id { get; protected set; }
```

This is a shorthand way to limit access to the `Id` property. Code outside of the `Product` class is unable to change the value of the `Id` property. However, NHibernate sets properties using highly optimized reflection, ignoring the `protected` restriction. This keeps your application from inadvertently altering this value.

Next, we create our mapping for the `Product` entity class. As a rule, all NHibernate mapping files end with a `.hbm.xml` extension and have a build action of **Embedded Resource**. NHibernate can search through the embedded resources in your assembly, loading each one with this extension.

One of the most common mistakes in mapping is forgetting to set the **Build Action** to **Embedded Resource**. This leads to the "No Persister for class" MappingException.

Let's break down this XML mapping. Every XML mapping document contains a single hibernate-mapping element.

The assembly attribute tells NHibernate, by default, which assembly contains our types. Similarly, the namespace attribute sets the default .NET namespace types in this mapping file. Together, they allow us to use the simple name Product instead of the full assembly qualified name of Eg.Core.Product, Eg.Core. Inside the hibernate-mapping element, we have a class element. The name attribute tells NHibernate that this class element defines the mapping for our entity class Product.

The Id element defines the POID. The name attribute refers to the Id property of our Product class. It is case-sensitive, just as in the C# language.

The generator element defines if and how NHibernate will generate POIDs. In this case, we have told NHibernate to use the guid.comb algorithm. Several other options exist.

The property elements define properties on our Product class. Each name attribute matches the name of a property on our Product class. By default, NHibernate allows null values. Adding not-null="true" tells NHibernate to disallow null values.

Avoid redundant mappings

In general, it's best to keep your mappings as short and concise as possible. NHibernate intelligently scans your model and combines this knowledge with the information provided in the mapping. In most cases, specifying the types of properties in your mappings only creates redundancies that have to be maintained. The default table name matches the class name, and each column name matches the corresponding property by default and it's not necessary to specify this information again. Similarly, you should avoid setting an attribute in your mapping when it matches an NHibernate default. For example, adding not-null="false" to each of your properties is redundant and makes your mapping difficult to read.

With this mapping, the Microsoft SQL Server database table used to store our `Product` entities appears as shown in the next screenshot. It may differ slightly for other databases:

Product

	Column Name	Data Type	Allow Nulls
🔑	Id	uniqueidentifier	☐
	Name	nvarchar(255)	☐
	Description	nvarchar(255)	☑
	UnitPrice	decimal(19, 5)	☐
			☐

In this recipe, we add the mappings to NHibernate's configuration in the overridden recipe method `Configure`. We simply call `cfg.AddAssembly(typeof(Product).Assembly)`, which instructs NHibernate to scan all the embedded resources in the specified assembly. In a normal application, this call will be added somewhere close to the other NHibernate configuration calls, as outlined in the *Chapter 1, The Configuration and Schema*.

There's more...

There are two main approaches to begin developing an NHibernate application:

- ▶ With the **code-first** approach, the path taken in this book, we create our entity classes, specify the needed mappings, and finally generate our database tables based on this setup. We treat the database as a storage and querying system only and structure the tables and columns accordingly.

- ▶ The **database-first** approach is only suggested when sharing an existing database with another application. Depending on the database design, this usually requires some advanced mapping techniques. Many NHibernate beginners travel down this path for fresh database applications and end up with mapping and modeling problems well beyond their experience level.

What happens to these mappings?

When it loads, NHibernate will deserialize each of our XML mappings into a graph of Hibernate mapping objects. NHibernate combines this data with metadata from the entity classes to create mapping metadata. This mapping metadata contains everything NHibernate must know about our model.

Surrogate keys and natural IDs

A **natural key** is an ID that has a semantic meaning or business value. It means something to people in the real world. A **surrogate key** is a system generated ID that has no semantic meaning; it's a value that identifies data in a database table in a unique manner. NHibernate strongly encourages the use of surrogate keys. There are two reasons for this:

- First, the use of natural keys inevitably leads to the use of composite keys. Composite keys are multi-field keys composed of the natural keys of other objects. Let's examine the model of a university's course schedule. The natural key for your term or semester entity may be Fall 2010. The natural key for the biology department may be BIOL. The natural key for an introductory biology course would be BIOL 101, a composite of the department's natural key and a course number, each stored in a separate field, with proper foreign keys. The natural key for a section or course offering would be the combination of the natural ids from the term, the course and a section number. You would have a key composed of four distinct pieces of information. The size of the key grows exponentially with each layer. This quickly leads to an incredible amount of complexity.

- Second, because natural keys have a real-world meaning, they must be allowed to change with the real world. Let's assume you have an `Account` class with a `UserName` property. While this may be unique, it's not a good candidate for use as a key. Suppose usernames are composed of the first initial followed by the last name. When someone changes their name, you'll have to update several foreign keys in your database. If, instead, you use an integer with no meaning for the POID, you only have to update a single `UserName` field.

However, `UserName` would be a great candidate for a natural id. A natural id is a property or set of properties that is unique and not null. Essentially, it is the natural key of an entity, though it is not used as the primary key. The mapping for a `natural-id` appears as shown in the following code:

```
<natural-id mutable="true">
  <property name="UserName" not-null="true" />
</natural-id>
```

The `natural-id` element has one attribute `mutable`. The default value is `false`, meaning that the property or properties contained in this natural id are immutable or constant. In our case, we want to allow our application to change the `UserName` of an account from time-to-time, so we set `mutable` to `true`.

Specifying a `natural-id` is optional. The difference it provides are some subtle improvements in caching and if NHibernate is used to create the database schema, the `natural-id` will be given a unique database index.

ID generator selection

NHibernate offers many options for generating POIDs. Some are better than others and generally fall under the following four categories:

▸ The assigned generator requires an application to assign an identifier before an object is persisted. This is typical when natural keys are used.

▸ Non-insert POID generators are the best option for new applications. These generators allow NHibernate to assign an identity to a persistent object without writing the object's data to the database, thus allowing it to delay writing until the business transaction is complete and reducing round trips to the database. The following POID generators fit in this category:

   ❑ `hilo`: This generates an integer using the Hi/Lo algorithm, where an entire range of integers is reserved and used as needed. Once they have all been used, another range is reserved because the identity reservation is managed using a database table, this POID generator is safe for use in a database cluster, web farm, client or server application, or other scenarios where a single database is shared by multiple applications or multiple instances of an application.

   ❑ `guid`: This generates a GUID by calling `System.Guid.NewGuid()`. All the GUID-based generators are safe for use in a shared database environment.

   ❑ `guid.comb`: This combines 10 bytes of a seemingly-random GUID, with six bytes representing the current date and time to form a new GUID. This algorithm reduces index fragmentation while maintaining high performance.

   ❑ `guid.native`: This gets a GUID from the database. Each generation requires a round trip to the database.

   ❑ `uuid.hex`: This generates a GUID and stores it as a human readable string of 32 hex digits, with or without dashes.

   ❑ `uuid.string`: This generates a GUID, converts each of the GUID instance 16 bytes to the binary equivalent character, and stores the resulting 16 characters as a string. Tshis is not readable by a human.

   ❑ `counter`: This is also known as `vm`. It is a simple incrementing integer. It's initialized from the system clock and counts up; it is not appropriate for shared database scenarios.

   ❑ `increment`: It is a simple incrementing integer, initialized by fetching the maximum primary key value from the database at start-up. It's not appropriate for shared database scenarios.

   ❑ `sequence`: This etches a single new ID from a database that supports named sequences, such as Oracle, DB2, and PostgreSQL. Each generation requires a round trip to the database. `seqhilo` performs better.

❑ `seqhilo`: This combines the Hi/Lo algorithm and sequences to provide better performance over the sequence generator.

❑ `foreign`: This simply copies keys across a one-to-one relationship. For example, if you have contact and customer associated by a one-to-one relationship, a foreign generator on customer would copy the ID from the matching contact.

▸ Post-insert POID generators require data to be persisted to the database for an ID to be generated. This affects the behavior of NHibernate in very subtle ways and disables some performance features. As such, use of these POID generators is strongly discouraged! They should be used only with existing databases where other applications rely on this behavior.

❑ `identity` returns a database-generated ID

❑ `select` performs a `SELECT` to fetch the ID from the row after the insert. It uses the natural id to find the correct row

❑ `sequence-identity` returns a database-generated ID for databases that support named sequences

❑ `trigger-identity` returns an ID generated by a database trigger

▸ Finally, the `native` generator maps to a different a POID generator, depending on the database product. For Microsoft SQL Server, DB2, Informix, MySQL, PostgreSQL, SQLite, and Sybase, it is equivalent to `identity`. For Oracle and Firebird, it's the same as `sequence`. On Ingres, it's `hilo`.

See also

▸ *Creating class hierarchy mappings*

▸ *Mapping a one-to-many relationship*

▸ *Setting up a base entity class*

▸ *Handling versioning and concurrency*

▸ *Creating mappings fluently*

Creating class hierarchy mappings

It's common to have an inheritance hierarchy of subclasses. In this example, we will show you one method for mapping inheritance with NHibernate, called table-per-class hierarchy.

Getting ready

Complete the previous *Mapping a class with XML* example.

How to do it...

1. Create a new class named `Book` with the following code:

```
namespace Eg.Core
{
  public class Book : Product
  {

    public virtual string ISBN { get; set; }
    public virtual string Author { get; set; }

  }
}
```

2. Create a new class named `Movie` with the following code:

```
namespace Eg.Core
{
  public class Movie : Product
  {

    public virtual string Director { get; set; }

  }
}
```

3. Change the `Product` mapping to match the XML shown in the following code:

```
<?xml version="1.0" encoding="utf-8" ?>
<hibernate-mapping xmlns="urn:nhibernate-mapping-2.2"
    assembly="Eg.Core"
    namespace="Eg.Core">
  <class name="Product">
    <id name="Id">
      <generator class="guid.comb" />
    </id>
    <discriminator column="ProductType" />
    <natural-id mutable="true">
      <property name="Name" not-null="true" />
    </natural-id>
    <property name="Description" />
    <property name="UnitPrice" not-null="true" />
  </class>
</hibernate-mapping>
```

4. Create a new embedded resource named `Book.hbm.xml` with the following XML:

```xml
<?xml version="1.0" encoding="utf-8" ?>
<hibernate-mapping xmlns="urn:nhibernate-mapping-2.2"
    assembly="Eg.Core"
    namespace="Eg.Core">
  <subclass name="Book" extends="Product">
    <property name="Author"/>
    <property name="ISBN"/>
  </subclass>
</hibernate-mapping>
```

5. Create another embedded resource named `Movie.hbm.xml` with the next XML:

```xml
<?xml version="1.0" encoding="utf-8" ?>
<hibernate-mapping xmlns="urn:nhibernate-mapping-2.2"
    assembly="Eg.Core"
    namespace="Eg.Core">
  <subclass name="Movie" extends="Product">
    <property name="Director" />
  </subclass>
</hibernate-mapping>
```

6. Create a new folder named `ClassHierarchy` in the `MappingRecipes` project.

7. Add a new class named `Recipe` to the folder:

```csharp
public class Recipe : BaseMappingRecipe
{
    protected override void Configure(Configuration cfg)
    {
      cfg.AddAssembly(typeof(Product).Assembly);
    }
    protected override void AddInitialData(
    ISession session)
    {
      session.Save(new Book
    {
      Name = "NHibernate Cookbook", ISBN = "12334"
    });
      session.Save(new Movie
      {
        Name = "Intouchables",
        Director = "Olivier Nakache"
      });
  }

      public override void RunQueries(ISession session)
    {
```

```
session.CreateQuery("from Product")
    .List<Product>();
    }
}
```

8. Run the `MappingRecipes` application and start the `ClassHierarchy` recipe.

9. Investigate the query log and the created tables.

How it works...

 In this example, we've mapped a table-per-class hierarchy, which means that the data for our entire hierarchy is stored in a single table, as shown in the following screenshot:

Product

	Column Name	Data Type	Allow Nulls
🔑	Id	uniqueidentifier	☐
	ProductType	nvarchar(255)	☐
	Name	nvarchar(255)	☐
	Description	nvarchar(255)	☑
	UnitPrice	decimal(19, 5)	☐
	Director	nvarchar(255)	☑
	Author	nvarchar(255)	☑
	ISBN	nvarchar(255)	☑
			☐

NHibernate uses a discriminator column, `ProductType` in this case, to distinguish among products, books, and movies. By default, the discriminator contains the class name. In this example, it would be `Eg.Core.Product`, `Eg.Core.Book`, or `Eg.Core.Movie`. These defaults can be overridden in the mappings using a `discriminator-value` attribute on our class and subclass elements.

In our `Book.hbm.xml` mapping, we have defined `Book` as a subclass of `Product` with `Author` and `ISBN` properties. In our `Movie.hbm.xml` mapping, we have defined `Movie` as a subclass of `Product` with a `Director` property.

With table-per-class-hierarchy, we cannot define any of our subclass properties as `not-null="true"` because this would create a not null constraint on those fields. For instance, if we set up the `Director` property as not null, we would not be able to insert `Product` or `Book` instances, because they do not define a `Director` property. If this is required, use one of the hierarchy mapping strategies that are listed in the next section.

There's more...

Java refugees may recognize the `extends` attribute, as `extends` is the Java keyword used to declare class inheritance. NHibernate first came to life as a port of Java's Hibernate ORM.

Table-per-class hierarchy is the suggested method for mapping class hierarchies, but NHibernate always gives us other options. However, mixing these options within the same class hierarchy is discouraged and only works in very limited circumstances.

Table per class

In table-per-class mappings, properties of the base class `Product` are stored in a shared table, while each subclass gets its own table for the subclass properties.

Table per subclass uses the `joined-subclass` element, which requires a key element to name the primary key column. As the name implies, NHibernate will use a join to query for this data. Also, notice that our `Product` table doesn't contain a `ProductType` column. Only table-per-class hierarchy uses discriminators. Using table-per-class, our `Movie` mapping would appear as the following code:

```xml
<?xml version="1.0" encoding="utf-8" ?>
<hibernate-mapping xmlns="urn:nhibernate-mapping-2.2"
    assembly="Eg.Core"
    namespace="Eg.Core">
  <joined-subclass name="Movie" extends="Product">
    <key column="Id" />
    <property name="Director" />
  </joined-subclass>
</hibernate-mapping>
```

Executing our recipe with table per class mapping would create three tables and execute the following queries:

- Inserting data:
  ```sql
  INSERT INTO Product(Name, Description, UnitPrice, Id)
  VALUES (@p0, @p1, @p2, @p3);
  INSERT INTO Book (Author, ISBN, Id)
  ```

```
VALUES (@p0, @p1, @p2);
INSERT INTO Product(Name, Description, UnitPrice, Id)
VALUES (@p0, @p1, @p2, @p3);
INSERT INTO Movie(Director, Id)
VALUES (@p0, @p1);
```

▶ Listing all products:

```
SELECT
        product0_.Id AS Id0_,
        product0_.Name AS Name0_,
        product0_.Description AS Descript3_0_,
        product0_.UnitPrice AS UnitPrice0_,
        product0_1_.Author AS Author1_,
        product0_1_.ISBN AS ISBN1_,
        product0_2_.Director AS Director2_,
        CASE
            WHEN product0_1_.Id IS NOT NULL THEN 1
            WHEN product0_2_.Id IS NOT NULL THEN 2
            WHEN product0_.Id IS NOT NULL THEN 0
        END AS clazz_
FROM
        Product product0_
LEFT OUTER JOIN
        Book product0_1_
            ON product0_.Id=product0_1_.Id
LEFT OUTER JOIN
        Movie product0_2_
            ON product0_.Id=product0_2_.Id
```

Note how the extra tables are joined (LEFT OUTER to be specific) and a CASE clause is used to return the clazz_ value, which indicates the return type to NHibernate.

Table per concrete class

In table-per-concrete-class mappings, each class gets its own table containing columns, for all properties of the class and the base class.

There is no duplication of data. That is, data from a book instance is written only in the Book table, not the Product table. To fetch Product data, NHibernate will use the SQL UNION operator to query all the three tables. Using table-per-concrete-class, our Movie mapping would appear as shown in the following code:

```xml
<?xml version="1.0" encoding="utf-8" ?>
<hibernate-mapping xmlns="urn:nhibernate-mapping-2.2"
    assembly="Eg.Core"
    namespace="Eg.Core">
  <union-subclass name="Movie" extends="Product">
    <property name="Director" />
  </union-subclass>
</hibernate-mapping>
```

Executing our recipe with table per concrete class mapping would result in the following queries:

- Inserting data:

```sql
INSERT INTO Book (Name, Description, UnitPrice, Author, ISBN, Id)
VALUES (@p0, @p1, @p2, @p3, @p4, @p5);
INSERT INTO Movie (Name, Description, UnitPrice, Director, Id)
VALUES (@p0, @p1, @p2, @p3, @p4);
```

- Listing all products:

```sql
SELECT
        product0_.Id AS Id0_,
        product0_.Name AS Name0_,
        product0_.Description AS Descript3_0_,
        product0_.UnitPrice AS UnitPrice0_,
        product0_.Author AS Author1_,
        product0_.ISBN AS ISBN1_,
        product0_.Director AS Director2_,
        product0_.clazz_ AS clazz_
    FROM
        (SELECT
            [columns snipped...]
            0 AS clazz_
        FROM
```

```
        Product
UNION
SELECT
        [columns snipped...]
        1 AS clazz_
FROM
        Book
UNION
SELECT
        [columns snipped...]
        2 AS clazz_
FROM
        Movie
) product0_
```

See also

▶ *Mapping a class with XML*

▶ *Mapping a one-to-many relationship*

▶ *Setting up a base entity class*

▶ *Handling versioning and concurrency*

▶ *Creating mappings fluently*

Creating class components

There are cases where a set of properties are used repeatedly. These properties may even have their own business logic, but they do not represent an entity in your application. They are value objects. In this recipe, we will tell you how to separate these properties and business logic into a component class without creating a separate entity.

Getting ready

Complete the *Getting ready* instructions at the beginning of this chapter.

How to do it...

1. Add a folder named `Components` to the `MappingRecipes` project.

2. In the folder, add an `Address` class with the following properties:

```
public virtual Guid Id { get; protected set; }
public virtual string Lines { get; set; }
public virtual string City { get; set; }
public virtual string State { get; set; }
public virtual string ZipCode { get; set; }
```

3. Add a `Customer` class with the following properties:

```
public virtual string Name { get; set; }
public virtual Address BillingAddress { get; set; }
public virtual Address ShippingAddress { get; set; }
```

4. Add the following embedded mapping document:

```xml
<?xml version="1.0" encoding="utf-8" ?>
<hibernate-mapping xmlns="urn:nhibernate-mapping-2.2"
    assembly="MappingRecipes"
    namespace=" MappingRecipes.Components">
  <class name="Customer">
    <id name="Id">
      <generator class="guid.comb" />
    </id>
    <property name="Name" not-null="true" />
    <component name="BillingAddress" class="Address">
      <property name="Lines" not-null="true"
                column="BillingLines" />
      <property name="City" not-null="true"
                column="BillingCity" />
      <property name="State" not-null="true"
                column="BillingState" />
      <property name ="ZipCode" not-null="true"
                column="BillingZipCode" />
    </component>
    <component name="ShippingAddress" class="Address">
      <property name="Lines" not-null="true"
                column="ShippingLines" />
      <property name="City" not-null="true"
                column="ShippingCity" />
      <property name="State" not-null="true"
                column="ShippingState" />
```

```
        <property name ="ZipCode" not-null="true"
                  column="ShippingZipCode" />
      </component>
    </class>
</hibernate-mapping>
```

5. Add the following `Recipe` class:

```csharp
using System;
using NH4CookbookHelpers;
using NHibernate;

namespace MappingRecipes.Components
{
  public class Recipe : HbmMappingRecipe
  {
    protected override void AddInitialData(ISession session)
    {
      session.Save(new Customer
      {
        Name = "Max Weinberg",
        BillingAddress = new Address
        {
          Lines = "E Street 1",
          City = "Belmar",
          State = "New Jersey",
          ZipCode = "123"
        },
        ShippingAddress = new Address
        {
          Lines = "Home street",
          City = "Newark",
          State = "New Jersey",
          ZipCode = "123"
        }
      });
    }

    public override void RunQueries(ISession session)
    {
      var customer = session.QueryOver<Customer>()
        .SingleOrDefault();
      Console.WriteLine(
```

```
       "Customer {0} has a billing address in {1}",
              customer.Name, customer.BillingAddress.City);
         }
       }
}
```

6.   Run the `MappingRecipes` application and start the `Components` recipe.

7.   Investigate the query log and the created tables.

How it works...

In this recipe, we can use the `Address` component class throughout our model without the overhead of maintaining a separate entity. We have used it in our `Customer` class for both billing and shipping address.

Our model looks like this:

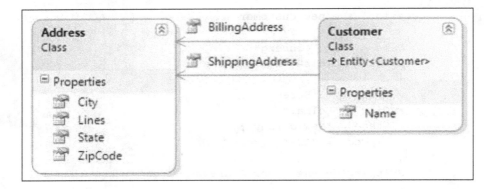

We get all the reuse benefits without the database work. The `Address` fields are included in every query for `Customer` and are automatically loaded.

Mapping a one-to-many relationship

It's usually necessary to relate an entity to other entities. For example, an order can be related to many order lines and to a customer. In this example, we'll show you how to map a one-to-many relationship between `Movie` and a new entity class, `ActorRole`.

Getting ready

Complete the previous *Creating class hierarchy mappings* recipe.

How to do it...

1. In `Eg.Core`, create a new class named `ActorRole` with the following code:

    ```csharp
    namespace Eg.Core
    {
      public class ActorRole : Entity
      {

        public virtual string Actor { get; set; }
        public virtual string Role { get; set; }

      }
    }
    ```

2. Create an embedded resource mapping for `ActorRole` with the following XML:

    ```xml
    <?xml version="1.0" encoding="utf-8" ?>
    <hibernate-mapping xmlns="urn:nhibernate-mapping-2.2"
        assembly="Eg.Core"
        namespace="Eg.Core">
      <class name="ActorRole">
        <id name="Id">
          <generator class="guid.comb" />
        </id>
        <property name="Actor" not-null="true" />
        <property name="Role" not-null="true" />
      </class>
    </hibernate-mapping>
    ```

3. Add this `Actors` property to the `Movie` class:

    ```csharp
    using System.Collections.Generic;

    namespace Eg.Core
    {
      public class Movie : Product
      {

        public virtual string Director { get; set; }
        public virtual IList<ActorRole> Actors { get; set; }

      }
    }
    ```

4. Add the following `list` element to our `Movie` mapping:

```
<subclass name="Movie" extends="Product">
  <property name="Director" />
  <list name="Actors" cascade="all-delete-orphan">
    <key column="MovieId" />
    <index column="ActorIndex" />
    <one-to-many class="ActorRole"/>
  </list>
</subclass>
```

5. Create a new folder named `OneToMany` in the `MappingRecipes` project.

6. Add a new class named `Recipe` to the folder:

```
public class Recipe : BaseMappingRecipe
{
    protected override void Configure(Configuration cfg)
    {
        cfg.AddAssembly(typeof(Product).Assembly);
    }
}
```

7. Add a new method to the `Recipe` class:

```
protected override void AddInitialData(ISession session)
{
    session.Save(new Movie
    {
        Name = "Hibernation",
        Description =
          "The countdown for the lift-off has begun",
        UnitPrice = 300,
        Actors=new List<ActorRole>
        {
            new ActorRole
            {
                Actor = "Adam Quintero",
                Role = "Joseph Wood"
            }
        }
    });
}
```

8. Start the application and run the `OneToMany` recipe. The query log will show something similar to this:

```
INSERT  INTO    Product    (Name, Description, UnitPrice, Director, ProductType, Id)  VALUES    (@p0, @p1, @p2, @p3, 'Eg.Core.Movie', @p4);
INSERT  INTO    ActorRole  (Actor, Role, Id)  VALUES    (@p0, @p1, @p2);
UPDATE  ActorRole  SET    MovieId = @p0,    ActorIndex = @p1  WHERE    Id = @p2;
```

How it works...

Our `ActorRole` mapping is simple. Check out mapping a class with XML for more information. `ActorRole` isn't a part of our `Product` hierarchy. In the database, it gets a table of its own, as shown in the next screenshot:

ActorRole		
Column Name	Data Type	Allow Nulls
Id	uniqueidentifier	☐
Actor	nvarchar(255)	☐
Role	nvarchar(255)	☐
MovieId	uniqueidentifier	☑
ActorIndex	int	☑
		☐

As expected, the `ActorRole` table has fields for the `Id`, `Actor`, and `Role` properties. The `MovieId` and `ActorIndex` columns come from the mapping of our actors list on `Movie`, not the `ActorRole` mapping.

The `Actors` property uses an `IList` collection. Another strong design choice with NHibernate and a good programming practice in general, is the liberal use of interfaces. This allows NHibernate to use its own list implementation to support features such as lazy loading, as discussed later in this recipe.

In our movie mapping, the `Actors` property is mapped with the `<list>` element. To associate an `ActorRole` with a `Movie` in the database, we store the movie's Id with each `ActorRole`. The `<key>` element tells NHibernate to store this in a column named `MovieId`.

We've defined `Actors` as a `list`, which implies that the order is significant. After all, actors in leading roles get top billing. Our `index` element defines the `ActorIndex` column to store the position of each element in the list. Finally, we tell NHibernate that `Actors` is a collection of `ActorRole` with `<one-to-many class="ActorRole" />`.

The `all-delete-orphan` value of the cascade attribute tells NHibernate to save the associated `ActorRole` objects automatically when it saves a movie, and delete them when it deletes a movie.

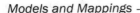

There's more...

A few items in this recipe are worth discussing. Note how the relationship isn't inserted at once. Instead an `UPDATE` at the end sets up the relationship. This is due to our unidirectional relationship. Only the `Movie` knows about its `ActorRole` and not the other way around. But, in order to persist the relationship, the `ActorRole` will first be saved.

This behavior is best circumvented by creating a bi-directional relationship (discussed later in this chapter), where the `ActorRole` is taking ownership of the relation. However, it is also possible to force NHibernate to insert to correct relationship keys at once, by simply adding `not-null="true"` to the `<key>` element:

```
<list name="Actors" cascade="all-delete-orphan" >
    <key column="MovieId" not-null="true"/>
    <index column="ActorIndex" />
    <one-to-many class="ActorRole"/>
</list>
```

The purpose of this is to avoid `NULL` values in the `MovieId` columns. It doesn't stop NHibernate from issuing the extra `UPDATE`. An added `update="false"` will do that, but with unfortunate side effects, especially when using `<list>` collections.

Lesson learned? Read up on bi-directional relationships.

Lazy loading collections

To improve application performance, NHibernate supports lazy loading. In short, data isn't loaded from the database until it is required by the application. Let's look at the steps that NHibernate will use when our application fetches a `Movie` from the database:

1. NHibernate fetches `Id`, `Name`, `Description`, `UnitPrice`, and `Director` data from the database for a `Movie` with a given `Id`; note that we do not load the `Actors` data. NHibernate uses the following SQL query:

```
select
    movie0_.Id as Id1_,
    movie0_.Name as Name1_,
    movie0_.Description as Descript4_1_,
    movie0_.UnitPrice as UnitPrice1_,
    movie0_.Director as Director1_
from Product movie0_
```

```
where
    movie0_.ProductType='Eg.Core.Movie' and
    movie0_.Id = 'a2c42861-9ff0-4546-85c1-9db700d6175e'
```

2. NHibernate creates an instance of the `Movie` object.

3. NHibernate sets the `Id`, `Name`, `Description`, `UnitPrice`, and `Director` properties of the `Movie` object with the data from the database.

4. NHibernate creates a special lazy loading object that implements `IList<ActorRole>` and assigns it to the `Actors` property of the `Movie` object. It is not a `List<ActorRoles>`, but rather a separate NHibernate-specific implementation of the `IList<ActorRole>` interface.

5. NHibernate returns the `Movie` object to our application.

Then, suppose our application contains the following code. Remember, we haven't loaded any `ActorRole` data:

```
foreach (var actor in movie.Actors)
    Console.WriteLine(actor.Actor);
```

The first time we enumerate the collection, the lazy loading object is initialized. It loads the associated `ActorRole` data from the database with a query, as shown:

```
SELECT
    actors0_.MovieId as MovieId1_,
    actors0_.Id as Id1_,
    actors0_.ActorIndex as ActorIndex1_,
    actors0_.Id as Id0_0_,
    actors0_.Actor as Actor0_0_,
    actors0_.Role as Role0_0_
FROM ActorRole actors0_
WHERE
    actors0_.MovieId='a2c42861-9ff0-4546-85c1-9db700d6175e'
```

We can disable lazy loading of a collection by adding the `lazy="false"` attribute to the `<list>` element of our mapping.

It's worth noting that lazy loading always uses the same NHibernate session as the one used to load the parent object. In other words, the session must stay open or the lazy loading will fail.

Lazy loading proxies

Suppose our `ActorRole` class had a reference back to `Movie`, similar to the following code:

```
public class ActorRole : Entity
{

  public virtual string Actor { get; set; }
  public virtual string Role { get; set; }
  public virtual Movie Movie { get; set; }


}
```

If we fetch an `ActorRole` from the database, NHibernate will build the `ActorRole` object as we expect, but it only knows the `Id` of the associated `Movie`. It won't have all the data necessary to construct the entire `Movie` object. Instead, it will create a proxy object to represent the `Movie` and enable lazy loading.

We can access the `Id` of this `Movie` proxy without loading the movie's data. If we access any other property or method on the proxy, NHibernate will immediately fetch all the data for this movie. Loading this data is completely transparent to the application. The proxy object behaves similar to a real `Movie` entity.

This proxy object is a subclass of `Movie`. NHibernate requires a few things from our `Movie` class to subclass `Movie` and intercept these calls to trigger lazy loading; they are:

- ▶ `Movie` cannot be a sealed class
- ▶ `Movie` must have a protected or public constructor without parameters
- ▶ All public members of `Movie` must be virtual; this includes methods

Why all members and not just the lazy properties? It is because NHibernate wants to ensure that the instance is fully initialized, as soon as something interacts with it. The proxy will need to override all the members and they have to be virtual for that.

By default, NHibernate creates these proxy objects using the `DefaultProxyFactory`. As the name implies, this factory can be replaced if you require special proxy functionalities, such as logging or integration with an IoC container.

If we specify `lazy="false"` on the class element of our `Movie` mapping, we can disable this behavior and NHibernate will never create a proxy of `Movie`. Instead, it forces NHibernate to load the associated movie's data as soon as it loads an `ActorRole`. Loading data unnecessarily like this can kill the performance of your application, and it should only be used in very specific and well-considered circumstances.

Collections

NHibernate supports several collection types. The most common types are as follows:

	Bag	Set	List	Map
Allows Duplicates	Yes	No	Yes	Keys must be unique. Values may be duplicated.
Order is significant	No	No	Yes	No
Property type	`IList<T>`	`ISet<T>`	`IList<T>`	`IDictionary<TKey,TValue>`
Suggested backing type	`List<T>`	`HashSet<T>`	`List<T>`	`Dictionary<TKey,TValue>`

All collections can use the `ICollection` type or a custom collection type implementing `NHibernate.UserType.IUserCollectionType`. Only bag and set can be used in bidirectional relationships. We will explore those in the *Bidirectional class relationships* recipe.

Bags

A bag collection allows duplicates and implies that order is not important. Let's consider a bag of `ActorRole` entities. The bag may contain actor role 1, actor role 2, actor role 3, actor role 1, actor role 4, and actor role 1. A typical bag mapping appears as shown in the following code:

```
<bag name="Actors">
  <key column="MovieId"/>
  <one-to-many class="ActorRole"/>
</bag>
```

The corresponding `Actors` property may be an `IList`, `ICollection` or even an `IEnumerable`.

In a one-to-many scenario, this behavior with duplicates is usually of limited consequence. Since `ActorRole` is an entity with an Id, duplicates can and will not be inserted, even if they have been added to the collection property. This would cause primary key violations in the database. However, in a many-to-many relationship, which we will discuss in the next recipe, the duplicates become a real issue (or opportunity). There is no way to identify an individual entry in the bag distinctly with a SQL statement. When an entry is removed, and the updated bag is persisted, all the rows representing the old bag contents are deleted, using a SQL statement, such as `delete from MovieActors where MovieId='1'`. After this, the entire contents of the bag are reinserted. For large bags, this can create performance issues.

To counter this issue, NHibernate also provides an `idBag` where each entry in the bag is assigned an Id by one of the POID generators. This allows NHibernate to address each bag entry uniquely with queries, such as:

```
delete from Actors where ActorRoleBagId='2'
```

The mapping for an `idBag` looks similar to the following code:

```
<idBag name="Actors">
  <collection-id column="ActorRoleBagId" type="Int64">
    <generator class="hilo" />
  </collection-id>
  <key column="MovieId"/>
  <one-to-many class="ActorRole"/>
</idBag>
```

Lists

A list collection also allows duplicates, but unlike a bag, the order is significant. Our list may contain actor role 1 at index 0, actor role 2 at index 1, actor role 3 at index 2, actor role 1 again at index 3, actor role 4 at index 4, and actor role 2 again at index 5. A typical list mapping looks similar to the following code:

```
<list name="Actors">
  <key column="MovieId" />
  <list-index column="ActorRoleIndex" />
  <one-to-many class="ActorRole"/>
</list>
```

The corresponding Actors property should be an `IList` because NHibernate maintains order with the `ActorRoleIndex` column; it can also uniquely identify individual list entries. However, because it maintains order, it also means that these indexes must be reset whenever the list contents change. For example, suppose we have a list of six actor roles and we remove the third actor role. NHibernate will then have to update the `ActorRoleIndex` of each list entry after the second. For large lists, this can cause real performance issues.

Sets

A set collection does not allow duplicates and the order of a set is not important. It may contain actor role 1, actor role 3, actor role 2, and actor role 4 but an attempt to add actor role 1 to the set again will fail. A typical set mapping appears as shown in the following code:

```
<set name="Actors">
  <key column="MovieId" />
  <one-to-many class="ActorRole"/>
</set>
```

The corresponding `Actors` property should be an `ISet` from `System.Collections. Generic`.

An attempt to add an item to an uninitialized lazy loaded set collection will cause the set to be loaded from the database. This is necessary to ensure uniqueness in the collection. To ensure proper uniqueness in a set, you should override the `Equals` and `GetHashCode` methods, as shown in the *Setting up a base entity class* recipe.

While it is very common to use `IList<T>` in .NET applications for any type of collection, an `ISet<T>` is actually the option that often represents the actual intent. No duplicates.

Map

Map is another term that crossed over when NHibernate was ported from Java. In .NET, it's known as a dictionary. Each collection entry is a key with a corresponding value. The keys must be unique, whereas the values can be valid instances of the value type:

```
<map name="Actors" >
  <key column="MovieId" />
  <map-key column="Role" type="string" />
  <element column="Actor" type="string"/>
</map>
```

As you may have guessed, the corresponding `Actors` property must be an `IDictionary<string, string>`, where the `key` is the name of the movie role, and the value is the actor's name. You are not limited to basic data types as shown here. NHibernate also allows entities for keys and values, as shown in the following code:

```
<map name="SomeProperty">
  <key column="Id" />
  <index-many-to-many class="KeyEntity"/>
  <many-to-many class="ValueEntity" />
</map>
```

See also

- ▸ *Mapping a class with XML*
- ▸ *Creating class hierarchy Mappings*
- ▸ *Mapping a many-to-many relationship*
- ▸ *Mapping collections of elements and components*
- ▸ *Setting up a base entity class*
- ▸ *Bidirectional class relationships*
- ▸ *Handling versioning and concurrency*
- ▸ *Creating mappings fluently*

Mapping a many-to-many relationship

A student often attends many classes and hopefully every class is attended by more than one student. This type of relationship is called many-to-many and in a relational database, an intermediate table usually represents it, with at least two columns referencing the keys of the participating entities.

NHibernate supports many-to-many relationships and does so without having to expose the intermediate table to the code.

Getting ready

Complete the *Getting ready* instructions at the beginning of this chapter.

How to do it...

1. Create a new folder named `ManyToMany` in the `MappingRecipes` project.

2. Add a new class `Student` to the folder:

```
public class Student
{
    public virtual Guid Id { get; protected set; }
    public virtual string Name { get; set; }
}
```

3. Create an embedded resource mapping named `Student.hbm.xml` (in the same folder) with the following XML:

```xml
<?xml version="1.0" encoding="utf-8" ?>
<hibernate-mapping xmlns="urn:nhibernate-mapping-2.2"
    assembly="MappingRecipes"
    namespace="MappingRecipes.ManyToMany">
  <class name="Student">
    <id name="Id">
      <generator class="guid.comb"/>
    </id>
    <property name="Name"/>
  </class>
</hibernate-mapping>
```

4. Add a new class `Course` to the folder:

```
public class Course
{
    public Course()
```

```
    {
        Students=new HashSet<Student>();
    }
    public virtual Guid Id { get; protected set; }
    public virtual string Name { get; set; }
    public virtual ISet<Student> Students { get; set; }
}
```

5. Create an embedded resource mapping named `Course.hbm.xml` with the following XML:

```xml
<?xml version="1.0" encoding="utf-8" ?>
<hibernate-mapping xmlns="urn:nhibernate-mapping-2.2"
    assembly="MappingRecipes"
    namespace="MappingRecipes.ManyToMany">
  <class name="Course">
    <id name="Id">
      <generator class="guid.comb"/>
    </id>
    <property name="Name"/>
    <set name="Students" table="CourseStudent">
      <key column="CourseId"/>
      <many-to-many class="Student" column="StudentId"/>
    </set>
  </class>
</hibernate-mapping>
```

6. Add a new class named `Recipe` to the folder:

```csharp
public class Recipe : HbmMappingRecipe
{
    private Guid _frenchId;

    protected override void AddInitialData(
    ISession session)
    {
        var anna = new Student { Name = "Anna" };
        var george = new Student { Name = "George" };

        var english = new Course { Name = "English" };
        var french = new Course { Name = "French" };

        english.Students.Add(anna);

        french.Students.Add(anna);
```

```
                    french.Students.Add(george);

                    session.Save(anna);
                    session.Save(george);

                    session.Save(english);
                    session.Save(french);

                    _frenchId = french.Id;
                }

                public override void RunQueries(ISession session)
                {
                    var course2 = session.Get<Course>(_frenchId);
                    Console.WriteLine("Course name: " + course2.Name);
                    Console.WriteLine("Student count: " +
                    course2.Students.Count());
                }
            }
```

7. Run the application and start the `ManyToMany` recipe. The query log will be similar to the following screenshot:

```
INSERT   INTO      Student        (Name, Id)    VALUES     (@p0, @p1);
INSERT   INTO      Student        (Name, Id)    VALUES     (@p0, @p1);
INSERT   INTO      Course         (Name, Id)    VALUES     (@p0, @p1);
INSERT   INTO      Course         (Name, Id)    VALUES     (@p0, @p1);
INSERT   INTO      CourseStudent  (CourseId, StudentId)    VALUES     (@p0, @p1);
INSERT   INTO      CourseStudent  (CourseId, StudentId)    VALUES     (@p0, @p1);
INSERT   INTO      CourseStudent  (CourseId, StudentId)    VALUES     (@p0, @p1);
SELECT   course0_.Id as Id0_0_,     course0_.Name as Name0_0_    FROM    Course course0_   WHERE     course0_.Id=@p0;
SELECT   students0_.CourseId as CourseId1_,     students0_.StudentId as StudentId1_,     student1_.Id as Id2_0_,     student1_.Name as Name2_0_     FROM
```

 The `Recipe` class in this example derives from the `HbmMappingRecipe` class. For convenience, this class automatically adds all embedded resources that are located in the same folder as the recipe class.

How it works...

As can be seen in the recipe, mapping a many-to-many relationship is easier than mapping a one-to-many relationship. NHibernate takes care of insertion and deletion of rows in the intermediate table.

In this recipe, we use an `ISet` type collection and a set mapping, as opposed to the list mapping used in the previous recipe. It makes sense to do so, since a `Student` can't be enrolled to a specific `Course` more than once (no duplicates allowed) and we don't really care about the order of the students in the collection (order is not significant). In addition, we didn't add any courses collection in the `Student` class. We certainly could have, but since such bi-directionality adds complexity, we'll dig deeper in the *Bidirectional class relationships recipe* instead.

In the `AddInitialData` method, we add two courses and two students and enroll the first student (Anna) to both courses and the second student (George) to only the French course. We save the students and the courses and, finally, store the newly assigned Id of the French course so that we can use it in the next method.

The saves will trigger four `INSERT` instances, to save the courses and the students and another three `INSERT` instances, will be triggered, to the intermediate table to store the relationships we added.

In `RunQueries`, we fetch the course in French, using the id we stored previously and output its name and the number of enrolled students. This will cause two queries to be executed. One to retrieve the course and one to retrieve the related students.

There's more...

For many-to-many relationships, the type of collection used becomes even more important than for one-to-many. We suggest you review the *Collections* section in the previous recipe for some meaty ingredients.

Mapping collections of elements and components

So far, we've shown how to use collections where an entity relates to a set of other entitities. However, a collection can also hold simple values, such as strings or components, that is, objects with properties but no id.

Getting ready

Complete the *Getting ready* instructions at the beginning of this chapter.

How to do it...

1. Add a new folder named `ComponentCollections` to the `MappingRecipes` project.

2. Add a new class named `Customer` to the folder:

```
public class Customer
{
    public Customer()
    {
        Addresses=new List<Address>();
        Tags=new HashSet<string>();
    }
    public virtual Guid Id { get; protected set; }
    public virtual string Name { get; set; }
    public virtual IList<Address> Addresses { get; set; }
    public virtual ISet<string> Tags { get; set; }
}
```

3. Add a new class named `Address` to the folder:

```
public class Address
{
    public string AddressLine1 { get; set; }
    public string AddressLine2 { get; set; }
    public string City { get; set; }
    public string PostalCode { get; set; }
}
```

4. Add an embedded mapping named `Customer.hbm.xml` to the folder:

```xml
<?xml version="1.0" encoding="utf-8" ?>
<hibernate-mapping xmlns="urn:nhibernate-mapping-2.2"
    assembly="MappingRecipes"
    namespace="MappingRecipes.ComponentCollections">
    <class name="Customer">
        <id name="Id">
            <generator class="guid.comb"/>
        </id>
        <property name="Name"/>
        <list name="Addresses" table="CustomerAddress">
            <key column="CustomerId"/>
            <index column="AddressIndex"/>
            <composite-element class="Address">
                <property name="AddressLine1"/>
```

```xml
                <property name="AddressLine2"/>
                <property name="City"/>
                <property name="PostalCode"/>
            </composite-element>
        </list>
        <set name="Tags" table="CustomerTag">
            <key column="CustomerId"/>
            <element column="Tag" type="string"/>
        </set>
    </class>
</hibernate-mapping>
```

5. Add a new class named `Recipe` to the folder:

```csharp
using NH4CookbookHelpers;
using NHibernate;

namespace MappingRecipes.ComponentCollections
{

    public class Recipe : HbmMappingRecipe
    {

        protected override void AddInitialData(ISession session)
        {

          session.Save(new Customer
          {

            Name = "Max Weinberg",
             Addresses =
            {

                new Address
                {

                  AddressLine1 = "E Street 1",
                  City = "Belmar, NJ"
                 },
                new Address
                {
                AddressLine1 = "Home street",
```

```
                                City = "Newark, NJ"
                            }
                    },
                    Tags = { "Drummer", "Bruce" }
                });
            }
        }
    }
```

6. Run the application and start the `ComponentCollections` recipe. The query log will look similar to this:

```
INSERT INTO    Customer      (Name, Id)   VALUES    (@p0, @p1);
INSERT INTO    CustomerAddress   (CustomerId, AddressIndex, AddressLine1, AddressLine2, City, PostalCode)   VALUES   (@p0, @p1, @p2, @p3, @p4, @p5);
INSERT INTO    CustomerAddress   (CustomerId, AddressIndex, AddressLine1, AddressLine2, City, PostalCode)   VALUES   (@p0, @p1, @p2, @p3, @p4, @p5);
INSERT INTO    CustomerTag    (CustomerId, Tag)   VALUES    (@p0, @p1);
INSERT INTO    CustomerTag    (CustomerId, Tag)   VALUES    (@p0, @p1);
```

How it works...

Mapping a collection of simple values or components is very similar to mapping a collection of entities. We can use the same type of collections - bags, lists, and sets - following the same rules regarding duplicates and ordering.

Since this kind of collection always is implicitly one-to-many, we cannot specify that in the mapping. Instead, we use `composite-element` for components, specifying the included component properties, or element for simple values. Both require that we specify a separate table where the values should be persisted.

Similar to how it is with the entity collections, a `set` mapping requires working overrides of `Equals` and `GetHashCode` to function properly. Simple value types, such as string, provide this by default. Components, such as `Address`, require a unique implementation.

There's more...

The component collections mapped using `composite-element` may look similar to `component` properties and they are; however, there are a few differences.

A component in a `composite-element` mapping can contain other nested components that should be specified using a `nested-composite-element` tag. However, unlike component properties, they cannot contain collections. The reason for this is simply that all collection relationships require some kind of Id on the parent side and components don't provide this.

Setting up a base entity class

In this recipe, we'll show how to set up a base class for your entities. The purpose of this class is to provide base implementations of potentially tricky `Equals` and `GetHashCode` methods.

How to do it...

1. We create a base class, where the type of `Id` is specified using a generic argument, as shown:

```
public abstract class Entity<TId>
{

  public virtual TId Id { get; protected set; }

  public override bool Equals(object obj)
  {
    return Equals(obj as Entity<TId>);
  }

  private static bool IsTransient(Entity<TId> obj)
  {
    return obj != null &&
           Equals(obj.Id, default(TId));
  }

  private Type GetUnproxiedType()
  {
    return GetType();
  }

  public virtual bool Equals(Entity<TId> other)
  {
    if (other == null)
      return false;

    if (ReferenceEquals(this, other))
      return true;

    if (!IsTransient(this) &&
        !IsTransient(other) &&
        Equals(Id, other.Id))
    {
```

```
            var otherType = other.GetUnproxiedType();
            var thisType = GetUnproxiedType();
            return thisType.IsAssignableFrom(otherType) ||
                    otherType.IsAssignableFrom(thisType);
        }

        return false;
    }

    public override int GetHashCode()
    {
        if (Equals(Id, default(TId)))
            return base.GetHashCode();
        return Id.GetHashCode();
    }

}
```

2. To use this class, our entity classes can simply derive from `Entity<TId>` to inherit the required functionality:

```
public class Employee : Entity<Guid>
{
    public virtual string FirstName {get;set;}
    public virtual string LastName {get;set;}
}
```

How it works...

NHibernate relies on the `Equals` method to determine equality. The default behavior defined in `System.Object` uses reference equality for reference types, including classes. In other words, `x.Equals(y)` is only true when `x` and `y` point to the same object instance. This default works well in most cases.

To support lazy loading, NHibernate uses proxy objects. As we learned in the previous recipe, these proxy objects are subclasses of the real entity class, with every member overridden to enable lazy loading.

This combination of proxy objects and the default `Equals` behavior can lead to subtle and unexpected bugs in your application. An application would not be aware of proxy objects and, therefore, would expect that a proxy and a real instance, representing the same entity, would be equal. A `Product` instance with an Id of 8 should be equal to a different `Product` instance or `Product` proxy with an Id of 8. To handle this, we must override the default `Equals` behavior.

On our entity base class, we override the `Equals` method to determine equality based on POID. In `Equals(Object obj)`, we simply call `Equals(Entity<TId> other)` to cast the object to Entity. If it can't be cast, `null` is passed instead.

If `other` is `null`, the objects are not equal. This serves two purposes. First, `x.Equals(null)` should always return `false`. Second, `someEntity.Equals(notAnEntity)` should also return `false`. Next, we compare references. Obviously, if two variables reference the same instance, they are equal. If `ReferenceEquals(this, other)` returns `true`, we return `true`.

Next, we compare the Ids to the default value to determine if the entities are transient. A transient object is an object that has not been persisted to the database. `default(TId)` returns, the default value, whatever it may be, for `TId`. For `Guid` instance, the default is `Guid.Empty`. For strings and all other reference types, it's `null`. For numeric types, it's zero. If the `Id` property equals the default value, the entity is transient. If one or both entities are transient, we give up and return `false`.

If both entities are persisted, they both have POIDs. We can compare these POIDs to determine equality. If the POIDs do not match, we know that the two entities are not equal and we return `false`.

Finally, we have one last check to do. We know that both entities are persistent and they have the same Id; however, this doesn't prove that they're equal. It's perfectly legal for an `ActorRole` entity to have the same POID as a `Product` entity. Our last check is to compare the types. If one type is assignable to the other type, then we know that the two are equal.

Suppose `other`, a proxy of `Product`, represents a book entity and `this` is an actual `Book` instance representing the same entity. Then, `this.Equals(other)` should return the `true` value because they both represent the same entity. Unfortunately, `other.GetType()` will return the `ProductProxy12398712938` type instead of the `Product` type. As `typeof(ProductProxy12398712938).IsAssignableFrom(typeof(Book))` returns `false`, our `Equals` will fail in this case. However, we can use `other.GetUnproxiedType()` to reach down through the proxy layer and return the entity type. However, since `typeof(Product).IsAssignableFrom(typeof(Book))` returns `true`, our `Equals` implementation works.

Since we have overridden `Equals`, we also need to override `GetHashCode` to satisfy the requirements of the .NET Framework. Specifically, if `x.Equals(y)`, then `x.GetHashCode()` and `y.GetHashCode()` should return the same value. The inverse is not necessarily true; however, `x` and `y` can share a hash code even when they're not equal. In our entity base class, we simply use the hash code of Id, as this is the basis of our equality check.

There's more...

For more information on `Equals` and `GetHashCode`, refer to the MSDN documentation for these methods at `http://msdn.microsoft.com/en-us/library/system.object.aspx`.

See also

> ▸ *Mapping a class with XML*
>
> ▸ *Creating class hierarchy mappings*
>
> ▸ *Mapping a one-to-many relationship*
>
> ▸ *Bidirectional one-to-many class relationships*
>
> ▸ *Handling versioning and concurrency*
>
> ▸ *Creating mappings fluently*

Handling versioning and concurrency

For any multiuser transactional system, you must decide how to handle concurrent updates and possible versioning issues. In this recipe, we will show you how to set up versioning and optimistic concurrency with NHibernate.

Getting ready

Complete the *Getting ready* instructions at the beginning of this chapter.

How to do it...

1. Add a new folder named `Versioning` to the `MappingRecipes` project.

2. Add a new class named `VersionedProduct` to the folder:

```
public class VersionedProduct
{
    public virtual int Id { get; protected set; }
    public virtual int Version { get; protected set; }
    public virtual string Name { get; set; }
    public virtual string Description { get; set; }
}
```

3. Add an embedded mapping named `VersionProduct.hbm.xml`:

```xml
<?xml version="1.0" encoding="utf-8" ?>
<hibernate-mapping xmlns="urn:nhibernate-mapping-2.2"
    assembly="MappingRecipes"
    namespace="MappingRecipes.Versioning">
    <class name="VersionedProduct">
        <id name="Id">
            <generator class="native"/>
        </id>
        <version name="Version" />
        <property name="Name"/>
        <property name="Description"/>
    </class>
</hibernate-mapping>
```

4. Add a new class named `Recipe` to the folder:

```csharp
public class Recipe : HbmMappingRecipe
{
 protected override void AddInitialData(ISession session)
 {
  session.Save(new VersionedProduct
  {
  Name = "Stuff",
   Description = "Cool"
  });
 }

 public override void RunQueries(
ISessionFactory sessionFactory)
 {
  try
  {
   using (var s1 = sessionFactory.OpenSession())
   using (var s2 = sessionFactory.OpenSession())
   using (var tx1 = s1.BeginTransaction())
   using (var tx2 = s2.BeginTransaction())
   {

    var product1 = s1.Get<VersionedProduct>(1);

    var product2 = s2.Get<VersionedProduct>(1);
```

```
        product1.Name = "Modified in session 1";

        product2.Name = "Modified in session 2";

        tx1.Commit();
        Console.WriteLine("Commit 1");
        //This should fail
        tx2.Commit();
        Console.WriteLine("Commit 2");

      }
    }
    catch (Exception ex)
    {
      Console.Error.WriteLine(ex);
    }
    }
  }
```

5. Run the application and start the `Versioning` recipe.

6. Investigate the output and the query log.

```
Commit 1
NHibernate.StaleObjectStateException: Row was updated or deleted by another transaction (or unsaved-value
mapping was incorrect): [MappingRecipes.Versioning.VersionedProduct#1]
   at NHibernate.Persister.Entity.AbstractEntityPersister.Update(Object id, Object[] fields, Object[]
oldFields, Object rowId, Boolean[] includeProperty, Int32 j, Object oldVersion, Object obj, SqlCommandInfo
sql, ISessionImplementor session)
   at NHibernate.Persister.Entity.AbstractEntityPersister.UpdateOrInsert(Object id, Object[] fields,
Object[] oldFields, Object rowId, Boolean[] includeProperty, Int32 j, Object oldVersion, Object obj,
SqlCommandInfo sql, ISessionImplementor session)
```

How it works...

Suppose you have a database application with two users, and user #1 and user #2 both pull up the same data on their screens and make changes. User #1 submits her changes to the database and a few moments later user #2 submits his changes. User #2's changes will silently overwrite user #1's changes without any concurrency check. There are two ways to prevent this: optimistic and pessimistic concurrency.

Optimistic concurrency is the process in which data is checked for changes before any update is executed. In this scenario, user #1 and user #2 both begin their changes. User #1 submits her changes but when user #2 submits his changes, his update will fail because the current data (after user #1's changes) doesn't match the data that user #2 originally read from the database.

In the example shown here, we use the version field to track changes to an entity. Update statements take the following form:

```
UPDATE  Versioned
SET     Version = 2,
        Name = 'Modified in session 1'
WHERE   Id = 1
        AND Version = 1
```

NHibernate checks whether the version is of the same value as when the entity was loaded from the database, and then increments the value. The version field will not be 1 if the entity was already updated and no rows are updated by this statement. NHibernate detects this and throws a StaleStateException, meaning the entity in memory is stale, or out of sync with the database.

Pessimistic concurrency is the process where a user obtains an exclusive lock on the data while they are editing it. It requires us to have the pessimistic view that, given the chance, user #2 will overwrite user #1's changes, so it's best not to let user #2 even look at the data. In this scenario, once user #1 pulls up the data, she has an exclusive lock. User #2 will not be able to read that data. His query will wait until user #1 drops the lock or the query times out. Inevitably, user #1 will take a phone call or step away for a cup of coffee while user #2 waits for access to the data. To implement this kind of locking with NHibernate, your application must call session.Lock within a transaction.

There's more...

In addition to integer version fields, NHibernate allows you to use DateTime based version fields. However, Micorosoft SQL Server has a DateTime resolution of about three milliseconds. This might fail when two updates occur almost simultaneously. We can use SQL Server 2008's DateTime2 data type, which has a resolution of 100 nanoseconds, or SQL Server's timestamp data type for the version field.

NHibernate allows you to use the more traditional form of optimistic concurrency through the optimistic-lock mapping attribute. A simple example would look similar to the following code:

```
<class name="Product"
       dynamic-update="true"
       optimistic-lock="dirty">
```

In this case, changing a `VersionedProduct` name from `Stuff` to `Junk` would generate SQL, as shown in the following code:

```
UPDATE VersionedProduct
SET     Name = 'Junk'
WHERE   Id = 1
        AND Name = 'Stuff'
```

This ensures that another user does not change the `Name` value because this user has already read the value. However, another user may have changed other properties of this entity.

Another alternative is to set `optimistic-lock` to `all`. In this case, an update would generate SQL similar to the following code:

```
UPDATE VersionedProduct
SET     Name = 'Junk' /* @p0 */
WHERE   Id = 1
        AND Name = 'Stuff'
        AND Description = 'Cool'
```

As you might have guessed, in this case, we check the values of all the properties.

When `optimistic-lock` is set to `dirty`, dynamic-update must be `true`. Dynamic update simply means that the `UPDATE` statement only updates dirty properties, or properties with changed values, instead of setting all properties explicitly.

See also

- ▶ *Mapping a class with XML*
- ▶ *Creating class hierarchy mappings*
- ▶ *Mapping a one-to-many relationship*
- ▶ *Setting up a base entity class*
- ▶ *Creating mappings fluently*

Mapping by code

XML files have been NHibernate's default approach to mapping since its inception. It's a platform neutral, flexible and easily parsed format. The mapping syntax for Java's Hibernate is virtually identical to NHibernate's.

NHibernate also allows you to specify the mappings using nothing but code. This gives us a couple of advantages, since the mapping code gets intricately connected to the classes it should map. There is no risk of misspelled class or property names and you can use runtime logic to customize the mappings.

Getting ready

Complete the *Getting ready* instructions given at the beginning of this chapter.

The recipe uses the entity classes that we created in `Eg.Core` in the preceding recipes of this chapter. However, for convenience, `NH4CookbookHelpers` also provide the same class model and we will use that model here. Feel free to modify the code (changing the `using` statements) to use `Eg.Core`, if that suits you better. You may have to add a `version` property (integer) to the `Product` class.

How to do it...

1. Add a new folder named `MappingByCode` to the `MappingRecipes` project.

2. Add a new class named `ProductMapping` to the folder:

```
using NH4CookbookHelpers.Mapping.Model;
using NHibernate.Mapping.ByCode;
using NHibernate.Mapping.ByCode.Conformist;

namespace MappingRecipes.MappingByCode
{
 public class ProductMapping : ClassMapping<Product>
 {
  public ProductMapping()
  {
   Table("Product");
   Id(x => x.Id, x => x.Generator(Generators.GuidComb));
   Version(p => p.Version, v => v.UnsavedValue(0));
   Discriminator(p=>p.Column("ProductType"));
   Property(p => p.Name);
   Property(p => p.Description);
   Property(p => p.UnitPrice);
  }
 }
}
```

3. Add a new class named `MovieMapping` to the folder:

```
using NH4CookbookHelpers.Mapping.Model;
using NHibernate.Mapping.ByCode;
using NHibernate.Mapping.ByCode.Conformist;

namespace MappingRecipes.MappingByCode
{
 public class MovieMapping : SubclassMapping<Movie>
 {
  public MovieMapping()
  {
   DiscriminatorValue("Movie");
   Property(x => x.Director);
   List(x => x.Actors, x =>
    {
     x.Key(k => k.Column("MovieId"));
     x.Index(i => i.Column("ActorIndex"));
     x.Cascade(Cascade.All | Cascade.DeleteOrphans);
    }
    , x => x.OneToMany()
   );
  }
 }
}
```

4. Add a new class named `BookMapping` to the folder:

```
using NH4CookbookHelpers.Mapping.Model;
using NHibernate.Mapping.ByCode.Conformist;

namespace MappingRecipes.MappingByCode
{
 public class BookMapping : SubclassMapping<Book>
 {
  public BookMapping()
  {
   DiscriminatorValue("Book");
   Property(x => x.Author);
   Property(x => x.ISBN);
  }
 }
}
```

5. Add a new class named `ActorRoleMapping` to the folder:

```
using NH4CookbookHelpers.Mapping.Model;
using NHibernate.Mapping.ByCode;
using NHibernate.Mapping.ByCode.Conformist;

namespace MappingRecipes.MappingByCode
{
 public class ActorRoleMapping : Class-Mapping<ActorRole>
 {
  public ActorRoleMapping()
  {
   Id(x => x.Id, x =>
x.Generator(new Generators.GuidComb));
   Property(x => x.Actor);
   Property(x => x.Role);
  }
 }
}
```

6. Add a new class named `Recipe` to the folder:

```
using System.Collections.Generic;
using NH4CookbookHelpers.Mapping;
using NH4CookbookHelpers.Mapping.Model;
using NHibernate;
using NHibernate.Cfg;
using NHibernate.Mapping.ByCode;

namespace MappingRecipes.MappingByCode
{
 public class Recipe : BaseMappingRecipe
 {
  protected override void Configure(Configuration cfg)
  {
   var mapper = new ModelMapper();
   mapper.AddMapping<ProductMapping>();
   mapper.AddMapping<MovieMapping>();
   mapper.AddMapping<BookMapping>();
   mapper.AddMapping<ActorRoleMapping>();

   var mapping =
```

```
mapper.CompileMappingForAllExplicitlyAddedEntities();
  cfg.AddMapping(mapping);
}

protected override void AddInitialData(ISession session)
{
 session.Save(new Movie
 {
  Name = "Mapping by code - the movie",
  Description = "An interesting documentary",
  UnitPrice = 300,
  Actors = new List<ActorRole> {
 new ActorRole {
 Actor = "You",
   Role = "The mapper"
   }
 }
 });
}
}
}
```

7. Run the application and start the `MappingByCode` recipe.

8. Investigate the query log.

How it works...

When NHibernate processes an XML-based mapping, it deserializes the XML into an in-memory structure of all the included mappings, called an `HbmMapping`. Using coded mappings, the same structure is produced from code without deserialization.

The `ModelMapper` is responsible for translating the `ClassMapping` and `SubclassMapping` classes into a well-structured `HbmMapping`. In this recipe, we added all the mappings explicitly, using the `AddMapping<T>` method, and therefore we could use the aptly named `CompileMappingForAllExplicitlyAddedEntities` method to generate the `HbmMapping`.

As you may have noticed, the naming of methods and properties in the mapping code very closely mimic that of elements and attributes in the HBM files. This was a deliberate design decision, to make it easy to translate HBM concepts and examples into coded mappings.

The following are a couple of examples:

XML mapping	Code mapping
`<property name="Author">`	`Property(x => x.Author)`

`<list name="Actors"`
`cascade=`
`"all-delete-orphan" >`
`    <key column="MovieId" />`
`    <index`
`column="ActorIndex" />`
`    <one-to-many`
`class="ActorRole"/>`
`</list>`
	`List(x => x.Actors, x =>{`
	`        x.Key(k =>`
	`k.Column("MovieId"));`
	`        x.Index(i =>`
	`i.Column("ActorIndex"));`
	`        x.Cascade(`
	`Cascade.All |`
	`Cascade.DeleteOrphans);`
	`    }`
	`    , x => x.OneToMany()`
	`)`

`<many-to-one`
`name="Publisher"`
`cascade="save-update">`
`    <column`
`name="PublisherId"/>`
`</many-to-one>`
	`ManyToOne(x => x.Author, x =>{`
	`    x.Column(`
	`"PublisherId");`
	`    x.Cascade(`
	`Cascade.Persist);`
	`});`

There's more...

It's not strictly necessary to use the separate mapping classes (`ClassMapping`, `SubclassMapping`, and so on.). These are just encapsulated ways to add mapping data to the model mapper. Mappings can also be added using the `Class<T>` or `Subclass<T>` methods:

```
var mapper = new ModelMapper();
mapper.Class<Product>(m =>
{
    m.Table("Product");
    m.Id(p => p.Id, p => p.Generator(Generators.GuidComb));
    m.Version(p => p.Version, v => v.UnsavedValue(0));
    m.Discriminator(p => p.Column("ProductType"));
    m.Property(p => p.Name);
    m.Property(p => p.Description);
    m.Property(p => p.UnitPrice);
});
```

Mapping a large object model like this tends to become unmanageable, but of course you could pass the `ModelMapper` instance around to different mapping contributors, if this is a syntax you prefer.

The `ModelMapper` exposes a large set of events that are fired when the mappings are generated. We can add handlers to those events, not just to inspect the process, but also to modify the mappings as they are generated. How these events are used is described in the next recipe.

See also

▸ *Mapping a class with XML*

▸ *Mapping by convention*

▸ *Creating mappings fluently*

Mapping by convention

In large object models, you will notice that many aspects of the mappings are repetitive. Maybe the Comb generator should generate all POIDs or all properties referencing a class without an Id property should be treated as a component mapping. By setting up mapping conventions, you can potentially avoid all explicit mappings and instead let the code structure do the work for you.

Getting ready

Complete the *Getting ready* instructions at the beginning of this chapter.

How to do it...

1. Add a folder named `MappingByConvention` to the `MappingRecipes` project.

2. Add a class named `MyModelMapper` to the folder:

```
using System.Collections.Generic;
using System.Linq;
using System.Reflection;
using NH4CookbookHelpers.Mapping.Model;
using NHibernate.Mapping.ByCode;

namespace MappingRecipes.MappingByConvention
{
  public class MyModelMapper : ConventionModelMapper
  {
    public MyModelMapper()
    {
      IsEntity((t, declared) =>
```

```
      typeof(Entity).IsAssignableFrom(t) &&
      typeof(Entity) != t);

  IsRootEntity((t, declared) =>
    t.BaseType == typeof(Entity));

  IsList((member, declared) =>
    member
      .GetPropertyOrFieldType()
      .IsGenericType &&
    member
      .GetPropertyOrFieldType()
      .GetGenericInterfaceTypeDefinitions()
      .Contains(typeof(IList<>)));


  IsVersion((member, declared) =>
    member.Name == "Version" &&
    member.MemberType == MemberTypes.Property &&
    member.GetPropertyOrFieldType() == typeof(int));

  IsTablePerClassHierarchy((t, declared) =>
    typeof(Product).IsAssignableFrom(t));

  BeforeMapSubclass += ConfigureDiscriminatorValue;
  BeforeMapClass += ConfigureDiscriminatorColumn;
  BeforeMapClass += ConfigurePoidGenerator;
  BeforeMapList += ConfigureListCascading;
}


private void ConfigureListCascading(
  IModelInspector modelInspector, PropertyPath member,
  IListPropertiesMapper propertyCustomizer)
{
  propertyCustomizer.Cascade(Cascade.All |
    Cascade.DeleteOrphans);
}

private void ConfigurePoidGenerator(
  IModelInspector modelInspector, System.Type type,
  IClassAttributesMapper classCustomizer)
{
```

```
        classCustomizer.Id(id =>
          id.Generator(Generators.GuidComb));
      }

    private void ConfigureDiscriminatorColumn(
      IModelInspector modelInspector, System.Type type,
      IClassAttributesMapper classCustomizer)
    {
      if (modelInspector.IsTablePerClassHierarchy(type))
      {
        classCustomizer.Discriminator(x =>
          x.Column(type.Name + "Type"));
      }
    }

    private void ConfigureDiscriminatorValue(
      IModelInspector modelInspector, System.Type type,
      ISubclassAttributesMapper subclassCustomizer)
    {
      subclassCustomizer.DiscriminatorValue(type.Name);
    }
  }
}
```

3. Add a new class named `Recipe` to the folder:

```
using System.Collections.Generic;
using System.Linq;
using NH4CookbookHelpers.Mapping;
using NH4CookbookHelpers.Mapping.Model;
using NHibernate;
using NHibernate.Cfg;

namespace MappingRecipes.MappingByConvention
{
 public class Recipe : BaseMappingRecipe
 {
  protected override void Configure(Configuration cfg)
  {
   var mapper = new MyModelMapper();
   var mapping = mapper
     .CompileMappingFor(typeof(Product).Assembly
     .GetExportedTypes()
```

```
.Where(x => x.Namespace == typeof(Product).Namespace));

  cfg.AddMapping(mapping);
}

protected override void AddInitialData(ISession session)
{
  session.Save(new Movie
  {
   Name = "Mapping by convention - the movie",
   Description = "An interesting documentary",
   UnitPrice = 300,
   Actors = new List<ActorRole> {
    new ActorRole {
     Actor = "NHibernate",
     Role = "The mapper"
    }
   }
  });
 }
}
}
```

4. Run the application and start the `MappingByConvention` recipe.

How it works...

Convention mapping in NHibernate has two main components.

▸ **The model inspector**: A model inspector, which is a class that implements the `IModelInspector` interface, is responsible for providing answers to questions that the mapping process asks about classes and properties:

    ❑ Is this a class that should be mapped?

    ❑ Is this collection property a list, a set or a bag?

    ❑ Is this class part of an inheritance hierarchy?

    ❑ Is this a version property?

    ...and many more.

▸ **The model mapper**: A model mapper is an instance of the `ModelMapper` class or a class deriving from it. It uses an assigned `IModelInspector` to investigate the entity classes and builds a `HbmMapping` instance. While it does that, it fires off a set of events, such as `BeforeMapClass` and `AfterMapProperty`, at different stages of the process. By adding handlers to these events, we can influence the outcome.

In the recipe, we created our own `ModelMapper`, by deriving it from `ConventionModelMapper`. This base class is convenient since it provides a set of useful defaults, and allows us to configure both the model inspection and the event handlers in the same place.

Our `MyModelMapper` starts by defining the classes that should be included in the mapping:

```
IsEntity((t, declared) => typeof(Entity).IsAssignableFrom(t) &&
typeof(Entity) != t);
```

We want all classes deriving from `Entity` to be included, but not `Entity` itself.

Next, we define which classes are `root` classes that are they are not subclasses of other mapped classes. In our example, `Product` is such a class, but `Movie` is not:

```
IsRootEntity((t, declared) => t.BaseType == typeof(Entity));
```

This will only return `true` for classes directly deriving from `Entity`. `Movie` and `Book` derives from `Product`, so they will not be considered `root` entities.

Next, comes a slightly more advanced check, which is supposed to identify whether a property (or a field) is an `IList<T>` and subsequently should be mapped as a `<list>`:

```
IsList((member, declared) =>
    member
        .GetPropertyOrFieldType()
        .IsGenericType &&
    member
        .GetPropertyOrFieldType()
        .GetGenericInterfaceTypeDefinitions()
        .Contains(typeof(IList<>)));
```

The `IsVersion` call should be rather self-explanatory. Any integer property named Version will be mapped as a version property:

```
IsVersion((member, declared) =>
                member.Name == "Version" &&
                member.MemberType == MemberTypes.Property &&
                member.GetPropertyOrFieldType() == typeof(int));
```

In order to specify that `Book` and `Movie` should be mapped as subclasses of `Product`, sharing the same table, we answer the following question:

```
IsTablePerClassHierarchy((t, declared) =>
typeof(Product).IsAssignableFrom(t));
```

Note that we return `true` for the base class itself.

Next come the event handlers and we set them up as shown:

```
BeforeMapSubclass += ConfigureDiscriminatorValue;
BeforeMapClass += ConfigureDiscriminatorColumn;
BeforeMapClass += ConfigurePoidGenerator;
BeforeMapList += ConfigureListCascading;
```

Note the `+=` operator, typical for events. We can add as many handlers to an event as we want and they will be invoked in the order they were added to the specific event. This makes it easy to keep the different handlers short and to the point. For example, in this recipe we have separated `ConfigureDiscriminatorColumn` and `ConfigurePoidGenerator`. Both are handlers for `BeforeMapClass`, but since they handle completely different aspects, we keep them separate.

Once we have set up our model mapper (and inspector), all we need to create and add the mappings are:

```
var mapper = new MyModelMapper();
var mapping = mapper.CompileMappingFor(typeof(Product).Assembly
    .GetExportedTypes()
    .Where(x => x.Namespace == typeof(Product).Namespace));
cfg.AddMapping(mapping);
```

Actually, this specific case was a bit more convoluted than usually necessary, since we only wanted the classes in the same namespace as `Product`. `CompileMappingFor` simply takes an enumerable of classes that it should include in the mapping.

There's more...

The model-mapping infrastructure is sufficiently powerful to accommodate almost any kind of conventions and customizations you may want to use. Consider, for instance, how to distinguish between the collections that should be mapped as `<set>` and the ones that should be mapped as `<bag>` or `<list>`. Our implementation of `IsSet`, `IsBag`, and `IsList` can check the property type (for example, mapping all `ISet<T>` as a `<set>`), but it can also use a property name convention, or perhaps even some kind of `IsSetAttribute`, applied to the property.

In a similar way, we could decide whether an instance should cascade changes to related entities, perhaps based on whether those entities belong to the same aggregate (root owning entity).

The event handlers we used were all of the before kind. These could be called default conventions, since they are applied before any implicit or explicit customizations (such as those inside the `ClassMappings` we created in the previous recipe) are performed. You can also add after handlers. They are applied at the very end, and can override any choices made. We could therefore call these enforced conventions.

Creating mappings fluently

Even before NHibernate added the possibility to provide mappings in code, the **Fluent NHibernate project** (**FNH**) delivered a strongly-typed, fluent syntax, as an alternative to XML mappings. It remains very popular and many NHibernate articles online show examples using FNH mappings. In this recipe, we will show you how to map our product model using Fluent NHibernate.

Getting ready

Complete the *Getting ready* instructions at the beginning of this chapter.

How to do it...

1. Add a new folder named `MappingWithFluent` to the `MappingRecipes` project.

2. Add a reference to the `FluentNHibernate` package using Nuget package manager console.

3. Create a new class named `ProductMap` with the following code:

```
using NH4CookbookHelpers.Mapping.Model;
using FluentNHibernate.Mapping;


namespace MappingRecipes.MappingWithFluent
{
 public class ProductMap : ClassMap<Product>
  {
   public ProductMap()
   {
     Id(p => p.Id).GeneratedBy.GuidComb();
     Version(x => x.Version);
     NaturalId().Property(p => p.Name).Not.ReadOnly();
     DiscriminateSubClassesOnColumn("ProductType");
     Map(p => p.Description);
     Map(p => p.UnitPrice);
   }
  }
}
```

4. Create a new class named `BookMap` with the following code:

```
using FluentNHibernate.Mapping;
using NH4CookbookHelpers.Mapping.Model;

namespace MappingRecipes.MappingWithFluent
{
 public class BookMap : SubclassMap<Book>
 {

  public BookMap()
  {
   DiscriminatorValue("Book");
   Map(p => p.Author);
   Map(p => p.ISBN);
  }
 }
}
```

5. Create a new class named `MovieMap` with the following code:

```
using FluentNHibernate.Mapping;
using NH4CookbookHelpers.Mapping.Model;

namespace MappingRecipes.MappingWithFluent
{
 public class MovieMap : SubclassMap<Movie>
 {
  public MovieMap()
  {
   DiscriminatorValue("Movie");
   Map(m => m.Director);
   HasMany(m => m.Actors)
     .KeyColumn("MovieId")
     .AsList(l => l.Column("ActorIndex"))
     .Cascade.AllDeleteOrphan();
  }
 }
}
```

6. Create a new class named `ActorRoleMap` with the following code:

```csharp
using FluentNHibernate.Mapping;
using NH4CookbookHelpers.Mapping.Model;

namespace MappingRecipes.MappingWithFluent
{
 public class ActorRoleMap : ClassMap<ActorRole>
 {

  public ActorRoleMap()
  {
   Id(ar => ar.Id).GeneratedBy.GuidComb();
   Map(ar => ar.Actor).Not.Nullable();
   Map(ar => ar.Role).Not.Nullable();
  }
 }
}
```

7. Add a new class named `Recipe` with the following code:

```csharp
using FluentNHibernate;
using NH4CookbookHelpers.Mapping;
using NH4CookbookHelpers.Mapping.Model;
using NHibernate;
using NHibernate.Cfg;

namespace MappingRecipes.MappingWithFluent
{
 public class Recipe : BaseMappingRecipe
 {
  protected override void Configure(Configuration cfg)
  {
   cfg.AddMappingsFromAssembly(GetType().Assembly);
  }

  protected override void AddInitialData(ISession session)
  {
   session.Save(new Movie()
   {
    Name = "Fluent mapping - the movie",
    Description = "Go with the flow.",
    UnitPrice = 300,
```

```
        Actors = { new ActorRole { Actor = "FNH", Role = "The mapper"
    } }
      });
    }
   }
  }
```

8. Run the application and start the `MappingWithFluent` recipe.

How it works...

Fluent NHibernate provides two methods for mappings: Fluent mapping syntax and `automapping`. In this recipe, we use the Fluent mapping syntax. Each entity class has a corresponding mapping class.

Mappings for `root` classes are inherited from `ClassMap` and subclasses in a class hierarchy inherit from `SubclassMap`. By default, Fluent NHibernate creates a table-per-subclass hierarchy. To use a table-per-class hierarchy instead, we specify `DiscriminateSubClassesOnColumn` in `Product`.

When mapping the natural id of `Product`, we specify `.Not.ReadOnly()`. This is the same as setting `mutable="true"` in the XML mapping.

Properties are mapped using the `Map()` method, which is equivalent to the `property` element in XML mappings.

One-to-many collections are mapped using the `HasMany()` method, followed by `AsMap()`, `AsBag()`, `AsSet()`, or `AsList()`. `AsList` uses the `Column()` method to specify a column name for the list index.

See also

▸ *Mapping a class with XML*

▸ *Creating class hierarchy mappings*

▸ *Mapping a one-to-many relationship*

▸ *Setting up a base entity class*

▸ *Bidirectional one-to-many class relationships*

▸ *Handling versioning and concurrency*

▸ *Creating mappings fluently*

Bidirectional one-to-many class relationships

It's often very useful to have a bidirectional relationship between entities. It also simplifies matters for NHibernate, which can often produce more efficient persistence queries when both sides of a relationship are involved.

In this recipe, we will show you how to set up a bidirectional one-to-many relationship between two entity classes.

How to do it...

1. Add a new folder named `Bidirectional` to the `MappingRecipes` project.

2. Add the following `Order` class:

```
public class Order
{
  private ISet<OrderItem> _items;
  private ISet<Project> _projects;

  public virtual Guid Id { get; protected set; }

  public Order()
  {
    _items = new HashSet<OrderItem>();
    _projects = new HashSet<Project>();
  }


  public virtual IEnumerable<OrderItem> Items
  {
    get
    {
      return _items;
    }
  }

  public virtual IEnumerable<Project> Projects
  {
    get
    {
```

```
      return _projects;
    }
  }

  public virtual bool AddItem(OrderItem newItem)
  {
    if (newItem != null && _items.Add(newItem))
    {
      newItem.SetOrder(this);
      return true;
    }
    return false;
  }

  public virtual bool RemoveItem(
    OrderItem itemToRemove)
  {
    if (itemToRemove != null &&
      _items.Remove(itemToRemove))
    {
      itemToRemove.SetOrder(null);
      return true;
    }
    return false;
  }

  public virtual bool ConnectProject(Project project)
  {
    if (project != null && _projects.Add(project))
    {
      project.ConnectOrder(this);
      return true;
    }
    return false;
  }

  public virtual bool DisconnectProject(Project project)
  {
    if (project != null && _projects.Contains(project))
    {
      _projects.Remove(project);
```

```
            project.DisconnectOrder(this);
            return true;
        }
        return false;
    }
}
```

3. Add the following `OrderItem` class:

```csharp
public class OrderItem
{
    protected OrderItem()
    {

    }

    public OrderItem(string name)
    {
        Name = name;
    }

    public virtual string Name { get; set; }

    public virtual Guid Id { get; protected set; }

    public virtual Order Order { get; protected set; }

    public virtual void SetOrder(Order newOrder)
    {
        var prevOrder = Order;

        if (newOrder == prevOrder)
            return;

        Order = newOrder;

        if (prevOrder != null)
            prevOrder.RemoveItem(this);

        if (newOrder != null)
            newOrder.AddItem(this);

    }
}
```

4. Add the following `Project` class:

```
public class Project
{
  private ISet<Order> _orders;

  public Project()
  {
    _orders = new HashSet<Order>();
  }
  public virtual Guid Id { get; protected set; }

  public virtual IEnumerable<Order> Orders
  {
    get
    {
      return _orders;
    }
  }

  public virtual bool ConnectOrder(Order order)
  {
    if (order != null && _orders.Add(order))
    {
      order.ConnectProject(this);
      return true;
    }
    return false;
  }

  public virtual bool DisconnectOrder(Order order)
  {
    if (order != null && _orders.Contains(order))
    {
      _orders.Remove(order);
      order.DisconnectProject(this);
      return true;
    }
    return false;
  }
}
```

5. Add the mapping for the three classes as an embedded resource named `Mapping.`
   `hbm.xml:`

```xml
<?xml version="1.0" encoding="utf-8" ?>
<hibernate-mapping xmlns="urn:nhibernate-mapping-2.2"
  assembly="MappingRecipes"
  namespace="MappingRecipes.Bidirectional">
  <class name="OrderItem">
    <id name="Id">
      <generator class="guid.comb" />
    </id>
    <property name="Name"/>
    <many-to-one name="Order" column="OrderId" />
  </class>
  <class name="Order" table="`Order`">
    <id name="Id">
      <generator class="guid.comb" />
    </id>
    <set name="Items"
      cascade="all-delete-orphan"
      inverse="true"
      access="field.camelcase-underscore">
      <key column="OrderId" />
      <one-to-many class="OrderItem"/>
    </set>
    <set name="Projects"
      inverse="true"
      access="field.camelcase-underscore"
      table="OrderProject">
      <key column="OrderId"/>
      <many-to-many class="Project" column="ProjectId"/>
    </set>
  </class>
  <class name="Project" table="Project">
    <id name="Id">
      <generator class="guid.comb" />
    </id>
    <set name="Orders"
      access="field.camelcase-underscore"
      table="OrderProject">
      <key column="ProjectId"/>
      <many-to-many class="Order" column="OrderId"/>
    </set>
  </class>
</hibernate-mapping>
```

6. Run the application and start the `Bidirectional` recipe:

```
INSERT  INTO    Project     (Id)    VALUES      (@p0);
INSERT  INTO    Project     (Id)    VALUES      (@p0);
INSERT  INTO    "Order"     (Id)    VALUES      (@p0);
INSERT  INTO    OrderItem       (Name, OrderId, Id)     VALUES      (@p0, @p1, @p2);
INSERT  INTO    "Order"     (Id)    VALUES      (@p0);
INSERT  INTO    OrderItem       (Name, OrderId, Id)     VALUES      (@p0, @p1, @p2);
INSERT  INTO    OrderItem       (Name, OrderId, Id)     VALUES      (@p0, @p1, @p2);
INSERT  INTO    OrderProject        (ProjectId, OrderId)    VALUES      (@p0, @p1);
INSERT  INTO    OrderProject        (ProjectId, OrderId)    VALUES      (@p0, @p1);
INSERT  INTO    OrderProject        (ProjectId, OrderId)    VALUES      (@p0, @p1);
SELECT      this_.Id as Id3_0_    FROM        Project this_
SELECT      orders0_.ProjectId as ProjectId1_,    orders0_.OrderId as OrderId1_,    order1_.Id as Id1_0_    FROM        OrderProject orders0_    left outer join
SELECT      items0_.OrderId as OrderId1_,    items0_.Id as Id1_,    items0_.Id as Id0_0_,    items0_.Name as Name0_0_,    items0_.OrderId as OrderId0_
SELECT      items0_.OrderId as OrderId1_,    items0_.Id as Id1_,    items0_.Id as Id0_0_,    items0_.Name as Name0_0_,    items0_.OrderId as OrderId0_
SELECT      orders0_.ProjectId as ProjectId1_,    orders0_.OrderId as OrderId1_,    order1_.Id as Id1_0_    FROM        OrderProject orders0_    left outer join
```

Note how all entities and relations are inserted at once, without the redundant UPDATE statements; this is one of the benefits of a properly set up bidirectional relationship.

How it works...

Object Relational Mapper (**ORM**) is designed to overcome the impedance mismatch between the object model in the application and the relational model in the database. This mismatch is especially evident when representing a bidirectional one-to-many relationship between entities. In the relational model, a single foreign key represents this bidirectional relationship. In the object model, the parent entity has a collection of children, and each child has a reference to its parent.

To work around this mismatch, NHibernate ignores one side of the bidirectional relationship. The foreign key in the database is populated based on either the OrderItems reference to the Order or the Orders collection of OrderItems, but not both. We determine which end of the relationship controls the foreign key using the inverse attribute on the collection. By default, the Order controls the foreign key. Saving a new Order with one OrderItem will result in the following three SQL statements:

```
INSERT INTO "Order" (Id) VALUES (@p0)

INSERT INTO OrderItem (Id) VALUES (@p0)

UPDATE OrderItem SET OrderId = @p0 WHERE Id = @p1
```

When we specify inverse="true", the OrderItem controls the foreign key. This is preferable because it eliminates the extra UPDATE statement, resulting in the following two SQL statements:

```
INSERT INTO "Order" (Id) VALUES (@p0)

INSERT INTO OrderItem (OrderId, Id) VALUES (@p0, @p1)
```

We are responsible for keeping both sides of our two-way relationship in sync. In a normal class, we would add code in the property setter or the collection's add or remove methods to update the other end of the relationship automatically. NHibernate, however, throws exceptions when an object is manipulated while NHibernate is initializing it.

For this reason, it's suggested that we prevent direct manipulation of either end of the relationship, and instead use methods specifically written for this purpose, as we've done here with `AddItem`, `RemoveItem`, and `SetOrder`. Note that we've mapped a set, which implies that the order is not significant, and that duplicates are not allowed.

There's more...

Notice the use of back ticks in our table name from the `Order` mapping as follows:

```
<class name="Order" table="`Order`">
```

In Microsoft SQL Server, `Order` is a keyword. If we want to use it as an identifier, a table name in this case, NHibernate will need to put quotes around it. The back ticks tell NHibernate to surround the identifier with whatever characters may be appropriate for the database you are using.

Mapping enumerations

An improperly mapped enumeration can lead to unnecessary updates. In this recipe, we'll discuss why and show you how to map an enumeration property to a string field.

How to do it...

1. Add a new folder named `Enumerations` to the `MappingRecipes` project.

2. Add the following `AccountTypes` enum to the folder:
```
public enum AccountTypes
{
    Consumer,
    Business,
    Corporate,
    NonProfit
}
```

3. Add the following `Account` class:
```
public class Account
{
    public virtual Guid Id { get; set; }
    public virtual AccountTypes AcctType { get; set; }
```

```
  public virtual string Number { get; set; }
  public virtual string Name { get; set; }
}
```

4. Add an embedded NHibernate mapping document named `Account.hbm.xml` with the following class mapping:

```xml
<class name="Account">
  <id name="Id">
    <generator class="guid.comb" />
  </id>
  <natural-id>
    <property name="Number" not-null="true"  />
  </natural-id>
  <property name="Name" not-null="true" />
  <property name="AcctType" not-null="true" />
</class>
```

5. On the `property` element for `AcctType`, add a `type` attribute with the following value:

```
NHibernate.Type.EnumStringType`1[[MappingRecipes.Enumerations.
AccountTypes, MappingRecipes]], NHibernate
```

6. Add the following `Recipe` class:

```csharp
using System;
using NH4CookbookHelpers.Mapping;
using NHibernate;

namespace MappingRecipes.Enumerations
{
  public class Recipe : HbmMappingRecipe
  {
    protected override void AddInitialData(ISession session)
    {
      session.Save(new Account
      {
        Name = "Test account",
        Number = "1",
        AcctType = AccountTypes.Consumer
      });
    }

    public override void RunQueries(ISession session)
    {
      var accounts=session.QueryOver<Account>()
```

```
            .OrderBy(x=>x.Name).Asc
            .List();

        foreach (var account in accounts)
        {
            Console.WriteLine("Account name: {0},type: {1}",account.
Name,account.AcctType);
        }
    }
  }
}
```

How it works...

By default, NHibernate will map an enumeration to a numeric field based on the enumeration's underlying type, typically an int. For example, if we set `AcctType` to `AccountTypes.Corporate`, the `AcctType` database field would hold the integer 2. This has two significant drawbacks. An integer value by itself doesn't describe the business meaning of the data. Also, if the order of the enum members change and they don't have assigned values, the wrong `AccountTypes` value will be returned for previously stored entities.

One solution, shown here, is to store the name of the enumeration value in a string field. For example, if we set `AcctType` to `AccountTypes.Corporate`, the `AcctType` database field would hold the string value `Corporate`.

By specifying a `type` attribute for `AcctType`, we tell NHibernate to use a custom class for conversion between .NET types and the database. NHibernate includes `EnumStringType<T>` to override the conversion of enumeration values to database values so that the string name is stored, not the numeric value.

The `type` value: `NHibenate.Type.EnumStringType`1[[MappingRecipes.Enumerations.AccountTypes, MappingRecipes]]`, `NHibernate` is the assembly qualified name for `NHibernate.Type.EnumStringType<AccountTypes>`.

Unnecessary updates

In the introduction to this recipe, we mentioned that an improperly mapped enum can lead to unnecessary updates. What did we mean by that? Let's try to introduce that error!

1. In the mapping document, remove the `not-null="true"` attribute on `AcctType`.

2. In the `Recipe` class' `AddInitialData` method, add this code to force an `Account` into the database via plain SQL:

```
session.CreateSQLQuery(
@"INSERT INTO Account (Id,Name,Number)
  VAlUES(:id,:name,:number)")
```

```
.SetGuid("id", Guid.NewGuid())
.SetString("name", "Test account 2")
.SetString("number", "2")
.ExecuteUpdate();
```

3. Start the recipe again and take note of the query log.

If things worked as expected, will we see an UPDATE query after the SELECT? Why on earth?

When we force inserted the Account via SQL, we omitted the AcctType column, resulting in a NULL value in that column. The query in RunQueries then loads this data from the database and maps it into new Account instances. Since the AcctType property is an enum, it tried to map the NULL into a valid enum member, which is not possible. Instead, it falls back to the first enum member, in this case Consumer. When the session is finally flushed (caused by the transaction commit), NHibernate sees that the persistable data for the Account instance is different from the way it looked when the data was loaded. The entity is classified as being dirty and NHibernate accordingly issues an UPDATE.

This problem is not unique to enums. It can happen any time you use a value type (int, decimal, Guid, and so on.) property and the corresponding database column allows NULL values. There are two solutions to this problem:

▶ Make the property nullable, for example using int? or AccountTypes?
▶ Modify the database to disallow NULL values.

See also

▶ *Using the Ghostbusters test*

Immutable entities

An immutable entity is an entity that never changes once it has been created. An example could be entries in event log. New log entries may be added all the time; however, once saved, they are not supposed to be modified.

This behavior could of course be enforced in code, or perhaps even in the database, but if we tell NHibernate to treat specific classes as immutable, we can both enforce the immutability and allow NHibernate optimize performance a bit.

Getting ready

Complete the *Getting ready* instructions at the beginning of this chapter.

How to do it...

1. Add a new folder named `ImmutableEntities` to the `MappingRecipes` project.

2. Add a new class named `LogEntry` to the folder:

```
using System;

namespace MappingRecipes.ImmutableEntities
{
  public class LogEntry
  {
    public virtual Guid Id { get; protected set; }
    public virtual string Message { get; set; }
  }
}
```

3. Add a new embedded mapping named `LogEntry.hbm.xml` to the folder:

```xml
<?xml version="1.0" encoding="utf-8" ?>
<hibernate-mapping xmlns="urn:nhibernate-mapping-2.2"
  assembly="MappingRecipes"
  namespace="MappingRecipes.ImmutableEntities">
  <class name="LogEntry" mutable="false">
    <id name="Id">
      <generator class="guid.comb"/>
    </id>
    <property name="Message"/>
  </class>
</hibernate-mapping>
```

4. Add a new class named `Recipe` to the folder:

```
using System;
using NH4CookbookHelpers.Mapping;
using NHibernate;

namespace MappingRecipes.ImmutableEntities
{
  public class Recipe : HbmMappingRecipe
  {
    protected override void AddInitialData(
      ISession session)
    {
      for (var i = 0; i < 10; i++)
      {
```

```
        session.Save(new LogEntry
        {
          Message = "Message " + i
        });
      }
    }

    public override void RunQueries(
      ISessionFactory sessionFactory)
    {
      using (var session = sessionFactory.OpenSession())
      {
        using (var tx = session.BeginTransaction())
        {
          var logEntries =
            session.QueryOver<LogEntry>().List();
          foreach (var logEntry in logEntries)
          {
            logEntry.Message = "Edited message";
          }
          tx.Commit();
        }
      }

      using (var session = sessionFactory.OpenSession())
      {
        using (var tx = session.BeginTransaction())
        {
          var logEntries = session.QueryOver<LogEntry>().List();
          foreach (var logEntry in logEntries)
          {
            Console.WriteLine(logEntry.Message);
          }
        }
      }
    }
  }
}
```

5. Run the application and start the `ImmutableEntities` recipe.

How it works...

In the recipe we tell NHibernate that the `LogEntry` class should be treated as immutable by adding `mutable="false"` to the class mapping. We can save a new entry to the database without issues, but if we later on try to modify that entry, nothing happens. NHibernate sees that the entity is immutable and silently ignores any updates that were made. Not only does this protect the entry from being modified, but it also reduces both processor and memory utilization, since no dirty check needs to be performed.

It would seem then that an immutable entity is just silently ignored when NHibernate updates the database. That is not entirely true, though. Some things may still happen:

- ▸ Immutable entities can be deleted
- ▸ If the immutable entity has a collection property (one-to-many or many-to-many), this collection will be persisted to the database if it is modified.
- ▸ If the entity is versioned, using the version mapping, a collection modification will cause the version to be updated.

NHibernate can also make entities read-only on demand. This can be useful when one part of the application is allowed to modify the entries, but another part, like the public front end of a web site, only should be used for reading and querying. We will dig deeper into that in *Chapter 5, Improving Performance*.

Mapping relations to non-primary keys

In legacy databases, sometimes data is stored in ways that doesn't quite map to an object model. One such scenario is when the relation between for example a `Customer` and its `ContactPersons` is controlled by a column other than the primary key in the `Customer` table. NHibernate provides a way to handle these relations, using the property-ref mapping attribute.

Getting ready

Complete the *Getting ready* instructions at the beginning of this chapter.

How to do it...

1. Add a new folder named `PropertyRefs` to the `MappingRecipes` project.
2. Add a class named `Customer` to the folder:

```
using System.Collections.Generic;

namespace MappingRecipes.PropertyRefs
{
```

```
   public class Customer
   {
     public Customer()
     {
       ContactPersons=new HashSet<ContactPerson>();
     }
     public virtual int Id { get; protected set; }
     public virtual string Name { get; set; }
     public virtual ISet<ContactPerson> ContactPersons
 {
   get;
   set;
 }
     public virtual int CompanyId { get; set; }


   }
 }
```

3. Add a class named `ContactPerson` to the folder:

```
namespace MappingRecipes.PropertyRefs
{
  public class ContactPerson
  {
    public virtual int Id { get; protected set; }
    public virtual string Name { get; set; }
    public virtual Customer Customer { get; set; }
  }
}
```

4. Add a new embedded mapping named `Mapping.hbm.xml` to the folder:

```xml
<?xml version="1.0" encoding="utf-8" ?>
<hibernate-mapping xmlns="urn:nhibernate-mapping-2.2"
  assembly="MappingRecipes"
  namespace="MappingRecipes.PropertyRefs">
  <class name="Customer">
    <id name="Id">
      <generator class="native"/>
    </id>
    <property name="Name"/>
    <property name="CompanyId" />
    <set name="ContactPersons"
      cascade="save-update"
      inverse="true">
      <key column="CompanyId"
```

```
              property-ref="CompanyId"/>
            <one-to-many class="ContactPerson"/>
          </set>
        </class>
        <class name="ContactPerson">
          <id name="Id">
            <generator class="native"/>
          </id>
          <property name="Name"/>
          <many-to-one name="Customer"
            class="Customer" column="CompanyId"
            property-ref="CompanyId" foreign-key="none"/>
        </class>
      </hibernate-mapping>
```

5. Add a class named Recipe to the folder:

```csharp
using System;
using NH4CookbookHelpers.Mapping;
using NHibernate;

namespace MappingRecipes.PropertyRefs
{
  public class Recipe : HbmMappingRecipe
  {
    protected override void AddInitialData(ISession session)
    {
      var customer = new Customer
      {
        Name = "The customer",
        CompanyId = 345
      };

      customer.ContactPersons.Add(
        new ContactPerson
        {
          Customer = customer,
          Name = "Person1"
        }
      );

      session.Save(customer);
    }

    public override void RunQueries(ISession session)
```

```
        {
            var customer = session.Get<ContactPerson>(1);
            Console.WriteLine("Customer:" + customer.Customer.Name);
        }
    }
}
```

6. Run the application and start the `PropertyRefs` recipe.

How it works...

In our scenario, the relation between the `Customer` and its `ContactPersons` is not expressed with a reference to the `Customer` table's `Id` column. Instead, we have a different column, with a legacy identifier, called `CompanyId`. To be able to use this setup in NHibernate, we specify `<key column="CompanyId"/>` in our set mapping. This is not enough, however. We also need to specify that it's the `CompanyId` and not the customer's `Id` that should be stored in that column; this is done by adding property `ref="CompanyId"`.

When the `Customer` is persisted, `INSERT` instance like the following will be executed:

```
INSERT INTO Customer (Name, CompanyId)
VALUES ('The customer', 345)
```

```
INSERT INTO ContactPerson (Name, CompanyId)
VALUES ('Person1', 345)
```

And when the `ContactPersons` are retrieved, for our only `Customer`, the `SELECT` looks like this:

```
SELECT [columns]
FROM ContactPerson
WHERE CompanyId=345
```

As promised, the relationship now is defined by the `CompanyId`, which in this case is `345`.

You may have noticed that we actually added the property-ref twice, once on the set in `Customer` and once on the many-to-one in `ContactPerson`. That's not always necessary, but in this case our relation was bidirectional, and NHibernate needs to know about the special relationship on both sides. Had the collection been unidirectional, only the `<key column="CompanyId" property-ref="CompanyId"/>` would have been needed. If there was no collection, but only a customer property on `ContactPerson`, the property-ref on the many-to-one would have sufficed.

We also specified in mapping that the `CompanyId` property should be unique. After all, we want that property to uniquely identify a `Customer`, even though it is not the primary key. NHibernate does not actively enforce this, but it's required in practice. This is what the documentation says about unique:

> *unique (optional): enables the DDL generation of a unique constraint for the columns. Also, allow this to be the target of a property-ref.*

There's more...

Property-ref is available on most kinds of relationships, such as one-to-one, one-to-many, many-to-one and many-to-many. It should be noted, though, that the purpose is only to support legacy scenarios, where an existing database schema requires it. For all scenarios where the database can be designed to fully support the object model, property-ref's should be avoided. They add unnecessary complexity and without proper database constraints in place (requiring the referenced property to be unique), there's a risk for unexpected behavior or exceptions.

Using lazy properties

Consider a class representing a scientific article, with properties for author, title, abstract, full text, and so on.

This looks simple enough, but having the full article text stored in the entity could cause serious issues. The text may be several megabytes in size and if we're, for example, just listing the available articles, it's very unnecessary to load all that from the database and storing it in memory.

Thankfully, NHibernate has a solution for this, called lazy properties. Just as with lazy loading of referenced entities and collections, this function will not load the data until it is accessed.

Getting ready

Complete the *Getting ready* instructions at the beginning of this chapter.

How to do it...

1. Add a new folder named `LazyProperties` to the `MappingRecipes` project.
2. Add a class named `Article` to the folder:

```
namespace MappingRecipes.LazyProperties
{
    public class Article
    {
```

```csharp
        public virtual int Id { get; protected set; }
        public virtual string Title { get; set; }
        public virtual string Abstract { get; set; }
        public virtual string Author { get; set; }
        public virtual string FullText { get; set; }
    }
}
```

3. Add a new embedded mapping named `Article.hbm.xml` to the folder:

```xml
<?xml version="1.0" encoding="utf-8" ?>
<hibernate-mapping xmlns="urn:nhibernate-mapping-2.2"
  assembly="MappingRecipes"
  namespace="MappingRecipes.LazyProperties">
  <class name="Article">
    <id name="Id">
      <generator class="native"/>
    </id>
    <property name="Title"/>
    <property name="Abstract"/>
    <property name="Author"/>
    <property name="FullText" lazy="true"/>
  </class>
</hibernate-mapping>
```

4. Add a class named `Recipe` to the folder:

```csharp
using System;
using NH4CookbookHelpers;
using NHibernate;

namespace MappingRecipes.LazyProperties
{
  public class Recipe : HbmMappingRecipe
  {
    protected override void AddInitialData(ISession session)
    {
      session.Save(new Article
      {
        Title = "Lazy properties",
        Author = "NHibernate",
        Abstract = "Supporting lazy properties is cool",
        FullText = "An enourmously long text"
      });
    }

    public override void RunQueries(ISession session)
```

```
        {
          var article = session.Get<Article>(1);
          Console.WriteLine("Title:" + article.Title);
          Console.WriteLine("Author:" + article.Author);
          Console.WriteLine("Abstract:" + article.Abstract);
          Console.WriteLine("Has fulltext been loaded: {0}",
            NHibernateUtil.IsPropertyInitialized(
                article,"FullText"));
          Console.WriteLine("Full text:" + article.FullText);

        }
      }
    }
```

5. Run the application and start the `LazyProperties` recipe.

How it works...

Lazy properties work similarly to how lazy loaded relations work. When the `Article` is loaded from the database, the `FullText` column and its data is ignored. Instead, it's loaded immediately when the `FullText` property is used for the first time.

NHibernate accomplishes this by instantiating the `Article` entity as a proxy class, in other words a dynamically generated subclass of `Article`. This proxy intercepts any call to the `FullText` property, and if necessary asks the session to load the text.

Mapping joins

In legacy databases, data is often spread across two or more tables, even though the rows represent one single entity. In SQL, such scenarios are handled using `JOIN` constructs in the queries, and NHibernate supports this.

Getting ready

Complete the *Getting ready* instructions at the beginning of this chapter.

How to do it...

1. Add a new folder named `MappingJoins` to the `MappingRecipes` project.

2. Add a class named `Article` to the folder:

```
namespace MappingRecipes.MappingJoins
{
  public class Article
```

```
    {
      public virtual int Id { get; protected set; }
      public virtual string Title { get; set; }
      public virtual string Abstract { get; set; }
      public virtual string Author { get; set; }
      public virtual string FullText { get; set; }
    }
}
```

3. Add a new embedded mapping named `Article.hbm.xml` to the folder:

```xml
<?xml version="1.0" encoding="utf-8" ?>
<hibernate-mapping xmlns="urn:nhibernate-mapping-2.2"
  assembly="MappingRecipes"
  namespace="MappingRecipes.MappingJoins">
  <class name="Article">
    <id name="Id">
      <generator class="native"/>
    </id>
    <property name="Title"/>
    <property name="Abstract"/>
    <property name="Author"/>
    <join table="ArticleFullText"
        optional="true">
      <key column="ArticleId" unique="true"/>
      <property name="FullText"/>
    </join>
  </class>
</hibernate-mapping>
```

4. Add a class named `Recipe` to the folder:

```csharp
using System;
using NH4CookbookHelpers;
using NHibernate;

namespace MappingRecipes.MappingJoins
{
  public class Recipe : HbmMappingRecipe
  {
    protected override void AddInitialData(
ISession session)
    {
      session.Save(new Article
      {
        Title = "Lazy properties",
```

```
            Author = "NHibernate",
            Abstract = "Supporting lazy properties is cool",
            FullText = "A really long article"
        });
    }

    public override void RunQueries(ISession session)
    {
        var article = session.Get<Article>(1);
        Console.WriteLine("Title:" + article.Title);
        Console.WriteLine("Author:" + article.Author);
        Console.WriteLine("Abstract:" + article.Abstract);
        Console.WriteLine("Full text:" + article.FullText);
    }
  }
}
```

5. Run the application and start the `MappingJoins` recipe.

How it works...

The `<join>` element in the mapping specifies that the mappings it contains belong to a different table than the one used for the mapped class. In the example, we have decided to store `FullText` in the joined table `ArticleFullText`, but we could just as well have added more properties and even related entities, collections, and so on. Running the recipe, the following queries are executed:

[screenshots]

The `optional="false"` setting (which is the default) tells NHibernate that we expect the `ArticleFullText` table to always contain a corresponding row. In other words, a full INNER JOIN can be used when data is retrieved. Had we specified `optional="true"`, an OUTER JOIN would be used, and rows will only be inserted if any of the joined properties contains a value (not null). You can try this out by changing the mapping to optional="true" and removing the line, which assigns the `FullText` property. The queries executed are now.

There's more...

The `<join>` functionality is very useful in legacy scenarios, where the database schema already has distributed entity data between two or more tables. However, we can also put it to good use in new models. One such incidence is when we use one table, in a table-per-class-hierarchy mapping, to handle inheritance hierarchies. Normally, we would have to add columns, for all properties of all classes in the hierarchy, to the single, common table. By using a `<join>` inside a subclass mapping, we can add an extra table, which will only hold the values specific to that subclass.

Using calculated properties

A property need not, always, be represented as a column value in the database. In plain SQL, we may have used built-in or custom functions, such as string length or encryption, or perhaps even a subquery, to project the data we want to expose. NHibernate allows you to map such a construct directly to a property.

Getting ready

Complete the *Getting ready* instructions at the beginning of this chapter.

How to do it...

1. Add a new folder named `CalculatedProperties` to the `MappingRecipes` project.

2. Add a class named `Invoice` to the folder:

```
using System;

namespace MappingRecipes.CalculatedProperties
{
  public class Invoice
  {
    public virtual Guid Id { get; protected set; }
    public virtual decimal Amount { get; set; }
    public virtual string Customer { get; set; }
    public virtual int InvoicesOnCustomer
{ get; protected set; }
  }
}
```

3. Add a new embedded mapping named `Invoice.hbm.xml` to the folder:

```
<?xml version="1.0" encoding="utf-8" ?>
<hibernate-mapping xmlns="urn:nhibernate-mapping-2.2"
  assembly="MappingRecipes"
  namespace="MappingRecipes.CalculatedProperties">
<class name="Invoice">
  <id name="Id">
    <generator class="guid.comb"/>
  </id>
  <property name="Amount"/>
  <property name="Customer"/>
```

```
        <property name="InvoicesOnCustomer" formula="(SELECT COUNT(*)
FROM Invoice i WHERE i.Customer=Customer)"/>
  </class>
</hibernate-mapping>
```

4. Add a class named `Recipe` to the folder:

```csharp
using System;
using NH4CookbookHelpers;
using NHibernate;

namespace MappingRecipes.CalculatedProperties
{
  public class Recipe : HbmMappingRecipe
  {
    protected override void AddInitialData(ISession
session)
    {
      session.Save(new Invoice { Amount = 200,
Customer = "A" });
      session.Save(new Invoice { Amount = 2000,
Customer = "A" });
      session.Save(new Invoice { Amount = 200,
Customer = "B" });
    }

    public override void RunQueries(ISession session)
    {
      var invoices = session.QueryOver<Invoice>().List();
      foreach (var invoice in invoices)
      {
        Console.WriteLine(@"Amount: {0},
InvoicesOnCustomer: {1}",
          invoice.Amount, invoice.InvoicesOnCustomer);
      }
    }
  }
}
```

5. Run the application and start the `CalculatedProperties` recipe.

How it works...

The formula attribute on the property element specifies that we want a SQL expression to be used to retrieve the property value, instead of a plain column reference. In this case we created the rather useless property `InvoicesOnCustomer`, which returns the COUNT of all invoices with the same `Customer` as the current row. Two things are worth noting here:

- The formula is specified using plain SQL. It may appear strange that we're not using something more abstracted, such as HQL, here. However, the formula mapping is handled at a lower level than the querying system, and it has no knowledge about the rest of the class model. The downside of this is that our mapping possibly becomes tied to the specific DBMS we're using. The upside is that we get easy access to core functions in SQL.

- We can reference the owning row in the SQL query. In our example we added WHERE `i.Customer=Customer` to the formula query. This may look strange from a plain SQL perspective. Where does the last Customer come from? Well, NHibernate doesn't leave the SQL expression completely untouched. Instead, it parses it and injects the owning row's alias to all column references which has no other alias.

Looking at the SELECT query executed by the recipe, we see this:

```
SELECT
    this_.Id as Id0_0_,
    this_.Amount as Amount0_0_,
    this_.Customer as Customer0_0_,
    (SELECT
        COUNT(*)
    FROM
        Invoice i
    WHERE
        i.Customer=this_.Customer) as formula0_0_
FROM
    Invoice this_
```

The SQL expression we specified has been included in the query, and the last reference to Customer has been prefixed with the currently used alias, in this case `this_`.

For obvious reasons, a formula mapping effectively becomes read only. Updates to the property value will be silently ignored. It's therefore recommended that the property write access is restricted as much possible.

There's more...

Formulas are not restricted to properties. They can be used in many mappings where a column reference is normally used. This includes the keys in `<one-to-one>`, `<many-to-one>` and `<many-to-many>` relations and even the discriminator value in a class hierarchy. Such a mapping would allow the subclass discrimination to be based on virtually anything, like the contents of a text field. The most likely scenario though, is a legacy database where many different values in a column should map to one specific subclass. Such a formula mapping could look like this:

```
<discriminator formula="CASE WHEN CustomerType IN ('Gold', 'Silver')
THEN 'Preferred' ELSE 'Normal' END" type="string"/>
```

Using serializable values

At some point you may need to store objects in the database that are either impossible to map using NHibernate (the object may be of a type you have no control over) or the resulting relational model would simply be too complex. As long as the objects are of a type that is serializable (using `BinaryFormatter`), NHibernate can save and retrieve them transparently.

In this recipe we'll show a crude NHibernate based error log, which stores raised `Exception`s, complete with any nested `InnerException`s.

Getting ready

Complete the *Getting ready* instructions at the beginning of this chapter.

How to do it...

1. Add a new folder named `SerializableValues` to the `MappingRecipes` project.

2. Add a new class named `Error` to the folder:
   ```
   public class Error
   {
     public virtual Guid Id { get; set; }
     public virtual DateTime ErrorDateTime { get; set; }
     public virtual Exception Exception { get; set; }
   }
   ```

3. Add an embedded mapping named `Error.hbm.xml` to the folder:

```xml
<?xml version="1.0" encoding="utf-8" ?>
<hibernate-mapping xmlns="urn:nhibernate-mapping-2.2"
  assembly="MappingRecipes"
  namespace="MappingRecipes.SerializableValues">
  <class name="Error">
    <id name="Id">
      <generator class="guid.comb"/>
    </id>
    <property name="ErrorDateTime" />
    <property name="Exception" type="Serializable"/>
  </class>
</hibernate-mapping>
```

4. Add a class named `Recipe` to the folder:

```csharp
using System;
using NH4CookbookHelpers;
using NHibernate;

namespace MappingRecipes.SerializableValues
{
  public class Recipe : HbmMappingRecipe
  {
    protected override void AddInitialData(
ISessionFactory sessionFactory)
    {
      try
      {
        throw new ApplicationException(
"Something happened",
          new NullReferenceException("Something was null")
          );
      }
      catch (Exception ex)
      {
        LogError(ex, sessionFactory);
      }
    }

    private void LogError(Exception exception,
ISessionFactory sessionFactory)
    {
      using (var session= sessionFactory
.OpenStatelessSession())
```

```
        {
          using (var tx = session.BeginTransaction())
          {
            session.Insert(new Error
            {
              ErrorDateTime = DateTime.Now,
              Exception = exception
            });
            tx.Commit();
          }
        }
      }

      public override void RunQueries(ISession session)
      {
        var error = session.QueryOver<Error>()
  .SingleOrDefault();
        if (error.Exception != null)
        {
          ShowException(error.Exception);
          Console.WriteLine("Stack trace:" +
  error.Exception.StackTrace);
        }
      }

      private void ShowException(Exception exception)
      {
        Console.WriteLine("Type: {0}, Message: {1}",
  exception.Message, exception.GetType());
        if (exception.InnerException != null)
        {
          ShowException(exception.InnerException);
        }
      }
    }
  }
```

5. Run the application and start the `SerializableValues` recipe.

How it works...

As long as an object can be serialized to a type which itself can be stored in the database, NHibernate can handle it.

In our example, we mapped the `Exception` property of the `Error` class as we do any other property. We added one little thing, though, with the attribute `type="Serializable"`. This tells NHibernate to use the type `NHibernate.Type.SerializableType` when persisting the object.

`SerializableType` stores its values using a binary column type in the database (the actual type will vary between DBMS:es) and it uses a `BinaryFormatter` to serialize and deserialize the mapped properties value to and from a byte array.

We expose our `Exception` property as a `System.Exception`. We could also have chosen `object` or `dynamic`, since the `BinaryFormatter` includes the type of the serialized object in the byte array data. It's therefore possible to map a property which can hold any type of serializable value and you can change and update values to different types, whenever you want.

There's more...

`SerializableType` is an implementation of an NHibernate `IType`, but you can also create a similar serializing and deserializing type, by implementing the `IUserType` interface. Such a type could store and retrieve complex values using JSON, BSON, Google protocol buffers or any other serialization technique which can convert an object into a string or a byte array.

The basics for creating a JSON serializing type, using the popular `JSON.NET` library, could be summed up in these two methods:

```
public object NullSafeGet(IDataReader rs, string[] names, object
owner)
{
  if (names.Length != 1)
    throw new InvalidOperationException("Invalid column count");

  var val = rs[names[0]] as string;

  if (val != null && !string.IsNullOrWhiteSpace(val))
  {
    return JsonConvert.DeserializeObject<T>(val);
  }

  return null;
```

```
    }

    public void NullSafeSet(IDbCommand cmd, object value, int index)
    {
      var parameter = (DbParameter)cmd.Parameters[index];

      if (value == null)
      {
        parameter.Value = DBNull.Value;
      }
      else
      {
        parameter.Value = JsonConvert.SerializeObject(value);
      }
    }
}
```

There's more to it than that, but that sums up the basics. For more on creating custom types, read the first two recipes in *Chapter 8, Extending NHibernate*.

Dynamic components

Sometimes there is a need to add more columns to a table, but the code model can't be updated to accommodate this. Can we still add the columns, persist, and query their values? Yes, NHibernate provides a way to do map table columns into a key-value IDictionary, instead of individual properties of the class. This is called a dynamic-component.

Getting ready

Complete the *Getting ready* instructions at the beginning of this chapter.

How to do it...

1. Add a new folder named DynamicComponents to the MappingRecipes project.

2. Add a new class named Contact to the folder:

   ```
   using System;
   using System.Collections;

   namespace MappingRecipes.DynamicComponents
   {
     public class Contact
     {
       public Contact()
   ```

```
    {
      Attributes=new Hashtable();
    }
    public virtual Guid Id { get; protected set; }
    public virtual IDictionary Attributes { get; set; }
  }
}
```

3. Add an embedded mapping named `Contact.hbm.xml` to the folder:

```xml
<?xml version="1.0" encoding="utf-8" ?>
<hibernate-mapping xmlns="urn:nhibernate-mapping-2.2"
  assembly="MappingRecipes"
  namespace="MappingRecipes.DynamicComponents">
  <class name="Contact">
    <id name="Id">
      <generator class="guid.comb"/>
    </id>
    <dynamic-component name="Attributes">
      <property name="FirstName" type="string"/>
      <property name="LastName" type="string"/>
      <property name="BirthDate" type="DateTime"/>
    </dynamic-component>
  </class>
</hibernate-mapping>
```

4. Add a new class named `Recipe` to the folder:

```csharp
using System;
using System.Linq;
using NH4CookbookHelpers;
using NHibernate;
using NHibernate.Linq;

namespace MappingRecipes.DynamicComponents
{
  public class Recipe : HbmMappingRecipe
  {
    protected override void AddInitialData(ISession session)
    {
      session.Save(new Contact
      {
        Attributes =
        {
          ["FirstName"] = "Dave",
```

```
          ["LastName"] = "Gahan",
          ["BirthDate"] = new DateTime(1962, 5, 9)
        }
      });
      session.Save(new Contact
      {
        Attributes =
        {
          ["FirstName"] = "Martin",
          ["LastName"] = "Gore",
          ["BirthDate"] = new DateTime(1961, 7, 23)
        }
      });
    }

    public override void RunQueries(ISession session)
    {
      var contactsBornInMay = session.Query<Contact>()
        .Where(x =>
((DateTime)x.Attributes["BirthDate"]).Month == 5)
        .ToList();
      foreach (var contact in contactsBornInMay)
      {
        Console.WriteLine("{0} {1} {2:d}",
          contact.Attributes["FirstName"],
          contact.Attributes["LastName"],
          contact.Attributes["BirthDate"]);
      }
    }
  }
}
```

5. Run the application and start the DynamicComponents recipe.

How it works...

Our Contact class currently doesn't contain much more than an Id property and an IDictionary called Attributes. Still, we are not only able to add data that is stored in specific column, we can also query the data, as if we had standard class properties.

The <dynamic-component> mapping can be said to change the scope, from the properties of the class, to named elements in an IDictionary. All the standard mappings are still available, so you are not limited to <property> elements, but can add <many-to-one>, collections and even nested dynamic components into the dictionary.

All the mappings within a dynamic component require that the mapped tables and columns exist, but the containing class never has to be modified in order to accommodate the new properties. Changes to the mapping and to the database can be performed without touching the code, for example by using non-embedded XML mapping files or by creating or modifying the mapping at runtime.

Storing the dynamic data could not be more straightforward. We simply add key value pairs to the IDictionary and persist the object. Here is one possible syntax, using the IDictionary initializer (which requires that the Attributes property is assigned in the constructor):

```
session.Save(new Contact
{
  Attributes =
  {
    ["FirstName"] = "Dave",
    ["LastName"] = "Gahan",
    ["BirthDate"] = new DateTime(1962, 5, 9)
  }
});
```

If unmapped keys are added to the dictionary, their values will be discarded, just as would happen to an unmapped property.

Querying is a bit different. In the recipe, we use LINQ and query the Attributes dictionary as is. We cast the value to a DateTime, but only so that we can get access to the Month sub property:

```
var contactsBornInMay = session.Query<Contact>()
  .Where(x => ((DateTime)x.Attributes["BirthDate"]).Month == 5)
  .ToList();
```

For HQL, CriteriaQueries, and QueryOver, we instead refer to the dynamic properties as if they were real properties. An HQL query would look like this:

```
var contactsBornInMay = session.CreateQuery(@"
    from Contact
    where month(Attributes.BirthDate)=:monthNumber")
  .SetInt32("monthNumber",5)
  .List<Contact>();
```

At the time of writing, NHibernate only provides support for the non-generic IDictionary type, meaning that both the keys and the values are effectively exposed as object. An upcoming update (possibly 4.1) will also provide support for IDictionary<string, TValue>.

There's more...

Multitenant applications are applications where many tenants (customers) share a common code base, and perhaps a common application process and database. If these tenants require custom properties on their entities, dynamic component mappings are a convenient way to provide just that. Adding a new property could involve these steps:

1. An integer property named `Points` is added, using a backend administration frontend.

2. The column is added to the database table, preferably using credentials with elevated permissions, which are not normally used by the application.

3. The property is added to the mapping, usually using mapping by code `ClassMapping` or Fluent NHibernate.

4. A new session factory `ISessionFactory` is created using the new mappings.

5. The currently used session factory is replaced with the new, and can then be disposed.

Step 2 can be omitted if you preconfigure the table with generically named spare columns of the right types. For example, you can have columns named `IntValue1`, `IntValue2` and so on, and map these using `<property name="Points" column="IntValue1" type="int"/>`. Just take care to add sensible default values (such as 0) to these columns, or remember that they may be empty or null.

Perhaps we do not want to modify the core tables of the application. We can avoid this by enclosing the `<dynamic-component>` mapping inside a `<join>` mapping. The core table will be untouched, and all the custom attributes can live in a table, which can be unique to the configuration/tenant:

```
<join table="ContactAttributesForTenant23">
  <key column="ContactId"/>
  <dynamic-component name="Attributes">
    <property name="FirstName" type="string"/>
    <property name="LastName" type="string"/>
    <property name="BirthDate" type="DateTime"/>
  </dynamic-component>
</join>
```

Mapping <subselect>

In the recipe *Using calculated properties* we learned how to use SQL expressions to provide custom calculations for specific properties. Using a <subselect> mapping we can to the same for an entire class.

Getting ready

Complete the *Getting ready* instructions at the beginning of this chapter.

How to do it...

1. Add a new folder named MappingSubselects to the MappingRecipes project.

2. Add a new class named PageHit to the folder:

```
using System;

namespace MappingRecipes.MappingSubselects
{
  public class PageHit
  {
    public virtual int Id { get; protected set; }
    public virtual string Url { get; set; }
    public virtual DateTime PageViewDateTime { get; set; }
  }
}
```

3. Add a new class named PageStatisticsEntry to the folder:

```
namespace MappingRecipes.MappingSubselects
{
  public class PageStatisticsEntry
  {
    public virtual string Url { get; protected set; }

    public virtual int ViewCount { get; protected set; }
  }
}
```

4. Add an embedded mapping named `Mappings.hbm.xml` to the folder:

```xml
<?xml version="1.0" encoding="utf-8" ?>
<hibernate-mapping xmlns="urn:nhibernate-mapping-2.2"
  assembly="MappingRecipes"
  namespace="MappingRecipes.MappingSubselects">
  <class name="PageHit">
    <id name="Id">
      <generator class="native"/>
    </id>
    <property name="Url" not-null="true"/>
  </class>
  <class name="PageStatisticsEntry" mutable="false">
    <subselect>
      SELECT Url, COUNT(*) as ViewCount
      FROM PageHit GROUP BY Url
    </subselect>
    <synchronize table="PageHit"/>
    <id name="Url"/>
    <property name="ViewCount"/>
  </class>
</hibernate-mapping>
```

5. Add a new class named `Recipe` to the folder:

```csharp
using System;
using NH4CookbookHelpers;
using NHibernate;

namespace MappingRecipes.MappingSubselects
{
  public class Recipe : HbmMappingRecipe
  {
    protected override void AddInitialData(
ISessionFactory sessionFactory)
    {
      var random = new Random();
      using (var session = sessionFactory
.OpenStatelessSession())
      {
        for (var i = 0; i < 100; i++)
        {
          session.Insert(new PageHit
          {
```

```
            Url = random.Next(10).ToString(),
            PageViewDateTime = DateTime.Now
        });
      }
    }
  }

  public override void RunQueries(ISession session)
  {
    var stats = session.QueryOver<PageStatisticsEntry>()
      .Where(x => x.ViewCount > 2)
      .OrderBy(x => x.ViewCount).Desc.List();

    foreach (var entry in stats)
    {
      Console.WriteLine("Url: {0}, View count: {1}",
        entry.Url, entry.ViewCount);
    }
  }
  }
}
```

6. Run the application and start the `MappingSubselects` recipe.

How it works...

Subselect mappings are in a way the full class version of a formula mapping, but a better description is perhaps that it works similar to a SQL VIEW. It defines a SQL query which takes the place of a table, and all the returned columns can be queried, as if they were actual columns on a table.

In our recipe, we created a `PageHit` table and mapping, and a `<subselect>` mapping using that very same table. However, it may just as well refer to tables which have not been included in any other mappings:

```
<class name="PageStatisticsEntry" mutable="false">
  <subselect>
    SELECT Url, COUNT(*) as ViewCount
    FROM PageHit GROUP BY Url
  </subselect>
  <synchronize table="PageHit"/>
  <id name="Url"/>
  <property name="ViewCount"/>
</class>
```

The `subselect` element is included in a regular class mapping, and takes the place of a table attribute. Instead, it defines the query that will be used as a table. One or more `<synchronize>` elements can be also added. They inform NHibernate of which tables are used in the query, which is crucial if we add caching to our application. If something modifies the `PageHit` table, any cached values for `PageStatisticsEntry` will be invalidated in the cache.

We also added `mutable="false"` to the mapping, to specify that we cannot update entities of this type. The resulting SQL would not make any sense.

3
Sessions and Transactions

In this chapter, we will cover the following topics:

- ▶ Setting up session-per-web request
- ▶ Setting up session-per-presenter
- ▶ Creating a session ASP.NET MVC action filter
- ▶ Creating a transaction ASP.NET MVC action filter
- ▶ Save entities to the database
- ▶ Using session.Merge
- ▶ Using session.Refresh
- ▶ Handle concurrency using session.Lock
- ▶ Using dictionaries as entities
- ▶ Using NHibernate with transaction scope

Introduction

NHibernate leaves session and transaction management up to the application. There are a number of different ways to manage sessions and transactions, and they depend greatly on the specific application architecture. In addition to a few interesting session methods, the recipes in this chapter show how to handle sessions and transactions for these different types of applications.

Setting up session-per-web request

Due to its simplicity, the most common pattern used in web applications for managing NHibernate sessions is session-per-request. In this recipe, we'll show you how to set up the session-per-request pattern using NHibernate's contextual sessions feature.

Getting ready

1. Create a new ASP.NET web forms or ASP.NET MVC application.
2. Add a reference to NHibernate using NuGet Package Manager Console.
3. If it doesn't exist already, add a new global application class Global.asax.
4. In Global.asax.cs, add these using statements:

```
using NHibernate;
using NHibernate.Cfg;
using NHibernate.Context;
```

5. Create a static property named SessionFactory:

```
public static ISessionFactory SessionFactory { get; private set; }
```

Now you have two choices. You can either use the companion library, NH4CookbookHelpers to set up the base configuration or set everything up manually.

Option 1: Using the companion library

1. Add a reference to NH4CookbookHelpers using NuGet Package Manager Console.
2. In the Application_Start method in Global.asax.cs, add the following code:

```
protected void Application_Start(object sender, EventArgs e)
{
  SessionFactory=ProductModel
    .CreateExampleSessionFactory(true, conf => {
    conf.SetProperty("current_session_context_class", "web");
  });
}
```

Option 2: Manual setup

1. In the web.config file, set up the NHibernate and log4net configuration sections. Refer to the *Configuring NHibernate with App.config* recipes in *Chapter 1, The Configuration and Schema*.

2. In the `hibernate-configuration` section of `web.config`, add the `current_session_context_class` property with a value of `web`.

3. In the `Application_Start` method in `Global.asax.cs`, add the following code:

```
protected void Application_Start(object sender, EventArgs e)
{
  var nhConfig = new Configuration().Configure();
  SessionFactory = nhConfig.BuildSessionFactory();
}
```

How to do it...

1. In the `Application_BeginRequest` method, add the following code:

```
protected void Application_BeginRequest(object sender, EventArgs e)
{
  var session = SessionFactory.OpenSession();
  CurrentSessionContext.Bind(session);
}
```

2. In the `Application_EndRequest` method, add the following code:

```
protected void Application_EndRequest(object sender,
EventArgs e)
{
  var session = CurrentSessionContext.Unbind(SessionFactory);
  session.Dispose();
}
```

How it works...

In web applications, it's common to use a session for each web request. We open the session when the request begins and close it when the request ends.

NHibernate's contextual session feature allows a session to be associated with application-specific scope that approximates a single unit of work. This context is configured with the `current_session_context_class` property, which specifies an implementation of `NHibernate.Context.ICurrentSessionContext`. In this case, we'll associate it with the web request. `web` is the short name for `NHibernate.Context.WebSessionContext`.

Even with contextual sessions, NHibernate does not open, close, or dispose the session for us. We have to associate and dissociate a session with the current web request using the `CurrentSessionContext.Bind` and `Unbind` methods.

There's more...

To get the NHibernate session for the current web request, we use `SessionFactory.GetCurrentSession()`. In our example web application, it might look something similar to this:

```
Guid productId = new Guid(Request["id"]);
Product product;
var session = Global.SessionFactory.GetCurrentSession();
using (var tran = session.BeginTransaction())
{
  product = session.Get<Product>(productId);
  tran.Commit();
}
Page.Title = product.Name;
Label1.Text = product.Name;
Label2.Text = product.Description;
```

This naive example fetches a product from the database and displays the name and description to the user. In a production-worthy application, we would probably use dependency injection rather than directly access the singleton.

> NHibernate sessions are extremely lightweight and cheap to make. Simply opening a session doesn't open a database connection. NHibernate makes every effort to avoid or delay opening of a connection. On the other hand, NHibernate goes through great effort to create the session factory. You should only create one session factory for the entire lifecycle of the application.

There are many implementations of session-per-request using inversion of control containers and even HTTP modules. Some use contextual sessions, while others manage the session without NHibernate's help. A complete session-per-request implementation has the following four characteristics:

- Create the one and only session factory when the application starts
- Open a session when the web request begins
- Close the session when the request ends
- Provide a standard way to access the current session throughout the data access layer

See also

- ▸ *Creating a session ASP.NET MVC action filter*
- ▸ *Creating a transaction ASP.NET MVC action filter*
- ▸ *Setting up session-per-presenter*

Setting up session-per-presenter

It's a good idea to use a session for each presenter in desktop applications using the **Model View Presenter** (**MVP**) pattern. This approach can also be adapted to the **Model View View Model** (**MVVM**) pattern. More information on these patterns is available at http://en.wikipedia.org/wiki/Model-view-presenter and http://en.wikipedia.org/wiki/Model-view-viewmodel.

In this recipe, we'll show you a crude implementation of this session-per-presenter pattern with dependency injection. While MVP and MVVM are more common in Windows Forms and WPF applications, we will just create a simple console application this time.

We will use an inversion of the control container, called Ninject, in this recipe. If you're not familiar with the dependency injection or Inversion of Control concepts, a free video tutorial is available at http://tinyurl.com/iocvideo.

 This recipe can be completed with other dependency injection frameworks. Just substitute the NinjectBindings class with an equivalent configuration for your favorite DI framework.

How to do it...

1. Add a new console project to the solution named SessionPerPresenter.
2. Add a reference to NH4CookbookHelpers, Ninject and Ninject.Extensions. NamedScope using NuGet Package Manager Console.
3. Add a folder to the new project named Data.
4. In the Data folder, create an IDao<TEntity> interface with the following code:

```
using System;
using System.Collections.Generic;

namespace SessionPerPresenter.Data
{
    public interface IDao<TEntity> : IDisposable
```

```
    where TEntity : class
    {
      IEnumerable<TEntity> GetAll();
    }
}
```

5. Create an implementation with the following code:

```
using System.Collections.Generic;

namespace SessionPerPresenter.Data
{
  public class Dao<TEntity> : IDao<TEntity>
  where TEntity : class
  {
    private readonly ISessionProvider _sessionProvider;
    public Dao(ISessionProvider sessionProvider)
    {
      _sessionProvider = sessionProvider;
    }
    public void Dispose()
    {
      _sessionProvider.Dispose();
    }
    public IEnumerable<TEntity> GetAll()
    {
      var session = _sessionProvider.GetCurrentSession();
      IEnumerable<TEntity> results;
      using (var tx = session.BeginTransaction())
      {
        results = session.QueryOver<TEntity>()
          .List<TEntity>();
        tx.Commit();
      }
      return results;
    }
  }
}
```

6. In the `Data` folder, create an `ISessionProvider` interface with the following code:

```
using System;
using NHibernate;

namespace SessionPerPresenter.Data
{
```

```
    public interface ISessionProvider : IDisposable
    {
      ISession GetCurrentSession();
      void DisposeCurrentSession();
    }
}
```

7. Create an implementation with the following code:

```
using System;
using NHibernate;

namespace SessionPerPresenter.Data
{
  public class SessionProvider : ISessionProvider
  {
    private readonly ISessionFactory _sessionFactory;
    private ISession _currentSession;
    public SessionProvider(ISessionFactory sessionFactory)
    {
      Console.WriteLine("Building session provider");
      _sessionFactory = sessionFactory;
    }
    public ISession GetCurrentSession()
    {
      if (null == _currentSession)
      {
        Console.WriteLine("Opening session");
        _currentSession = _sessionFactory.OpenSession();
      }
      return _currentSession;
    }
    public void DisposeCurrentSession()
    {
      _currentSession.Dispose();
      _currentSession = null;
    }
    public void Dispose()
    {
      if (_currentSession != null)
      {
        Console.WriteLine("Disposing session");
        _currentSession.Dispose();
      }
      _currentSession = null;
    }
  }
}
```

8. Create a `ProductListView` class with the following code:

```
using System;
using System.Collections.Generic;
using NH4CookbookHelpers.Queries.Model;

namespace SessionPerPresenter
{
  public class ProductListView
  {
    private readonly string _description;
    private readonly IEnumerable<Product> _products;
    public ProductListView(
      string description,
      IEnumerable<Product> products)
    {
      _description = description;
      _products = products;
    }
    public void Show()
    {
      Console.WriteLine(_description);
      foreach (var p in _products)
        Console.WriteLine(" * {0}", p.Name);
    }
  }
}
```

9. Create a public `IPresenter` interface inherited from `IDisposable`. This interface can be left empty:

```
using System;

namespace SessionPerPresenter
{
  public interface IPresenter : IDisposable
  {
  }
}
```

10. Create a `MediaPresenter` class with the following code:

```
using System.Linq;
using NH4CookbookHelpers.Queries.Model;
using SessionPerPresenter.Data;

namespace SessionPerPresenter
{
```

```
public class MediaPresenter : IPresenter
{
  private readonly IDao<Movie> _movieDao;
  private readonly IDao<Book> _bookDao;
  public MediaPresenter(IDao<Movie> movieDao,
    IDao<Book> bookDao)
  {
    _movieDao = movieDao;
    _bookDao = bookDao;
  }
  public ProductListView ShowBooks()
  {
    return new ProductListView("All Books",
      _bookDao.GetAll().OfType<Product>());
  }
  public ProductListView ShowMovies()
  {
    return new ProductListView("All Movies",
      _movieDao.GetAll().OfType<Product>());
  }
  public void Dispose()
  {
    _movieDao.Dispose();
    _bookDao.Dispose();
  }
}
}
```

11. Create a `ProductPresenter` class with the following code:

```
using NH4CookbookHelpers.Queries.Model;
using SessionPerPresenter.Data;

namespace SessionPerPresenter
{
  public class ProductPresenter : IPresenter
  {
    private readonly IDao<Product> _productDao;
    public ProductPresenter(IDao<Product> productDao)
    {
      _productDao = productDao;
    }
    public ProductListView ShowAllProducts()
    {
      return new ProductListView("All Products",
        _productDao.GetAll());
```

```
      }
      public virtual void Dispose()
      {
        _productDao.Dispose();
      }
    }
  }
```

12. In the root of our project, create a class named `NinjectBindings` with the following code:

```
using System.Linq;
using Ninject.Extensions.NamedScope;
using Ninject.Modules;
using SessionPerPresenter.Data;

namespace SessionPerPresenter
{
  public class NinjectBindings : NinjectModule
  {
    public override void Load()
    {
      const string presenterScope = "PresenterScope";
      var asm = GetType().Assembly;
      var presenters =
        from t in asm.GetTypes()
        where typeof(IPresenter).IsAssignableFrom(t) &&
          t.IsClass && !t.IsAbstract
        select t;
      foreach (var presenterType in presenters)
        Kernel.Bind(presenterType)
          .ToSelf()
          .DefinesNamedScope(presenterScope);
      Kernel.Bind<ISessionProvider>()
        .To<SessionProvider>()
        .InNamedScope(presenterScope);
      Kernel.Bind(typeof(IDao<>))
        .To(typeof(Dao<>));
    }
  }
}
```

13. In `Program.cs`, add the following code in the `Main` method:

```
var sessionFactory = ProductModel
  .CreateExampleSessionFactory(true);
var kernel = new StandardKernel();
kernel.Load(new NinjectBindings());
kernel.Bind<ISessionFactory>()
.ToConstant(sessionFactory);

var media1 = kernel.Get<MediaPresenter>();
var media2 = kernel.Get<MediaPresenter>();

media1.ShowBooks().Show();
media2.ShowMovies().Show();

media1.Dispose();
media2.Dispose();

using (var product = kernel.Get<ProductPresenter>())
{
  product.ShowAllProducts().Show();
}

Console.WriteLine("Press any key");
Console.ReadKey();
```

14. Build and run your application. You will see the following output:

How it works...

There are several interesting items in this recipe to discuss. First, we've set up a slightly complex object graph. For each instance of `MediaPresenter`, our graph appears as shown in the following figure:

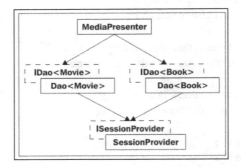

In the previous figure, one instance of session provider is shared by both data access objects. This is accomplished with the configuration of Ninject, our dependency injection framework.

In our `NinjectBindings`, we match up our service interfaces to their matching implementations. We bind the open generic `IDao<>` interface to `Dao<>`, so that requests for `IDao<Book>` are resolved to `Dao<Book>`, `IDao<Movie>` to `Dao<Movie>`, and so on.

One session-per-presenter is accomplished with the use of `DefinedNamedScope` and `InNamedScope`. We find all of the `IPresenter` implementations in the assembly. Each presenter is bound and defines the `PresenterScope`. When we bind `ISessionProvider` to `SessionProviderImpl`, we use `InNamedScope("PresenterScope")` to indicate that we will have only one session provider per presenter.

A simple call to `Kernel.Get<MediaPresenter>()` will return a new presenter instance all wired up and ready to use. It will have two data access objects sharing a common session provider. To close the session and release any lingering database connections, be sure to call `Dispose()` when you're finished with the presenter.

A typical `Save` method on a Dao may look something similar to this:

```
var session = _sessionProvider.GetCurrentSession();
try
{
  session.SaveOrUpdate(entity);
}
catch (StaleObjectStateException)
{
  _sessionProvider.DisposeCurrentSession();
  throw;
}
```

Note how we are immediately throwing away the session (not the provider itself) in the `catch` block. When NHibernate throws an exception from inside a session call, the session's state is undefined. The only remaining operation you can safely perform on that session is `Dispose()`. This allows us to recover gracefully from any exceptions, as the exploded session is already thrown away, so a fresh session can take its place.

You should also take care with entities still associated with this failed session. It's usually a good idea to attach them to the new session, as any operation, including lazy loading, against the failed session will cause further exceptions. The *session.Merge* recipe mentioned later in this chapter discusses a method for accomplishing this.

There's More...

Since the boundaries are not as well-defined as in a web application, there are two very common anti-patterns for handling NHibernate sessions in desktop applications. The first, a singleton session, has the following problems:

▶ Undefined point for flushing the session to the database

▶ Interactions, which cannot be tested, between unrelated parts of the application

▶ It is impossible to recover gracefully from a `StaleObjectExceptions` or other session-exploding exceptions

▶ A stateful singleton is always bad architecture, since consuming code can't rely on the state being consistent between calls

The second, a micro-session, where a session is opened to perform a single operation and then quickly closed, loses all of the benefits of the unit of work, most notably the session cache. Entities will be constantly re-fetched from the database.

See also

▶ *Using session.Merge*

Creating a session ASP.NET MVC action filter

Often, a unit of work maps neatly on to a single controller action. I'll show you how to create an action filter to manage our NHibernate sessions in an ASP.NET MVC or Web API 2 application.

Getting ready

Follow the instructions in the *Getting ready* section of the *Setting up session-per-web request* recipe in the beginning of this chapter. You can name the project `ActionFilterExample`.

How to do it...

1. Add the `NHibernateSessionAttribute` class as shown in the following code:

```
[AttributeUsage(AttributeTargets.Method,
AllowMultiple=false)]
public class NHibernateSessionAttribute
  : ActionFilterAttribute
{
  public NHibernateSessionAttribute()
  {
    Order = 100;
  }
  protected ISessionFactory sessionFactory
  {
    get
    {
      return MvcApplication.SessionFactory;
    }
  }
  public override void OnActionExecuting(
    ActionExecutingContext filterContext)
  {
    var session = sessionFactory.OpenSession();
    CurrentSessionContext.Bind(session);
  }
  public override void OnActionExecuted(
    ActionExecutedContext filterContext)
  {
    var session = CurrentSessionContext
.Unbind(sessionFactory);
    session.Close();
  }
}
```

2. Create a new model class (in the `Models` folder) named `BookModel`:

```
public class BookModel
{
  public int Id { get; set; }
  public string Name { get; set; }
  public string Author { get; set; }
}
```

3. Create a new MVC controller called `BooksController`:

```
public class BooksController : Controller
{
  [NHibernateSession]
  public ActionResult Index()
  {
    var books = DataAccessLayer.GetBooks()
        .Select(x=>new BookModel {
Id=x.Id,
Name=x.Name,
Author= x.Author});
    return View(books);
  }
}
```

4. Create a dummy data access layer with this code:

```
public static class DataAccessLayer
{
  public static IEnumerable<Book> GetBooks()
  {
    var session = MvcApplication.SessionFactory
      .GetCurrentSession();
    using (var tx = session.BeginTransaction())
    {
      var books = session.QueryOver<Book>()
        .List();
      tx.Commit();
      return books;
    }
  }
}
```

5. Inside the `Views` folder, create a folder named `Books`.

6. In the `Books` folder, add a view named `Index.cshtml`:

```
@model IEnumerable<ActionFilterExample.Models.BookModel>

@{
  ViewBag.Title = "Books";
}

<h2>Books</h2>
<ul>
  @foreach (var book in Model)
  {
<li>@book.Name - @book.Author</li>
  }
</ul>
```

7. Build and run your application. You will see the following web page:

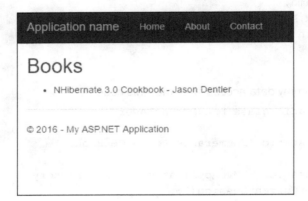

How it works...

The concept behind this recipe builds on the session-per-request recipe at the beginning of the chapter.

Before the `Index()` controller action is executed, ASP.NET MVC will run our filter's `OnActionExecuting` method. In `OnActionExecuting`, our action filter opens a session and binds it to this web request using NHibernate's contextual sessions feature. An option here would be just keep a reference to the session instance inside the controller.

Similarly, ASP.NET MVC will run our filter's `OnActionExecuted` when `Index()` returns. In `OnActionExecuted`, the filter unbinds the session and closes it. Then, ASP.NET MVC processes the action result. In this case, it renders a view to display a list of books.

The `Order` property of an action filter determines in what order that action filter executes. For `Executing` events, all action filters with an unspecified `Order` are executed first. Then, those with a specific `Order` are executed, starting with zero, in ascending order. For `Executed` events, the process works in reverse. Essentially, it allows us to stack action filters as last in, first out. This provides a determinate order, so we can combine it with session-dependent filters with higher `Order` values.

What about Web API?

We can apply exactly the same concept to Web API, since that framework uses an almost identical action filter model. Instead of deriving from `System.Web.Mvc.ActionFilterAttribute` we go for the `System.Web.Http.Filters.ActionFilterAttribute` and override the corresponding methods:

```
public override void OnActionExecuting(HttpActionContext
  actionContext)
{
  var session = sessionFactory.OpenSession();
  CurrentSessionContext.Bind(session);
}

public override void OnActionExecuted(HttpActionExecutedContext
 actionExecutedContext)
{
  var session = CurrentSessionContext.Unbind(sessionFactory);
  session.Close();
}
```

This attribute can now be applied to any `ApiController` that requires an NHibernate session.

There's more...

NHibernate requires an NHibernate transaction around every database interaction, whether it be a direct method call on the session or an action that triggers lazy loading. With this implementation, it is very difficult to capture lazy loading calls in a transaction. As we will see in the next recipe, we can combine the proper use of sessions and transactions in a single action filter to allow for lazy loading elsewhere in the controller action.

Make sure that the action loads all of the data required by the view. The session is not open anymore when the action result (a view, in this case) is rendered.

 Because the session has already been closed, if a view attempts to access a lazy-loaded collection that wasn't loaded by the controller action, you will get a `LazyInitializationException`.

Even with lenient implementations, it's not recommended to access the database from the view. Views are usually dynamic and difficult to test.

View models

To avoid this issue and many others, many ASP.NET MVC applications use view models. A view model class is defined for each view, and contains exactly the data required by that view, and nothing more. Think of it as a data-transfer object between the controller and the view.

Rather than writing pages of plumbing code to copy data from entities to view models, you can use an open source project, `AutoMapper`. When combined with an action filter attribute, this process becomes dead simple.

Pay attention to the `Order` property on the `AutoMapper` attribute. To allow for lazy loading when translating from entities to view models, the `Order` should be even higher than our session attribute. This ensures that the session is open when `AutoMapper` is translating.

See also

▸ *Setting up session-per-web request*

▸ *Creating a transaction ASP.NET MVC action filter*

Creating a transaction ASP.NET MVC action filter

We can extend the concepts of the previous recipe to NHibernate transactions as well. In this recipe, we'll show you how to create an action filter to manage our NHibernate sessions and transactions in an MVC or Web API 2 application.

Getting ready

Complete the previous recipe, *Creating a session ASP.NET MVC action filter*.

How to do it...

1. Add the `NeedsPersistenceAttribute` class:

```
public class NeedsPersistenceAttribute
    : NHibernateSessionAttribute
{

    protected ISession session
    {
```

```
    get
    {
      return sessionFactory.GetCurrentSession();
    }
  }

  public override void OnActionExecuting(
    ActionExecutingContext filterContext)
  {
    base.OnActionExecuting(filterContext);
    session.BeginTransaction();
  }

  public override void OnActionExecuted(
    ActionExecutedContext filterContext)
  {

    var tx = session.Transaction;
    if (tx != null && tx.IsActive)
    {
      var noUnhandledException =
        filterContext.Exception == null ||
        filterContext.ExceptionHandled;

      if (noUnhandledException &&
      filterContext.Controller.ViewData.ModelState.IsValid)
      {
        session.Transaction.Commit();
      }
      else
      {
        session.Transaction.Rollback();
      }
    }

    base.OnActionExecuted(filterContext);
  }

}
```

2. Decorate your controller actions with the `NeedsPersistence` attribute as shown in the following lines of code:

```
public class BooksController : Controller
{
[NeedsPersistence]
  public ActionResult Index()
  {
    var books = DataAccessLayer.GetBooks()
        .Select(x=>new BookModel {
                Id=x.Id,
          Name=x.Name,
          Author= x.Author});
    return View(books);
  }
}
```

3. Update the `DataAccessLayer.GetBooks()` method to use the following code:

```
var session = MvcApplication.SessionFactory
  .GetCurrentSession();
var books = session.QueryOver<Book>()
  .List();
return books;
```

How it works...

Before ASP.NET MVC executes the controller action, our `NeedsPersistence` action filter starts a new session and NHibernate transaction. If everything goes as planned, as soon as the action is completed, the filter commits the transaction. However, if an exception is thrown or if some kind of model validation error is present, the transaction will be rolled back. Note that we no longer need to use a transaction in our data access layer, as the entire controller action is wrapped in a transaction.

There's more...

This attribute inherits from our session action filter defined in the previous recipe. If you're managing your session differently, such as session-per-request, inherit from `ActionFilterAttribute` instead.

Just as in the previous recipe, we can adapt this filter for use with ASP.NET Web API, just by deriving from a different base class.

Save entities to the database

Clearly we have saved entities to the database in many of the previous recipes, but it's time to dig a bit deeper into how that actually works. This recipe will explore different ways of saving and what happens behind the scenes.

Getting ready

1. Create a new Windows forms project named `SessionRecipes`, in Visual Studio.
2. Add a reference to `NHibernate` using NuGet Packet Manager Console:

   `Install-Package NHibernate -project SessionRecipes`

3. Also add a reference to `NH4CookbookHelpers`:

   `Install-Package NH4CookbookHelpers -project SessionRecipes`

4. Remove the class `Form1.cs` from the project.
5. Add `using NH4CookbookHelpers;` to the top of `Program.cs`.
6. Edit `Program.cs` so that the last line in `Main` reads:

   `Application.Run(new WindowsFormsRunner());`

Using `NHCookbookHelpers` you don't even have to have a database server available, since it uses an in-memory SQLite database by default. If you want to use something else, like a local SQL server, you can specify a configuration instance to be used. Perhaps the most convenient way is to use a coded configuration, as described in *Chapter 1*, *The Configuration and Schema*.

Specify the default configuration before the last line in `Main`:

```
RecipeLoader.DefaultConfiguration = new Configuration()
.DataBaseIntegration(db =>
{
    db.Dialect<MsSql2012Dialect>();
    db.Driver<Sql2008ClientDriver>();
    db.ConnectionString =
      @"Server=.\SQLEXPRESS;Database=NHCookbook;
Trusted_Connection=True;";
});
```

Note that the database used in the recipes will be tinkered with, so don't use a database with data that you need to stay intact.

How to do it...

1. Add a new folder named `SavingEntities` to the `SessionRecipes` project.

2. Add a new class named `Recipe` to the folder:

```csharp
using System;
using NH4CookbookHelpers.Queries;
using NH4CookbookHelpers.Queries.Model;
using NHibernate;

namespace SessionRecipes.SavingEntities
{
  public class Recipe : QueryRecipe
  {
    protected override void Run(ISessionFactory
      sessionFactory)
    {
      PerformSave(sessionFactory);
      PerformUpdate(sessionFactory);

      TestFlushMode(sessionFactory, FlushMode.Auto);
      TestFlushMode(sessionFactory, FlushMode.Commit);
      TestFlushMode(sessionFactory, FlushMode.Never);
    }

    private void PerformSave(ISessionFactory
      sessionFactory)
    {
      Console.WriteLine("PerformSave");

      var product = new Product { Name = "PerformSave" };

      using (var session = sessionFactory.OpenSession())
      {
        using (var tx = session.BeginTransaction())
        {

          session.Save(product);
          Console.WriteLine("Id:{0}", product.Id);
          tx.Commit();
        }
```

```csharp
    }
  }

private void PerformUpdate(ISessionFactory
  sessionFactory)
{
  Console.WriteLine("PerformUpdate");
  Product product;

  using (var firstSession = sessionFactory
    .OpenSession())
  {
    using (var tx = firstSession.BeginTransaction())
    {
      product = firstSession.Get<Product>(1);
      tx.Commit();
    }
  }

  product.Description += "-Updated by PerformUpdate";

  using (var secondSession = sessionFactory
    .OpenSession())
  {
    using (var tx = secondSession.BeginTransaction())
    {
      secondSession.Update(product);
      tx.Commit();
    }
  }
}

private void TestFlushMode(ISessionFactory
  sessionFactory, FlushMode flushMode)
{
  var name = "TestPublisher" + flushMode;

  using (var session = sessionFactory.OpenSession())
  {
    session.FlushMode = flushMode;

    using (var tx = session.BeginTransaction())
```

```
        {
          var publisher = new Publisher { Name = name};
          Console.WriteLine("Saving {0}", name);
          session.Save(publisher);

          Console.WriteLine("Searching for {0}", name);

          var searchPublisher = session
            .QueryOver<Publisher>()
            .Where(x => x.Name == name)
            .SingleOrDefault();

          Console.WriteLine(searchPublisher != null ?
"Found it!" : "Didn't find it!");

          tx.Commit();
        }

        using (var tx = session.BeginTransaction())
        {
          Console.WriteLine(
"Searching for {0} again", name);

          var searchPublisher = session
            .QueryOver<Publisher>()
            .Where(x => x.Name == name)
            .SingleOrDefault();

          Console.WriteLine(searchPublisher != null ?
"Found it!" : "Didn't find it!");
        }
      }
    }
  }
}
```

3. Run the application and start the `SavingEntities` recipe. You should be able to see the following output:

```
PerformSave
Id:4
PerformUpdate
Saving TestPublisherAuto
Searching for TestPublisherAuto
Found it!
Searching for TestPublisherAuto again
Found it!
Saving TestPublisherCommit
Searching for TestPublisherCommit
Didn't find it!
Searching for TestPublisherCommit again
Found it!
Saving TestPublisherNever
Searching for TestPublisherNever
Didn't find it!
Searching for TestPublisherNever again
Didn't find it!
```

How it works...

In the preceding recipe, we use a couple of different session methods to insert and update entities in the database.

Save

This is probably the method you will use most frequently. It's used when you have a fresh new entity that you want to save to the database. To summarize what it does:

- Attach the entity to the session
- Assign the Id to the entity, even if that requires a database roundtrip which possibly saves the entire entity
- Follow any cascading rules for related entities
- Return the assigned Id
- When the session is flushed, if still necessary, insert the entity into the database

Calling `Save` more than once with the same entity and the same session works just fine, but is basically pointless. However, saving the same entity in more than one session will actually cause multiple database inserts.

Update

We're updating entities all the time, so isn't this the most frequently used method? No, probably not. As we will discuss later in this recipe, updates are usually handled automatically when the session is flushed. So, what's the purpose of `Update` then? It can be used if you have an entity that was loaded in one session but the update is delayed and performed later in another session. In short:

- ▶ Attach the entity to the session and mark is as existing
- ▶ Follow any cascading rules for related entities
- ▶ When the session is flushed, update the entity in the database

Calling `Update` more than once for the same entity will cause an exception to be thrown.

SaveOrUpdate

You probably guessed it. `SaveOrUpdate` is a combination of the previous methods. If the session determines that the entity was already saved, it will trigger an `Update`, otherwise a `Save`.

Persist

This method is very similar to `Save`, but with a few differences. Most notably, it's a void method that does not return the assigned Id as `Save` does. `Session.Persist` doesn't guarantee that it will assign the Id to the entity. In theory, it can delay that action until the session is flushed. Another difference is that `Persist` will throw an exception if you pass a detached entity to it (an entity that was already saved but no longer connected to a session).

Using different flush modes

We have mentioned the term **session flush** a couple of times now. Maybe it's time we describe what it means.

NHibernate normally doesn't execute inserts, updates, and deletes as a response to explicit method calls. Instead it keeps the initial state of each loaded entity in memory and whenever a flush is triggered, this state is compared to the current state. Modified states will cause updates, new states will cause inserts and deleted states will cause deletes. This means that we don't have to ask NHibernate to update an entity. If it has been modified since it was loaded, the flushing process will pick this up and acts accordingly.

It may, however, be useful to control when this process occurs. Do we want it to happen automatically or should an explicit method call be necessary? For this purpose we can set the session's `FlushMode` property to one of several enum values.

Commit

When using this flush mode, changes are applied to the database when the current transaction is committed.

Auto

This is the default flush mode, but also the most advanced. Not only does it flush the session when a transaction is committed, it also attempts to deduce the entities or tables that are used in a query. If required, the session will be flushed before the query is executed, in order to make the query results reflect the state of the database, including all pending inserts, updates, and deletes.

Always

This flush mode acts similarly to `Auto`, but no query scanning logic is applied. The session will be flushed before every query. This mode is rarely used, but it does provide the best protection against consistency problems. While the `Auto` mode is very clever, there are occasions when NHibernate won't be able to extract the tables used, especially for native SQL queries. If you use such queries often and still want the consistency support offered by automatic flushing, the `Always` mode is a good choice.

Never

It does what it says on the box. Nothing is flushed to the database, unless explicitly triggered by calling `session.Flush()`. This is useful when we want to ensure that nothing is written to the database, unless we say so. An example can be a long running business process, perhaps spanning multiple sessions, which should be finalized only after several steps have been executed.

In the recipe, use the `Publisher` entity to show the behaviour of the different flush modes. If we instead use the `Product` entity, the searches will always return the entity. Why the difference? It's simply because `Product` has an integer Id, which is generated by the `Native` POID generator. In order to properly assign an Id to the new entity, the database must be contacted and when that is done, NHibernate might as well save the entity too. The Publisher class, on the other hand, has a `Guid` Id, which is assigned by NHibernate's comb generator. No roundtrip to the database is required and nothing will be saved until the session is flushed.

Using session.Merge

`Session.Merge` is perhaps one of the most misunderstood features in NHibernate. In this recipe, we'll show you how to use `session.Merge` to associate a dirty, detached entity with a new session. This is particularly handy when recovering from `StaleObjectStateException`s.

Getting ready

Follow the Getting ready step in the *Save entities to the database* recipe in this chapter.

How to do it...

1. Add a new folder named `MergingEntities` to the `SessionRecipes` project.

2. Add a class named `Recipe` to the folder:

```csharp
using System;
using NH4CookbookHelpers.Queries;
using NH4CookbookHelpers.Queries.Model;
using NHibernate;

namespace SessionRecipes.MergingEntities
{
  public class Recipe : QueryRecipe
  {
    protected override void Run(ISessionFactory sessionFactory)
    {
      var book = CreateAndSaveBook(sessionFactory);
      book.Name = "Dormice in Action";
      book.Description = "Hibernation of the Hazel Dormouse";
      book.UnitPrice = 0.83M;
      book.ISBN = "0123";

      using (var session = sessionFactory.OpenSession())
      {
        using (var tx = session.BeginTransaction())
        {
          var mergedBook = (Book)session.Merge(book);
          tx.Commit();

          Console.WriteLine(
            ReferenceEquals(book, mergedBook));
        }
      }
    }

    private static Book CreateAndSaveBook(
  ISessionFactory sessionFactory)
    {
      var book = new Book()
      {
        Name = "The book of awesomeness",
        Description = "Pure Awesome",
        UnitPrice = 50.0M,
        ISBN = "3043",
```

```
        Author = "Awe Some",
      };

      using (var session = sessionFactory.OpenSession())
      {
        using (var tx = session.BeginTransaction())
        {
          session.Save(book);
          tx.Commit();
          session.Evict(book);
        }
      }
      return book;
    }
  }
}
```

3. Run the application and start the MergingEntities recipe. Inspect the query log.

How it works...

In `CreateAndSaveBook`, we create a book and save it to the database. We commit our transaction, evict the book from session, close the session, and return the book. This sets up our problem. We now have an entity without a session. Changes to this entity are not being tracked. It's just a plain ordinary book object.

We continue to change the book object and now we want to save those changes. NHibernate doesn't know what we've done to this book. It could have been passed through other layers or tiers of a large application. We don't know the session with which it's associated, if any. We may not even know if the book exists in the database.

`Session.Merge` handles all of this uncertainty for us. If the current session has a book with this ID, data from our book is copied on to the persistent book object in the session and the persistent book object is returned.

If the current session doesn't have a book with this ID, NHibernate loads it from the database. The changes are copied on to the persistent book object that was just loaded in to the session. The persistent book object is returned.

If NHibernate didn't find a book with that ID in the database, it copies data from our book object on to a new persistent book associated with the session and returns the new persistent book object.

The end result of `session.Merge` is the same. The book it returns is not the same instance we passed it in, but it contains all of our changes and is associated with the current session. When we commit our transaction, those changes are written to the database.

The book we passed in is not associated with the current session.

See also

▶ *Using session.Refresh*

Using session.Refresh

Especially in desktop applications, it may be necessary to reload an entity to reflect recent changes made in a different session. In this recipe, we'll use `session.Refresh` to refresh an entity's data as it is being manipulated by two sessions.

Getting ready

Follow the Getting ready step in the *Save entities to the database* recipe in this chapter.

How to do it...

1. Add a new folder named `SessionRefresh` to the `SessionRecipes` project.

2. Add a class named `Recipe` to the folder:

```
using System;
using NH4CookbookHelpers;
using NH4CookbookHelpers.Queries.Model;
using NHibernate;

namespace SessionRecipes.SessionRefresh
{
  public class Recipe : QueryRecipe
  {
    protected override void Run(ISessionFactory sessionFactory)
    {
      using (var sessionA = sessionFactory.OpenSession())
      using (var sessionB = sessionFactory.OpenSession())
      {

        int productId;
```

```csharp
var productA = new Product()
{
  Name = "Lawn Chair",
  Description = "Lime Green, Comfortable",
  UnitPrice = 10.00M
};

using (var tx = sessionA.BeginTransaction())
{
  Console.WriteLine("Saving product in session A.");
  productId = (int)sessionA.Save(productA);
  tx.Commit();
}

using (var tx = sessionB.BeginTransaction())
{
  Console.WriteLine("Changing price in session B.");
  var productB = sessionB.Get<Product>(productId);
  productB.UnitPrice = 15.00M;
  tx.Commit();
}

using (var tx = sessionA.BeginTransaction())
{
  Console.WriteLine("Price was {0:c}",
    productA.UnitPrice);

  Console.WriteLine("Refreshing");

  sessionA.Refresh(productA);

  Console.WriteLine("Price is {0:c}",
    productA.UnitPrice);
  tx.Commit();
}
        }
      }
    }
  }
}
```

3. Run your application and start the `SessionRefresh` recipe. You will see the following output:

```
Saving product in session A.
Changing price in session B.
Price was 10,00 kr
Refreshing
Price is 15,00 kr
```

How it works...

In this contrived example, we open two sessions and manipulate two instances of the same entity. In `session A`, we save a newly created product – a $10 lime green lawn chair. Then in `session B`, we get the very same lawn chair. We now have two instances of the same entity. One is associated with `session A` and the other with `session B`.

We change the price of `session B`'s lawn chair to $15. Notice that we don't call any method to save or update the database. Because `session B` loaded the lawn chair, it is tracking the changes and will automatically update the database when the session is flushed. This happens automatically when we commit the transaction. This is called **automatic dirty checking**. `Session A`'s instance of lawn chair is still priced at $10.

When we call `sessionA.Refresh`, NHibernate will update session A's lawn chair with fresh data from the database. Now `session A`'s lawn chair shows the new $15 price.

There's more...

`session.Refresh` is especially important in desktop applications, where we may have several sessions running simultaneously to handle multiple databound forms, and we want our saved changes on one form to be reflected immediately on another form displaying the same entity.

In this scenario, you will most likely set up some sort of message publishing between forms so that saving an entity on one form broadcasts an "I saved this entity" message to other forms displaying the same entity. When a form receives such a message, it calls `session.Refresh` to get the new data.

A `session.Refresh` will also cascade to associated entities, if the association's mapping has `cascade="refresh"` specified (it's implied by `cascade="all"`). In that case, Refresh might trigger multiple database queries!

See also

▶ *Setting up session-per-presenter*

Handle concurrency using session.Lock

It's often important to handle scenarios where two or more clients may try to work with the same entities, concurrently. In *Chapter 2, Models and Mappings*, in section: *Handling versioning and concurrency* we discussed how to handle that using versioning and optimistic concurrency. A more aggressive approach is to use pessimistic concurrency, where specific rows in the database are explicitly locked for certain operations. Many DBMSes, such as SQL Server, has a good support for this and in this recipe we'll show how NHibernate can use that functionality.

Getting ready

Follow the Getting ready step in the *Save entities to the database* recipe in this chapter.

How to do it...

Since this recipe requires specific database support, you can't run it using the SQLite database, which is the default in NH4CookbookHelpers. Reconfigure the recipe runner by setting the RecipeLoader.DefaultConfiguration property or simply override the Configure method in the Recipe class to provide a database configuration specific to this recipe.

1. Create a new folder named SessionLock in the project.

2. Add a new class named Recipe to the folder:

```
using System;
using System.Threading;
using NH4CookbookHelpers.Queries;
using NH4CookbookHelpers.Queries.Model;
using NHibernate;

namespace SessionRecipes.SessionLock
{
  public class Recipe : QueryRecipe
  {
    protected override void Run(ISessionFactory
      sessionFactory)
    {
```

```
    ExecuteWithLockMode(sessionFactory,
      LockMode.None,
      LockMode.None);

    ExecuteWithLockMode(sessionFactory,
      LockMode.Upgrade,
      LockMode.Upgrade);

    ExecuteWithLockMode(sessionFactory,
      LockMode.UpgradeNoWait,
      LockMode.UpgradeNoWait);
}

private void ExecuteWithLockMode(ISessionFactory
  sessionFactory, LockMode lockMode1,
  LockMode lockMode2)
{
  Console.WriteLine("Executing with {0} and {1}",
    lockMode1, lockMode2);
  Console.WriteLine();

  var thread1 = new Thread(() =>
    GetAndChangeProductInLock(sessionFactory,
      lockMode1, 3000)) {
      Name = "Thread1"
  };

  var thread2 = new Thread(() =>
    GetAndChangeProductInLock(sessionFactory,
      lockMode2, 0)) {
      Name = "Thread2"
  };

  thread1.Start();

  Thread.Sleep(300);

  thread2.Start();

  thread1.Join();
  thread2.Join();
```

```csharp
        Console.WriteLine();
    }

    private void GetAndChangeProductInLock(ISessionFactory
      sessionFactory, LockMode lockMode, int sleepTime)
    {
      try
      {
        using (var session = sessionFactory.OpenSession())
        {
          using (var tx = session.BeginTransaction())
          {
            var product = session.Get<Product>(1);
            Console.WriteLine("{0} acquiring lock",
            Thread.CurrentThread.Name);

            session.Lock(product, lockMode);

            Console.WriteLine("{0} acquired lock",
            Thread.CurrentThread.Name);

            product.Description =
              string.Format("Updated in LockMode.{0}",
                lockMode);

            Thread.Sleep(sleepTime);

            Console.WriteLine("{0} committing",
              Thread.CurrentThread.Name);

            tx.Commit();

            Console.WriteLine("{0} committed",
              Thread.CurrentThread.Name);
          }
        }
      }
      catch (Exception ex)
      {
        Console.WriteLine("Exception in {0}:{1}",
          Thread.CurrentThread.Name, ex.Message);
      }
    }
  }
}
```

3. Run the application and start the `SessionLock` recipe. You should be able to see this output:

```
Executing with None and None

Thread1 acquiring lock
Thread1 acquired lock
Thread2 acquiring lock
Thread2 acquired lock
Thread2 committed
Thread1 committed

Executing with Upgrade and Upgrade

Thread1 acquiring lock
Thread1 acquired lock
Thread2 acquiring lock
Thread1 committed
Thread2 acquired lock
Thread2 committed

Executing with UpgradeNoWait and UpgradeNoWait

Thread1 acquiring lock
Thread1 acquired lock
Thread2 acquiring lock
Exception in Thread2:could not lock: [NH4CookbookHelpers.Queries.Model.Movie#1][SQL: SELECT Id FROM Product
with (updlock, rowlock, nowait) WHERE Id = ?]
Thread1 committed
```

How it works...

`Session.Lock` uses database specific methods to acquire locks on specific rows, in order to prevent concurrent access to the same entities from multiple clients. In our recipe, we try to simulate this scenario, using two separate threads executing almost simultaneously. The first thread will sleep for three seconds before it commits its transaction, and the second thread will have to act accordingly. How it acts depends on the `LockMode` used.

None

This is the default lock mode. No specific lock is required. However, if the database becomes involved (the object was not found in any cache), a read lock may be acquired.

Read

This is a shared lock, which will be acquired implicitly if the transaction's serialization level is `RepeatableRead` or serializable.

Upgrade

When this lock mode is used, NHibernate will issue a SELECT WITH (updlock,rowlock) query. This query will not return anything until any previous locks have been released. This can be seen in the recipe output, where the second thread doesn't acquire its lock until the first thread has committed its transaction:

- ▶ Thread1 acquiring lock
- ▶ Thread1 acquired lock
- ▶ Thread2 acquiring lock
- ▶ Thread1 committed
- ▶ Thread2 acquired lock
- ▶ Thread2 committed

If the transaction owning the lock takes a lot of time to complete, a timeout exception may be thrown in the transaction which tries to acquire the new lock.

UpgradeNoWait

This lock mode, which requires specific database support, behaves similarly to Upgrade. However, instead of waiting for a previous lock to be released, it will fail immediately if the lock couldn't be acquired.

- ▶ Thread1 acquiring lock
- ▶ Thread1 acquired lock
- ▶ Thread2 acquiring lock

Exception in Thread2:could not lock: [NH4CookbookHelpers.Queries.Model. Movie#1] [SQL: SELECT Id FROM Product with (updlock, rowlock, nowait) WHERE Id = ?]

Thread1 committed

There's more...

Session.Lock is not the only way these lock modes can be used. We can also use overloads on session.Load or session.Get.

```
var product = session.Load<Product>(1, LockMode.Upgrade);
```

Note that LockMode.Upgrade or LockMode.UpgradeNoWait changes the behavior of session.Load. Normally it will not call the database, until the loaded entity is being used. When a lock is required, the database must be involved and the entity will be loaded immediately.

We can also specify the lock mode on a query, effectively acquiring locks on all the entities it returns. For an HQL query it looks similar to this:

```
session.CreateQuery("from Movie m where m.Director = :director")
  .SetString("director", directorName)
  .SetLockMode("m",LockMode.Upgrade)
  .List<Movie>();
```

Using dictionaries as entities

A little-known feature of NHibernate is `EntityMode.Map`. In this recipe, I'll show you how we can use this feature to persist entities without classes.

Getting ready

Follow the Getting ready step in the *Save entities to the database* recipe in this chapter.

How to do it...

1. Add a new folder named `EntityModeMap` to the `SessionRecipes` project.

2. Add a new class named `Recipe` to the folder:

```csharp
using System;
using System.Collections;
using System.Collections.Generic;
using System.Linq;
using NH4CookbookHelpers;
using NHibernate;
using NHibernate.Cfg;

namespace SessionRecipes.EntityModeMap
{
  public class Recipe : HbmMappingRecipe
  {

    protected override void Configure(Configuration cfg)
    {
      cfg.SetProperty("default_entity_mode", "dynamic-map");
    }

    protected override void AddInitialData(ISession session)
    {
      var movieActors = new List<Dictionary<string, object>>()
      {
```

```
      new Dictionary<string, object>() {
        {"Actor","Keanu Reeves"},
        {"Role","Neo"}
      },
      new Dictionary<string, object>() {
        {"Actor", "Carrie-Ann Moss"},
        {"Role", "Trinity"}
      }
    };

    var movie = new Dictionary<string, object>()
    {
     {"Name", "The Matrix"},
     {"Description", "Sci-Fi Action film"},
     {"UnitPrice", 18.99M},
     {"Director", "Wachowski Brothers"},
     {"Actors", movieActors}
    };

    session.Save("Movie", movie);
  }

  public override void RunQueries(ISession session)
  {
    var movies = session
      .CreateQuery("from Movie").List<IDictionary>();
    foreach (var movie in movies)
    {
      Console.WriteLine("Movie:{0}", movie["Name"]);
      Console.WriteLine("Actors");
      foreach (var actor in ((IEnumerable)movie["Actors"]).
OfType<IDictionary>())
        {
          Console.WriteLine("{0} as {1}", actor["Actor"],
actor["Role"]);
        }
    }
  }
 }
}
```

3. Add a new `Product.hbm.xml` mapping file to the folder:

```xml
<?xml version="1.0" encoding="utf-8" ?>
<hibernate-mapping xmlns="urn:nhibernate-mapping-2.2">
  <class entity-name="Product"
      discriminator-value="Product">
    <id name="Id" type="Guid">
      <generator class="guid.comb" />
    </id>
    <discriminator column="ProductType" type="String" />
    <natural-id mutable="true">
      <property name="Name" not-null="true"
          type="String" />
    </natural-id>
    <version name="Version" type="Int32"/>
    <property name="Description" type="String" />
    <property name="UnitPrice" not-null="true"
        type="Currency" />
  </class>
</hibernate-mapping>
```

4. Again, create a mapping file named `Movie.hbm.xml` with the following mapping:

```xml
<?xml version="1.0" encoding="utf-8" ?>
<hibernate-mapping xmlns="urn:nhibernate-mapping-2.2">
  <subclass entity-name="Movie" extends="Product"
      discriminator-value="Movie">
    <property name="Director" type="String" />
    <bag name="Actors" cascade="all-delete-orphan">
      <key column="MovieId" />
      <one-to-many class="ActorRole"/>
    </bag>
  </subclass>
</hibernate-mapping>
```

5. Finally, create a mapping file named `ActorRole.hbm.xml` with the following mapping:

```xml
<?xml version="1.0" encoding="utf-8" ?>
<hibernate-mapping xmlns="urn:nhibernate-mapping-2.2">

  <class entity-name="ActorRole">
    <id name="Id" type="Guid">
      <generator class="guid.comb" />
    </id>
```

```
<version name="Version" type="Int32" />
<property name="Actor" type="String"
    not-null="true" />
<property name="Role" type="String"
    not-null="true" />
    </class>
</hibernate-mapping>
```

6. Don't forget to set your mapping files as embedded resources.

7. Run the application and start the `EntityModeMap` recipe.

8. Check the database's `Product` and `ActorRole` tables.

How it works...

`EntityMode.Map` allows us to define entities as dictionaries, instead of statically typed objects. There are three key pieces to this approach.

First, instead of creating sessions using the default `EntityMode.Poco` where NHibernate expects us to interact with it using plain old class objects. We've told NHibernate to use `EntityMode.Map` by setting `default_entity_mode` to `dynamic-map`. Remember from *Chapter 1, The Configuration and Schema* that, because of NHibernate's Java roots, NHibernate uses the term map in place of dictionary.

Next, we've made slight changes to our mappings. First, you'll notice that we've set an `entity-name` instead of a `classname`. This allows us to specify an entity by name, instead of allowing NHibernate to decide based on the type of object we pass in. Next, you'll note that we specify types for all of our properties. We don't have classes that NHibernate can reflect to guess our data types, we have to declare it. Finally, we specify discriminator values. You'll recollect from *Chapter 2, Models and Mappings* that the default discriminator value is the type's `FullName`. The default discriminator is actually the entity-name, which defaults to the type's `FullName`. In this case, we don't have a type and if we used our entity-names, the data wouldn't match our normal mappings. We override the values simply so the data will match perfectly with the data from our other recipes.

Finally, we interact with the session using dictionaries (maps) and entity-name strings instead of objects with types.

While this example may seem a bit academic, with the release of the dynamic language runtime and the new `dynamic` feature of C# 4.0, this type of scenario will undoubtedly prove useful in bridging the gap between NHibernate and the dynamic language world.

Partially dynamic

It's rarely desirable to use `EntityMode.Map` throughout your application, as shown in this recipe. Instead, you may want to use it only in a specific case, where you would rather not create matching classes. In this scenario, we will not set the `default_entity_mode` property and instead open a child session in map mode. The code to accomplish this is as follows:

```
using (var pocoSession = sessionFactory.OpenSession())
{
  using (var childSession =
  pocoSession.GetSession(EntityMode.Map))
  {
    // Do something here
  }
}
```

Using NHibernate with transaction scope

Reliable integration with other systems is a common business requirement. When these systems report error conditions, it's necessary to roll back not only the local database work, but perhaps the work of multiple transactional resources. In this recipe, we'll show you how to use Microsoft's transaction scope and NHibernate to achieve this goal.

Getting ready

Follow the Getting ready step in the *Save entities to the database* recipe in this chapter.

How to do it...

1. Add a reference to `System.Transaction`.
2. Add a folder named `UsingTransactionScope` to the project.

3. Add a public interface named `IReceiveProductUpdates` to the folder:

```
using NH4CookbookHelpers.Queries.Model;

namespace SessionRecipes.UsingTransactionScope
{
  public interface IReceiveProductUpdates
  {
    void Add(Product product);
    void Update(Product product);
    void Remove(Product product);
  }
}
```

4. Add a public class named `WarehouseFacade` with this code:

```
public class WarehouseFacade : IReceiveProductUpdates
{

  public void Add(Product product)
  {
    Console.WriteLine("Adding {0} to warehouse system.",
              product.Name);
  }

  public void Update(Product product)
  {
    Console.WriteLine("Updating {0} in warehouse system.",
                product.Name);
  }

  public void Remove(Product product)
  {
    Console.WriteLine("Removing {0} from warehouse system.",
                product.Name);
    var message = string.Format(
"Warehouse still has inventory of {0}.",
      product.Name);
    throw new ApplicationException(message);
  }

}
```

5. Add a public class named `ProductCatalog` with this code:

```
public class ProductCatalog : IReceiveProductUpdates
{

  private readonly ISessionFactory _sessionFactory;

  public ProductCatalog(ISessionFactory sessionFactory)
  {
    _sessionFactory = sessionFactory;
  }

  public void Add(Product product)
  {
    Console.WriteLine("Adding {0} to product catalog.",
                      product.Name);
    using (var session = _sessionFactory.OpenSession())
    using (var tx = session.BeginTransaction())
    {
      session.Save(product);
      tx.Commit();
    }
  }

  public void Update(Product product)
  {
    Console.WriteLine("Updating {0} in product catalog.",
                      product.Name);
    using (var session = _sessionFactory.OpenSession())
    using (var tx = session.BeginTransaction())
    {
      session.Update(product);
      tx.Commit();
    }
  }

  public void Remove(Product product)
  {
    Console.WriteLine("Removing {0} from product catalog.",
                      product.Name);
    using (var session = _sessionFactory.OpenSession())
    using (var tx = session.BeginTransaction())
    {
      session.Delete(product);
```

```
      tx.Commit();
    }
  }

}
```

6. Add a class named `ProductApp` with the following code:

```
using System;
using System.Transactions;
using NH4CookbookHelpers.Queries.Model;

namespace SessionRecipes.UsingTransactionScope
{
  public class ProductApp
  {
    private readonly IReceiveProductUpdates[] _services;

    public ProductApp(params IReceiveProductUpdates[] services)
    {
      _services = services;
    }

    public void AddProduct(Product newProduct)
    {
      Console.WriteLine("Adding {0}.", newProduct.Name);
      try
      {
        using (var scope = new TransactionScope())
        {
          foreach (var service in _services)
            service.Add(newProduct);
          scope.Complete();
        }
      }
      catch (Exception ex)
      {
        Console.WriteLine("Product could not be added.");
        Console.WriteLine(ex.Message);
      }

    }

    public void UpdateProduct(Product changedProduct)
```

```
    {
      Console.WriteLine("Updating {0}.",
        changedProduct.Name);
      try
      {
        using (var scope = new TransactionScope())
        {
          foreach (var service in _services)
            service.Update(changedProduct);
          scope.Complete();
        }
      }
      catch (Exception ex)
      {
        Console.WriteLine("Product could not be updated.");
        Console.WriteLine(ex.Message);
      }
    }

    public void RemoveProduct(Product oldProduct)
    {
      Console.WriteLine("Removing {0}.",
        oldProduct.Name);
      try
      {
        using (var scope = new TransactionScope())
        {
          foreach (var service in _services)
            service.Remove(oldProduct);
          scope.Complete();
        }
      }
      catch (Exception ex)
      {
        Console.WriteLine("Product could not be removed.");
        Console.WriteLine(ex.Message);
      }
    }
  }
}
```

7. Add a new class named `Recipe` to the folder:

```
using NH4CookbookHelpers.Queries;
using NH4CookbookHelpers.Queries.Model;
using NHibernate;

namespace SessionRecipes.UsingTransactionScope
{
  public class Recipe : QueryRecipe
  {
    protected override void Run(ISessionFactory sessionFactory)
    {
      var catalog = new ProductCatalog(sessionFactory);
      var warehouse = new WarehouseFacade();

      var p = new ProductApp(catalog, warehouse);

      var sprockets = new Product()
      {
        Name = "Sprockets",
        Description = "12 pack, metal",
        UnitPrice = 14.99M
      };

      p.AddProduct(sprockets);

      sprockets.UnitPrice = 9.99M;
      p.UpdateProduct(sprockets);

      p.RemoveProduct(sprockets);
    }
  }
}
```

8. Run the application and start the `UsingTransactionScope` recipe. You should see this output:

```
Adding Sprockets.
Adding Sprockets to product catalog.
Adding Sprockets to warehouse system.
Updating Sprockets.
Updating Sprockets in product catalog.
Updating Sprockets in warehouse system.
Removing Sprockets.
Removing Sprockets from product cata-log.
Removing Sprockets from warehouse system.
Product could not be removed.
Warehouse still has inventory of Sprockets.
```

9. Check the database (in the tables tab). You should find a `Product` row for `Sprocket` with a unit price of $9.99.

How it works...

In this recipe, we work with two services that receive product updates. The first, a "product catalog that uses NHibernate to store product data. The second, a small facade, is not as well-defined. It could use a number of different technologies to integrate our application with the larger warehouse system it represents.

Our services allow us to add, update, and remove products in these two systems. By wrapping these changes in a `TransactionScope`, we gain the ability to roll back the product catalog changes if the warehouse system fails, maintaining a consistent state.

Remember that NHibernate requires NHibernate transactions when interacting with the database. `TransactionScope` is not a substitute. As illustrated in the following figure, the `TransactionScope` should completely surround both the session and NHibernate transactions. The call to `TransactionScope.Complete()` should occur after the session has been disposed. Any other order will most likely lead to nasty, production crashing bugs, such as connection leaks.

When we attempt to remove a product, our `WarehouseFacade` throws an exception, and things get a little strange. We committed the NHibernate transaction, so why didn't our delete happen? It did, but it was rolled back by the `TransactionScope`. When we started our NHibernate transaction, NHibernate detected the ambient transaction created by the `TransactionScope` and enlisted. The underlying connection and database transaction were held until the `TransactionScope` committed, or in this case, rolled back.

See also

- ▸ *Creating a session ASP.NET MVC action filter*
- ▸ *Creating a transaction ASP.NET MVC action filter*

4

Queries

In this chapter, we will cover the following recipes:

- ▶ Query entities by ID
- ▶ Using LINQ to NHibernate
- ▶ Using CriteriaQueries
- ▶ Using QueryOver
- ▶ Using QueryOver projections and aggregates
- ▶ Using the Hibernate Query Language
- ▶ Using native SQL
- ▶ Eager loading with LINQ
- ▶ Eager loading with Criteria
- ▶ Eager loading with QueryOver
- ▶ Eager loading with HQL
- ▶ Eager loading with SQL
- ▶ Using named queries
- ▶ Using detached queries
- ▶ Using HQL for bulk data changes
- ▶ Filtering collections
- ▶ Using result transformers
- ▶ Extra lazy collections

Introduction

Since all the recipes in this chapter deal with querying, we have provided the necessary setup and data using the NH4CookbookHelpers library. You can easily adapt the recipes to your own liking, but if you want to only test the queries, the supplied setup will work just fine.

Getting ready

1. Create a new Windows Forms project named QueryRecipes in Visual Studio.

2. Add a reference to NHibernate using NuGet Packet Manager Console:

    Install-Package NHibernate

3. Also, add a reference to NH4CookbookHelpers.

4. Remove the class Form1.cs from the project.

5. Add using NH4CookbookHelpers; to the top of Program.cs.

6. Edit Program.cs so that the last line in Main reads:

    Application.Run(new WindowsFormsRunner());

If you use NH4CookbookHelpers, you don't even have to have a database server available, since it uses an in-memory SQLite database by default. If you want to use something else, like a local SQL Server, you can specify a Configuration instance to be used. Perhaps the most convenient way is to use a coded configuration, as described in *Chapter 1, The Configuration and Schema*.

Somewhere prior to the last line in Main, specify a default configuration, as shown:

```
RecipeLoader.DefaultConfiguration = () => new Configuration()
.DataBaseIntegration(db =>
{
    db.Dialect<MsSql2012Dialect>();
    db.Driver<Sql2008ClientDriver>();
    db.ConnectionString =
      "Server=.\SQLEXPRESS;Database=NHCookbook;Trusted_
Connection=True;";
});
```

Please be advised that the database used in the recipes will be tinkered with, so don't use a database with data that you need to stay intact.

Query entities by ID

Loading a specific identified entity from the database is a very common operation in the majority of NHibernate applications. Just querying for an entity by its Id or primary key may seem like the obvious thing to do, but as we'll see in this recipe, there's a bit more to it.

Getting ready

Complete the _Getting Ready_ section at the beginning of this chapter.

How to do it...

1. Add a new folder named `QueryById` to the project.

2. Add a new class named `Recipe` to the folder, containing the following code:

```
using NH4CookbookHelpers;
using NH4CookbookHelpers.Queries.Model;
using NHibernate;

namespace QueryRecipes.QueryById
{
    public class Recipe : QueryRecipe
    {
        protected override void Run(ISession session)
        {
            var product1 = session.Get<Product>(1);

            ShowNumberOfQueriesExecuted();
            ShowProduct(product1);
            ShowNumberOfQueriesExecuted();

            var product2 = session.Load<Product>(2);

            ShowProduct(product2);
            ShowNumberOfQueriesExecuted();

            var movie2 = session.Load<Movie>(2);

            ShowProduct(movie2);
            ShowNumberOfQueriesExecuted();
        }
    }
}
```

3. Run the application.

4. Follow the instructions in the *Query entities by ID* recipe.

How it works...

NHibernate provides three ways to fetch an entity by its Id. The most obvious way is to simply use one of the query syntaxes to find an entity where the Id property is equal to a specified value. That method, however, should rarely be used, since is misses out on a lot of the functionality provided by NHibernate's caching mechanisms.

In this recipe, we will focus on the two methods `Load` and `Get`, which look similar but have very specific and different behaviors.

Session.Get

We retrieve our first entity using `session.Get<Product>(1)`, where 1 is the Id of one of the Movie entities we have added to the database. On the next line we output the number of queries executed so far. As expected, one query has been executed:

```
SELECT
        product0_.Id as Id0_0_,
        product0_.Name as Name0_0_,
        product0_.Description as Descript4_0_0_,
        product0_.UnitPrice as UnitPrice0_0_,
        product0_.ISBN as ISBN0_0_,
        product0_.Author as Author0_0_,
        product0_.Director as Director0_0_,
        product0_.ProductType as ProductT2_0_0_
FROM
        Product product0_
WHERE
        product0_.Id=1
```

Session.Load

The next entity is retrieved used `session.Load<Product>(2)` and immediately we output the number of queries executed. Still only one? Yes, a call to `Load` will never trigger a query. Instead it returns a proxy object (in this case, `ProductProxy`) with only the value of the `Id` populated. The rest of the data isn't requested until we start accessing the other properties. In this case, that happens in the call to `ShowProduct`.

The session cache jumps in

We continue with `session.Get<Movie>(2)`, which should have the same entity as the `Product` we just loaded. As we hoped, no extra query was executed. The session realizes that it has already loaded this entity and returns the same `ProductProxy` instance, as in the previous `session.Load` section.

Using LINQ to NHibernate

Since version 3.0 NHibernate has included a LINQ provider. In this recipe, we'll show you how to execute LINQ queries with NHibernate.

Getting ready

Complete the *Getting Ready* section given at the beginning of this chapter.

How to do it...

1. Add a new folder named `QueryByLinq` to the project.
2. Add a new class named `LinqQueries` to the folder:

```
using System.Collections.Generic;
using System.Linq;
using NH4CookbookHelpers.Queries;
using NH4CookbookHelpers.Queries.Model;
using NHibernate;
using NHibernate.Linq;

namespace QueryRecipes.QueryByLinq
{
  public class LinqQueries : IQueries
  {
    private readonly ISession _session;

    public LinqQueries(ISession session)
    {
      _session = session;
    }

    public IEnumerable<Movie> GetMoviesDirectedBy(
      string directorName)
    {
      return _session.Query<Movie>()
```

```
                    .Where(x => x.Director == directorName)
                    .ToList();
            }

        public IEnumerable<Movie> GetMoviesWith(
            string actorName)
        {
            return _session.Query<Movie>()
                .Where(x => x.Actors.Any(ar =>
                        ar.Actor == actorName))
                .ToList();
        }

        public Book GetBookByISBN(string isbn)
        {
            return _session.Query<Book>()
                .FirstOrDefault(x => x.ISBN == isbn);
        }

        public IEnumerable<Product> GetProductsByPrice(
            decimal minPrice, decimal maxPrice)
        {
            return
            _session.Query<Product>()
                .Where(x =>
                    x.UnitPrice >= minPrice &&
                    x.UnitPrice <= maxPrice
                )
                .OrderBy(x => x.UnitPrice)
                .ToList();
        }
    }
}
```

3. Add a new `class` named `Recipe` to the folder:

```
using NH4CookbookHelpers;
using NHibernate;

namespace QueryRecipes.QueryByLinq
{
```

```
public class Recipe : QueryRecipe
{
    protected override void Run(ISession session)
    {
        var queries = new LinqQueries(session);
        ShowQueryResults(queries);
    }
}
```

4. Run the application.

5. Start the *QueryByLinq* recipe.

How it works...

The entry point to LINQ querying in NHibernate is always the `session.Query<T>()` extension method, which returns an `IQueryable<T>` instance for further processing. If you want to retrieve all the entities of a certain type, you could use this instance directly:

```
foreach(var movie in session.Query<Movie>())
{
    //Do something with the movie
}
```

The real power is revealed by adding criteria and other restrictions to the query, such as `Where` and `OrderBy` expressions.

As with any LINQ query, its execution is deferred, meaning that it will not be executed until the results are needed. Use the following code:

```
var query=session.Query<Movie>();
query = query.Where(x=>x.Name.StartsWith("Raiders "));
query = query.Where(x=>x.Name.EndsWith("the Lost Ark"));
//No query will be executed until the next line runs.
var movie = query.FirstOrDefault();
```

This means that you can add a criteria dynamically, based on application logic, and the query sent to the database will be a composition of all the added restrictions.

Let's go through the following four queries in the recipe:

▶ `GetMoviesDirectedBy` query:

```
return _session.Query<Movie>()
    .Where(x => x.Director == directorName)
    .ToList();
```

This should be rather obvious. We are fetching the `IQueryable<Movie>` and apply a `Where` restriction to it. But why the `ToList` call? Well, since the `IQueries` interface specified that it expected an `IEnumerable<Movie>` to be returned, we don't want to cause confusion and problems by returning the `IQueryable<Movie>` (although it implements `IEnumerable<Movie>`), which at that point has not yet been executed.

The following SQL query will be executed:

```
SELECT    this_.Id           as Id1_0_,
          this_.Name         as Name1_0_,
          this_.Description   as Descript4_1_0_,
          this_.UnitPrice    as UnitPrice1_0_,
          this_.Director     as Director1_0_
FROM      Product this_
WHERE     this_.ProductType = 'Movie'
AND       this_.Director = 'Steven Spielberg'
```

Note that an extra criterion was added to the query, in order to make sure that we only query on Movie entities.

▶ `GetMoviesWith` query:

```
_session.Query<Movie>()
    .Where(x => x.Actors.Any(ar=>ar.Actor==actorName))
    .ToList();
```

Again, we use the `Movie` queryable, but this time we want the restriction to apply to the `Actors` list on the `Movie` entity. You could read the query as:

Return all movies where any of the actors' name is equal to the `actorName` parameter.

The query executed looks something similar to this:

```
SELECT
        movie0_.Id as Id0_,
        movie0_.Name as Name0_,
        movie0_.Description as Descript4_0_,
        movie0_.UnitPrice as UnitPrice0_,
        movie0_.Director as Director0_
    FROM
```

```
        Product movie0_
WHERE
    movie0_.ProductType='Movie'
    AND (
        EXISTS (
            SELECT
                actors1_.Id
            FROM
                ActorRole actors1_
            WHERE
                movie0_.Id=actors1_.MovieId
                AND actors1_.Actor='Morgan Freeman'
        )
    );
```

Here, the WHERE clause contains an EXISTS subquery on the ActorRole table, restricted by the actor name we supplied, and the movie Id from the outer query.

In the next few recipes, you will see the same queries getting implemented using a JOIN instead of a subquery. Why didn't we do that here?

For starters, while LINQ provides a Join method, its syntax quickly becomes a bit convoluted and it requires the collection entity (ActorRole in this case) to expose a property that can be used to join the two entities. Also, unless we apply Distinct to the query result, a join can potentially return duplicates, for example if Morgan Freeman played more than one role in a movie.

For reference, a LINQ Join query would look similar to the following code:

```
_session.Query<Movie>()
    .Join(
        _session.Query<ActorRole>(),
        movie => movie,
        actorRole => actorRole.Movie,
        (movie, actorRole) => new
        {
            Movie = movie,
            ActorRole = actorRole
        })
    .Where(ar => ar.ActorRole.Actor==actorName)
    .Select(ar => ar.Movie)
    .Distinct()
    .ToList();
```

► `GetBookByISBN` query:

```
_session.Query<Book>()
    .FirstOrDefault(x => x.ISBN == isbn);
```

In this query, we're searching for a particular book by its ISBN. We could have used the Where method to specify the criterion, followed by an empty `FirstOrDefault()`, but this terser format will result in exactly the same query.

Since `FirstOrDefault` means "only the first result, return null if nothing is found", NHibernate can apply a limit to the number of rows it requests.

The resulting SQL Server query looks similar to this:

```
SELECT
        book0_.Id as Id0_,
        book0_.Name as Name0_,
        book0_.Description as Descript4_0_,
        book0_.UnitPrice as UnitPrice0_,
        book0_.ISBN as ISBN0_,
        book0_.Author as Author0_
FROM
        Product book0_
WHERE
        book0_.ProductType='Book'
        and book0_.ISBN='978-1-849513-04-3'
ORDER BY
        CURRENT_TIMESTAMP
OFFSET 0 ROWS FETCH FIRST 1 ROWS ONLY
```

NHibernate applies the limit using the recommended syntax of the configured database. In this case, an `OFFSET/FETCH` in the `ORDER BY` clause is used and since we didn't specify a sort order in the query, `CURRENT_TIMESTAMP` is used as a fallback. Other databases can use other constructs, such as `SELECT TOP` or `LIMIT`.

If `Single` or `SingleOrDefault` had been used instead of `FirstOrDefault`, an exception is expected if the query returns more than one row. In that scenario, no limit will be added to the query, potentially leading to the consumption of more resources.

► `GetProductByPrice` query:

```
_session.Query<Product>()
    .Where(x =>
        x.UnitPrice >= minPrice &&
        x.UnitPrice <= maxPrice
    )
    .OrderBy(x=>x.UnitPrice)
    .ToList();
```

Just like `GetMoviesDirectedBy`, this query is very straightforward. The requested restriction is simply expressed in the `Where` expression and we also order the results by `UnitPrice` (ascending).

SQL Server executes the following query:

```
SELECT
        product0_.Id as Id0_,
        product0_.Name as Name0_,
        product0_.Description as Descript4_0_,
        product0_.UnitPrice as UnitPrice0_,
        product0_.ISBN as ISBN0_,
        product0_.Author as Author0_,
        product0_.Director as Director0_,
        product0_.ProductType as ProductT2_0_
    FROM
        Product product0_
    WHERE
        product0_.UnitPrice>=0
        and product0_.UnitPrice<=15
    ORDER BY
        product0_.UnitPrice ASC
```

Since the query was on the base class `Product`, no restriction on the `ProductType` column is present. Instead it is included in the `SELECT` clause, together with all the properties required for both `Movie` and `Book`.

There's more...

In this recipe, we let the `Queries` class implement the interface `IQueries`. That interface doesn't, yet, provide us with much, but we will use it in few of the upcoming recipes, to show that that we can provide the same results in many ways.

Under the hood, the NHibernate LINQ provider will transform the query expressions into **Hibernate Query Language** (**HQL**) syntax trees, which means that virtually everything that can be accomplished using HQL can also be done with LINQ. This may sound limiting, but in reality it rarely is. In addition, NHibernate provides ways to extend HQL with new functionality and this power can also be harnessed in LINQ. Read the recipe *Extending LINQ Provider* in *Chapter 8, Extending NHibernate* for further details.

See also

- ▶ *Eager loading with LINQ*
- ▶ *Using custom functions in LINQ*
- ▶ *Extending LINQ Provider*

Using CriteriaQueries

In the last chapter, we fetched our entities by their Id. In this recipe, we'll show you a few basic criteria queries to fetch entities by other properties.

Getting ready

Complete the *Getting Ready* section at the beginning of this chapter.

How to do it...

1. Add a new folder named QueryByCriteria to the project.

2. Add a new class CriteriaQueries to the folder:

```
using System.Collections.Generic;
using NH4CookbookHelpers.Queries;
using NH4CookbookHelpers.Queries.Model;
using NHibernate;
using NHibernate.Criterion;
using NHibernate.SqlCommand;

namespace QueryRecipes.QueryByCriteria
{
    public class CriteriaQueries : IQueries
    {
        private readonly ISession _session;

        public CriteriaQueries(ISession session)
        {
            _session = session;
        }

        public IEnumerable<Movie>
GetMoviesDirectedBy(string directorName)
        {
            return _session.CreateCriteria<Movie>()
              .Add(Restrictions.Eq("Director",
              directorName))
              .List<Movie>();
        }
```

```csharp
        public IEnumerable<Movie>
GetMoviesWith(string actorName)
        {
            return _session.CreateCriteria<Movie>()
              .CreateCriteria("Actors", JoinType.InnerJoin)
              .Add(Restrictions.Eq("Actor", actorName))
              .List<Movie>();
        }


        public Book GetBookByISBN(string isbn)
        {
            return _session.CreateCriteria<Book>()
              .Add(Restrictions.Eq("ISBN", isbn))
              .UniqueResult<Book>();
        }


        public IEnumerable<Product>
GetProductsByPrice(decimal minPrice,
decimal maxPrice)
        {
            return _session.CreateCriteria<Product>()
              .Add(Restrictions.And(
                Restrictions.Ge("UnitPrice", minPrice),
                Restrictions.Le("UnitPrice", maxPrice)
                    ))
              .AddOrder(Order.Asc("UnitPrice"))
              .List<Product>();
        }
    }
}
```

3. Add a new `class` Recipe to the folder.

```csharp
using NH4CookbookHelpers.Queries;
using NHibernate;

namespace QueryRecipes.QueryByCriteria
{
    public class Recipe : QueryRecipe
    {
        protected override void Run(ISession session)
        {
            var queries=new CriteriaQueries(session);
            ShowQueryResults(queries);
```

```
            }
        }
    }
```

4. Build and run your application.

5. Follow the instructions in the *Using CriteriaQueries* recipe.

6. You should see the following output:

```
Movies directed by Spielberg:
9,59 kr Raiders of the Lost Ark starring Harrison Ford & Karen Allen

Movies with Morgan Freeman:
15,00 kr The Bucket List starring Jack Nicholson & Morgan Freeman

This book:
50,00 kr NHibernate 3.0 Cookbook  - Packt Publishing (ISBN 978-1-849513-04-3)

Cheap products:
9,59 kr Raiders of the Lost Ark starring Harrison Ford & Karen Allen
15,00 kr The Bucket List starring Jack Nicholson & Morgan Freeman
```

How it works...

Again, let's work through each of these four queries individually:

- `GetMoviesDirectedBy` query:

```
_session.CreateCriteria<Movie>()
        .Add(Restrictions.Eq("Director", directorName))
        .List<Movie>();
```

In the preceding code, we use `session.CreateCriteria` to get an `ICriteria` object. Our generic parameter, `Movie`, tells NHibernate that we're going to query on movies. In the second line, we restrict the movies to only those directed by *n*. Finally, we call the `List` method, which executes the query and returns our `Steven Spielberg` movies. Due to the generic parameter `Movie`, NHibernate returns a strongly typed `IList<Movie>` instead of an `IList`.

This results in the following SQL query:

```
SELECT  this_.Id           as Id1_0_,
        this_.Name         as Name1_0_,
        this_.Description   as Descript4_1_0_,
        this_.UnitPrice     as UnitPrice1_0_,
```

```
            this_.Director      as Director1_0_
FROM        Product this_
WHERE       this_.ProductType = 'Movie'
            AND this_.Director = 'Steven Spielberg'
```

▶ GetMoviesWith query:

```
_session.CreateCriteria<Movie>()
        .CreateCriteria("Actors", JoinType.InnerJoin)
        .Add(Restrictions.Eq("Actor", actorName))
        .List<Movie>();
```

We are again querying movies, but in this example, we are querying based on a child collection. We want all the *Morgan Freeman's* movies. In terms of our model, we want to return all of the `Movies` with an associated `ActorRole` object where the `Actor` property equals the string `'Morgan Freeman'`.

The second line sets up an inner join between `Movies` and `ActorRoles` based on the contents of a `Movie`'s `Actors` collection. In SQL an inner join only returns the rows with a match. `CreateCriteria` also changes the context of the query from `Movie` to `ActorRole`. This allows us to filter our `ActorRoles` further on the third line.

On the third line, we simply filter the `ActorRole` objects down to only *Morgan Freeman's* roles. Because of the inner join, this also filters the `Movies`. Finally, we execute the query and get the results with a call to `List<Movie>`.

Here is the resulting SQL query:

```
SELECT this_.Id            as Id1_1_,
       this_.Version       as Version1_1_,
       this_.Name          as Name1_1_,
       this_.Description    as Descript5_1_1_,
       this_.UnitPrice      as UnitPrice1_1_,
       this_.Director       as Director1_1_,
       actorrole1_.Id       as Id0_0_,
       actorrole1_.Version  as Version0_0_,
       actorrole1_.Actor    as Actor0_0_,
       actorrole1_.Role     as Role0_0_
FROM   Product this_
       inner join ActorRole actorrole1_
         on this_.Id = actorrole1_.MovieId
WHERE  this_.ProductType = 'Movie'
       AND actorrole1_.Actor = 'Morgan Freeman'
```

▶ `GetBookByISBN` query:

```
_session.CreateCriteria<Book>()
        .Add(Restrictions.Eq("ISBN", isbn))
        .UniqueResult<Book>();
```

In this criteria query, we're searching for a particular book by its ISBN. However, since we use `UniqueResult<Book>` instead of `List<Book>`, NHibernate returns a single `Book` object or null if it's not found. This query assumes that `ISBN` is unique.

We get this simple SQL query:

```
SELECT this_.Id           as Id1_0_,
       this_.Name         as Name1_0_,
       this_.Description   as Descript4_1_0_,
       this_.UnitPrice     as UnitPrice1_0_,
       this_.Author        as Author1_0_,
       this_.ISBN          as ISBN1_0_
FROM   Product this_
WHERE  this_.ProductType = 'Eg.Core.Book'
       AND this_.ISBN = '3043'
```

▶ `GetProductByPrice` query:

```
_session.CreateCriteria<Product>()
        .Add(Restrictions.And(
          Restrictions.Ge("UnitPrice", minPrice),
          Restrictions.Le("UnitPrice", maxPrice)
               ))
        .AddOrder(Order.Asc("UnitPrice"))
        .List<Product>()
```

With this criteria query, we combine a *greater than or equal to* operation and a *less than or equal to* operation using an `And` operation to return products priced between two values. The `And` restriction takes two child restrictions as parameters.

We can also use the `Between` restriction to create an equivalent criteria query, such as this:

```
.Add(Restrictions.Between("UnitPrice", minPrice, maxPrice))
```

We use the `AddOrder` method to sort our product results by ascending unit price.

Here's the resulting SQL query:

```
SELECT    this_.Id           as Id1_0_,
          this_.Name         as Name1_0_,
          this_.Description   as Descript4_1_0_,
          this_.UnitPrice     as UnitPrice1_0_,
          this_.Director      as Director1_0_,
          this_.Author        as Author1_0_,
```

```
            this_.ISBN          as ISBN1_0_,
            this_.ProductType as ProductT2_1_0_
FROM        Product this_
WHERE       (this_.UnitPrice >= 0 /* @p0 */
             and this_.UnitPrice <= 15 /* @p1 */)
ORDER BY this_.UnitPrice asc
```

There's more...

The criteria API is intended for dynamically built queries, such as the advanced search feature we see on retail websites, where the user may choose any number of filters and sort criteria. However, these queries must be parsed and compiled on the fly.

For relatively static queries, with a set of well-known parameters, it is preferable to use named HQL queries, as these are precompiled when we build the session factory.

The criteria API suffers from the magic strings problem, where strings refer to properties and classes in our application. With strongly typed APIs, we can easily change a property name using the refactoring tools of Visual Studio or ReSharper. With the criteria API, when we change a property name in our model, we have to find and update every criteria query that uses the property. As we will see in the next recipe, the new QueryOver API helps solve this problem.

See also

- ▶ *Using QueryOver*
- ▶ *Using QueryOver projections and aggregates*
- ▶ *Using MultiCriteria*
- ▶ *Using named queries*
- ▶ *Using detached queries*

Using QueryOver

NHibernate 3.0 added a new fluent syntax to criteria queries. Although it's not an actual LINQ provider, it does bring the familiar lambda syntax to criteria queries, eliminating the magic strings problem. In this recipe, we'll show you the QueryOver syntax for the criteria queries from our last recipe.

Getting ready

Complete the *Getting Ready* instructions at the beginning of this chapter.

How to do it...

1. Add a new folder named `QueryByQueryOver` to the project.

2. Add a new class named `QueryOverQueries` to the folder:

```csharp
using System.Collections.Generic;
using NH4CookbookHelpers.Queries;
using NH4CookbookHelpers.Queries.Model;
using NHibernate;

namespace QueryRecipes.QueryByQueryOver
{
    public class QueryOverQueries : IQueries
    {
        private readonly ISession _session;

        public QueryOverQueries(ISession session)
        {
            _session = session;
        }
    }
}
```

3. Add the following method to the `QueryOverQueries` class:

```csharp
public IEnumerable<Movie> GetMoviesDirectedBy(string directorName)
{
    return _session.QueryOver<Movie>()
        .Where(m => m.Director == directorName)
        .List();
}
```

4. In the `QueryOverQueries` class, add the following method to query for movies by actor's name:

```csharp
public IEnumerable<Movie> GetMoviesWith(string actorName)
{
    return _session.QueryOver<Movie>()
        .OrderBy(m => m.UnitPrice).Asc
        .Inner.JoinQueryOver<ActorRole>(m => m.Actors)
        .Where(a => a.Actor == actorName)
        .List();
}
```

5. So we can query for a book by its ISBN by adding the following method:

```
public Book GetBookByISBN(string isbn)
{
  return _session.QueryOver<Book>()
    .Where(b => b.ISBN == isbn)
    .SingleOrDefault();
}
```

6. Add the following method to find all the products in a price range:

```
public IEnumerable<Product> GetProductsByPrice(
  decimal minPrice,
  decimal maxPrice)
{
  return _session.QueryOver<Product>()
    .Where(p => p.UnitPrice >= minPrice
             && p.UnitPrice <= maxPrice)
    .OrderBy(p => p.UnitPrice).Asc
    .List();
}
```

7. Add a new class named `Recipe` to the folder:

```
using NH4CookbookHelpers.Queries;
using NHibernate;

namespace QueryRecipes.QueryByQueryOver
{
    public class Recipe : QueryRecipe
    {
        protected override void Run(ISession session)
        {
            var queries = new QueryOverQueries(session);
            ShowQueryResults(queries);
        }
    }
}
```

8. Build and run your application. You should see the same screen as in the previous recipe.

How it works...

In the preceding code, we've implemented the queries from the last recipe using NHibernate's `QueryOver` syntax. Using this syntax, most restrictions can be represented using the `Where` method, which takes a lambda expression as input. For example, to filter our movies by director's name, we use `.Where(m => m.Director == directorName)`. In many cases, we can combine multiple restrictions in a single `Where`. To get products within a particular price range, we can write this:

```
.Where(p => p.UnitPrice >= minPrice)
.And(p => p.UnitPrice <= maxPrice)
```

We can also combine it into one `Where` clause, as shown:

```
.Where(p => p.UnitPrice >= minPrice && p.UnitPrice <= maxPrice)
```

Some restrictions, such as `Between`, don't have equivalent lambda expressions. For these operations, we begin with `WhereRestrictionOn` to specify the property we'll use. Then, we follow it with a call to the restriction's method. For example, we could write this same price range filter using criteria's `Between` restriction:

```
.WhereRestrictionOn(p => p.UnitPrice)
.IsBetween(minPrice).And(maxPrice)
```

To create a join, we use `JoinQueryOver`, as shown:

```
.Inner.JoinQueryOver<ActorRole>(m => m.Actors)
```

In `QueryOver`, `UniqueResult` is replaced with the LINQ-like `SingleOrDefault`.

There's more...

`QueryOver` is built on top of NHibernate's existing criteria queries. Should we need to use the criteria API directly, we can get to the criteria query inside through the `QueryOver` objects's `UnderlyingCriteria` property.

See also

- ▶ *Using QueryOver projections and aggregates*
- ▶ *Using CriteriaQueries*
- ▶ *Using MultiCriteria*
- ▶ *Using named queries*
- ▶ *Using detached queries*

Using QueryOver projections and aggregates

In some cases, we only need specific properties of an entity. In other cases, we may need the results of an aggregate function, such as average or count. In this recipe, we'll show you how to write `QueryOver` queries with projections and aggregates.

Getting ready

Complete the *Getting Ready* instructions at the beginning of this chapter.

How to do it...

1. Add a new folder named `QueryOverProjections` to the project.

2. Add a new class named `QueryOverAggregateQueries` to the folder, having the following code:

```
using System;
using System.Collections.Generic;
using System.Linq;
using NH4CookbookHelpers.Queries;
using NH4CookbookHelpers.Queries.Model;
using NHibernate;
using NHibernate.Criterion;

namespace QueryRecipes.QueryOverProjections
{
  public class QueryOverAggregateQueries :
    IAggregateQueries
  {
    private readonly ISession _session;

    public QueryOverAggregateQueries(ISession session)
    {
      _session = session;
    }
  }
}
```

3. Add the following method to the class:

```
public IEnumerable<NameAndPrice> GetMoviePriceList()
{
    return _session.QueryOver<Movie>()
      .Select(m => m.Name, m => m.UnitPrice)
      .List<object[]>()
      .Select(props =>
        new NameAndPrice()
        {
          Name = (string)props[0],
          Price = (decimal)props[1]
        });
}
```

4. Add the following method to the class to fetch a simple average of movie prices:

```
public decimal GetAverageMoviePrice()
{
    var result = _session.QueryOver<Movie>()
      .Select(Projections.Avg<Movie>(m => m.UnitPrice))
      .SingleOrDefault<double>();
    return Convert.ToDecimal(result);
}
```

5. Add the following method to get a list of directors and the average price of their movies:

```
public IEnumerable<NameAndPrice> GetAvgDirectorPrice()
{
    return _session.QueryOver<Movie>()
      .Select(list => list
        .SelectGroup(m => m.Director)
        .SelectAvg(m => m.UnitPrice)
      )
      .List<object[]>()
      .Select(props =>
        new NameAndPrice()
        {
          Name = (string)props[0],
          Price = Convert.ToDecimal(props[1])
        });
}
```

6. Add a new `class` named `Recipe` to the folder:

```
using NH4CookbookHelpers;
using NHibernate;

namespace QueryRecipes.QueryOverProjections
{
  public class Recipe : QueryRecipe
  {
    protected override void Run(ISession session)
    {
      var queries = new QueryOverAggregateQueries(session);
      ShowAggregateQueryResults(queries);
    }
  }
}
```

7. Build and run your application. You should see the following output:

```
Movie Price List:
9,59 kr Raiders of the Lost Ark
15,00 kr The Bucket List

Average Movie Price:
12,30 kr

Average Price by Director:
15,00 kr Rob Reiner
9,59 kr Steven Spielberg
```

How it works...

Again, we'll discuss each query separately. The queries are as follows:

► `GetMoviePriceList` query:

Here's the code we used for our `Movie Price List` query:

```
_session.QueryOver<Movie>()
.Select(m => m.Name, m => m.UnitPrice)
.List<object[]>()
.Select(props =>
  new NameAndPrice()
  {
    Name = (string)props[0],
    Price = (decimal)props[1]
  });
```

In this query, we want to return a list containing only movie names and their prices. To accomplish this, we project two properties from our `Movie` object: `Name` and `UnitPrice`. We do this using `QueryOver` objects `Select` method. Our `QueryOver` ends with a call to `List`. As we are returning the values of individual properties instead of entire `Movie` objects, our generic argument specifies that we'll return a list of object arrays. Each element in the list represents a row in our query results. The first element of each of those object arrays is the movie's `Name`. The second is the movie's `UnitPrice`.

The resulting SQL query for Microsoft SQL Server is as follows:

```
SELECT this_.Name      as y0_,
       this_.UnitPrice as y1_
FROM   Product this_
WHERE  this_.ProductType = 'Eg.Core.Movie'
```

To return a list of strongly typed objects instead of these object arrays, we use a standard LINQ to Objects `Select` from `System.Linq` to put our query results into neat `NameAndPrice` objects.

▶ `GetAverageMoviePrice` query:

```
_session.QueryOver<Movie>()
.Select(Projections.Avg<Movie>(m => m.UnitPrice))
.SingleOrDefault<double>();
```

In the preceding code, we query for the average price of all movies in the database. We call our aggregate functions through `Projections.Avg` and then project the result.

Since we have projected a single aggregate result, we execute the query and get the result with a call to `.SingleOrDefault<double>()`. We expect a `double` to be returned by the average aggregate function. However, because we're dealing with money, we'll convert it to a `decimal` before returning it to our application.

This `QueryOver` query results in the following SQL query:

```
SELECT avg(cast(this_.UnitPrice as DOUBLE PRECISION)) as y0_
FROM   Product this_
WHERE  this_.ProductType = 'Eg.Core.Movie'
```

▶ `GetAvgDirectorPrice` query:

With the following code, we query for a list of movie directors and the average price of their movies:

```
_session.QueryOver<Movie>()
.Select(list => list
  .SelectGroup(m => m.Director)
  .SelectAvg(m => m.UnitPrice)
)
```

```
.List<object[]>()
.Select(props =>
  new NameAndPrice()
  {
    Name = (string)props[0],
    Price = Convert.ToDecimal(props[1])
  });
```

In this case, we will group and project the `Director` property and the average `UnitPrice` using the following syntax:

```
.Select(list => list
  .SelectGroup(m => m.Director)
  .SelectAvg(m => m.UnitPrice)
)
```

Just as we did in our first query, we return a list of object arrays and then transform them into a list of `NameAndPrice` objects with LINQ to Objects.

Here is the resulting SQL query:

```
SELECT     this_.Director as y0_,
           avg(cast(this_.UnitPrice as DOUBLE PRECISION)) as y1_
FROM       Product this_
WHERE      this_.ProductType = 'Eg.Core.Movie'
GROUP BY this_.Director
```

See also

- ▸ *Using CriteriaQueries*
- ▸ *Using QueryOver*
- ▸ *Using MultiCriteria*
- ▸ *Using named queries*
- ▸ *Using detached queries*

Using the Hibernate Query Language

So far, we've covered various queries using LINQ, the Criteria API and its sibling, the `QueryOver` syntax. NHibernate provides another, more powerful, query method named Hibernate Query Language, which is a domain-specific language that blends familiar SQL-like syntax with Object-Oriented thinking. In this recipe, we'll show you how to use the Hibernate Query Language to perform the same queries as in the previous recipes.

Complete the *Getting Ready* section at the beginning of this chapter.

1. Add a new folder named `QueryByHql` to the project.
2. Add a new class named `HqlQueries` to the folder:

```
using System.Collections.Generic;
using NH4CookbookHelpers.Queries;
using NH4CookbookHelpers.Queries.Model;
using NHibernate;

namespace QueryRecipes.QueryByHql
{
  public class HqlQueries : IQueries, IAggregateQueries
  {
    private readonly ISession _session;

    public HqlQueries(ISession session)
    {
      _session = session;
    }

    public IEnumerable<Movie> GetMoviesDirectedBy(
      string directorName)
    {
      var hql = @"from Movie m
        where m.Director = :director";
      return _session.CreateQuery(hql)
        .SetString("director", directorName)
        .SetLockMode("m",LockMode.Upgrade)
        .List<Movie>();
    }

    public IEnumerable<Movie> GetMoviesWith(
      string actorName)
    {
      var hql = @"select m
        from Movie m
        inner join m.Actors as ar
        where ar.Actor = :actorName";
```

```
  return _session.CreateQuery(hql)
    .SetString("actorName", actorName)
    .List<Movie>();
}

public Book GetBookByISBN(string isbn)
{
  var hql = @"from Book b
    where b.ISBN = :isbn";
  return _session.CreateQuery(hql)
    .SetString("isbn", isbn)
    .UniqueResult<Book>();
}

public IEnumerable<Product> GetProductsByPrice(
  decimal minPrice,
  decimal maxPrice)
{
  var hql = @"from Product p
    where p.UnitPrice >= :minPrice
    and p.UnitPrice <= :maxPrice
    order by p.UnitPrice asc";

  return _session.CreateQuery(hql)
    .SetDecimal("minPrice", minPrice)
    .SetDecimal("maxPrice", maxPrice)
    .List<Product>();
}

public IEnumerable<NameAndPrice> GetMoviePriceList()
{
  var hql = @"select new NameAndPrice(
    m.Name, m.UnitPrice)
    from Movie m";
  return _session.CreateQuery(hql)
    .List<NameAndPrice>();

}

public decimal GetAverageMoviePrice()
{
  var hql = @"select Cast(avg(m.UnitPrice)
    as Currency)
    from Movie m";
```

```
          return _session.CreateQuery(hql)
            .UniqueResult<decimal>();

      }

      public IEnumerable<NameAndPrice> GetAvgDirectorPrice()
      {
        var hql = @"select new NameAndPrice(
          m.Director,
          Cast(avg(m.UnitPrice) as Currency)
          )
          from Movie m
          group by m.Director";
        return _session.CreateQuery(hql)
          .List<NameAndPrice>();

      }
    }
  }
```

3. Add a new class named `Recipe` to the folder:

```
using NH4CookbookHelpers;
using NH4CookbookHelpers.Queries.Model;
using NHibernate;
using NHibernate.Cfg;
using NHibernate.Mapping.ByCode;

namespace QueryRecipes.QueryByHql
{
  public class Recipe : QueryRecipe
  {
    protected override void Configure(
      Configuration nhConfig)
    {
      var modelMapper = new ModelMapper();
      modelMapper.Import<NameAndPrice>();
      var mapping = modelMapper.
        CompileMappingForAllExplicitlyAddedEntities();
      nhConfig.AddMapping(mapping);
    }

    protected override void Run(ISession session)
    {
```

```
        var queries = new HqlQueries(session);
        ShowQueryResults(queries);
        ShowAggregateQueryResults(queries);
    }
  }
}
```

4. Run the application and start the `QueryByHql` recipe. You should be able to see the following output:

```
Movies directed by Spielberg:
9,59 kr Raiders of the Lost Ark starring Harrison Ford & Karen Allen

Movies with Morgan Freeman:
15,00 kr The Bucket List starring Jack Nicholson & Morgan Freeman

This book:
50,00 kr NHibernate 3.0 Cookbook  - Packt Publishing (ISBN 978-1-849513-04-3)

Cheap products:
9,59 kr Raiders of the Lost Ark starring Harrison Ford & Karen Allen
15,00 kr The Bucket List starring Jack Nicholson & Morgan Freeman

Movie Price List:
9,59 kr Raiders of the Lost Ark
15,00 kr The Bucket List

Average Movie Price:
12,30 kr

Average Price by Director:
15,00 kr Rob Reiner
9,59 kr Steven Spielberg
```

How it works...

Hibernate Query Language syntax resembles SQL in many ways, but operates at an object level. We build all of our queries as strings. Much like `DbCommands` in ADO.NET, we create `IQuery` objects around those query strings, set the parameter values, and execute our queries with `List` or `UniqueResult`. Similar to the *at* sign (@) in Microsoft SQL Server queries, in HQL, we prepend our parameter names with a colon (:) in the query string. When we set the parameter value, we don't include the colon:

▶ `GetMoviesDirectedBy` query:

We have a very basic HQL query, as shown:

```
from Movie m
where m.Director = :director
```

For brevity, we've aliased our movies as simply m. In this case, there is an implied select m to project our movies. We have a single parameter, director, which we use to filter our movies.

▶ GetMoviesWith query:

```
select m
from Movie m
inner join m.Actors as ar
where ar.Actor = :actorName
```

In this query, we join from movies to their actor roles. Note that unlike SQL, we don't need to specify ActorRoles or set up a comparison with an ON clause explicitly. NHibernate already understands the relationships between our entities. We filter those actor roles based on the actor name. Just as with SQL, because we use an inner join, this filter on actor role effectively filters our movies as well.

▶ GetProductByPrice query:

```
from Product p
where p.UnitPrice >= :minPrice
and p.UnitPrice <= :maxPrice
order by p.UnitPrice asc
```

In this query, we filter our Product based on a price range defined by the two parameters, minPrice and maxPrice. This query could also be written using HQL's between:

```
from Product p
where p.UnitPrice between
:minPrice and :maxPrice
order by p.UnitPrice asc
```

As with SQL, the order by clause sorts our products by unit price.

▶ GetMoviePriceList query:

We have this simple query:

```
select new NameAndPrice(m.Name, m.UnitPrice)
from Movie m
```

When working with HQL, think in terms of objects and properties, not tables and columns. This query passes the Name and UnitPrice properties into this constructor of our NameAndPrice class:

```
public NameAndPrice(string name, decimal unitPrice)
```

Then it projects the resulting NameAndPrice instances. To make NHibernate aware of this class, we can use the following import mapping:

```
<import class="NameAndPrice"/>
```

In the recipe, we used mapping by code to do the same thing, as it can be seen in the `Configure` method.

```
var modelMapper = new ModelMapper();
modelMapper.Import<NameAndPrice>();
var mapping = modelMapper.
  CompileMappingForAllExplicitlyAddedEntities();
nhConfig.AddMapping(mapping);
```

As an alternative, just as with `Criteria` and `QueryOver`, we could simply project `Name` and `UnitPrice`, return a list of object arrays and then use LINQ to `Objects` to transform those object arrays into `NameAndPrice` instances, as shown in the following code:

```
var hql = @"select m.Name, m.UnitPrice
            from Movie m";
var query = session.CreateQuery(hql);
return query.List<object[]>()
  .Select(props =>
    new NameAndPrice(
      (string)props[0],
      (decimal)props[1]));
```

In this case, we wouldn't need to import our `NameAndPrice` class.

▶ `GetAverageMoviePrice` query:

```
select Cast(avg(m.UnitPrice) as Currency)
from Movie m
```

In this query, we use the aggregate function average. This returns a scalar value of type `double`, so we cast it back to NHibernate's `Currency` type. The equivalent `.NET` type is `decimal`, so we execute the query using `UniqueResult<decimal>()`.

▶ `GetAvgDirectorPrice` query:

```
select new NameAndPrice(
    m.Director,
    Cast(avg(m.UnitPrice) as Currency)
)
from Movie m
group by m.Director
```

In this query, we group by `Director`. We then pass `Director` and our average `UnitPrice` into the constructor of `NameAndPrice`. Just as before, because `avg` returns a `double`, we'll need to `Cast` it back to `Currency` first.

There's more...

In addition to the mapped properties and collections on our entities, HQL allows you to query on two implied and special properties:

▶ The `property` class is the full name of the type of our entity. For example, to query for books, we could write the following:

```
from Product p where p.class='Eg.Core.Book'
```

▶ The property `id` always represents the POID of the entity, regardless of what we may name it in our entity. We can query for three books at a time with this query:

```
from Book b where b.id in (@id0, @id1, @id2)
```

See also

▶ *Using CriteriaQueries*

▶ *Using QueryOver*

▶ *Using MultiQuery*

▶ *Using named queries*

▶ *Using detached queries*

Using native SQL

At some point in the development of your application, you may find that none of the NHibernate specific querying techniques really does the trick. Maybe you need to write a query with a very specific SQL, so that it performs optimally, or maybe there's a function or stored procedure that you need to use. Thankfully, NHibernate allows you to use plain SQL queries in the native dialect of your target database and dropping out to SQL doesn't mean dropping out of NHibernate.

Getting ready

Complete the *Getting Ready* section at the beginning of this chapter.

How to do it...

1. Add a new folder named `QueryBySql` to the project.

2. Add a new class named `SqlQueries` to the folder:

```
using System.Collections.Generic;
using NH4CookbookHelpers.Queries;
```

```csharp
using NH4CookbookHelpers.Queries.Model;
using NHibernate;

namespace QueryRecipes.QueryBySql
{
  public class SqlQueries : IQueries
  {
    private readonly ISession _session;

    public SqlQueries(ISession session)
    {
      _session = session;
    }

    public IEnumerable<Movie> GetMoviesDirectedBy(
      string directorName)
    {
      var sql = @"select * from Product
        where ProductType = 'Movie'
        and Director = :director";
      return _session.CreateSQLQuery(sql)
        .AddEntity(typeof(Movie))
        .SetString("director", directorName)
        .List<Movie>();
    }

    public IEnumerable<Movie> GetMoviesWith(
      string actorName)
    {
      var sql = @"select m.*
        from Product m
        inner join ActorRole as ar on ar.MovieId=m.Id
        where ar.Actor = :actorName";
      return _session.CreateSQLQuery(sql)
        .AddEntity(typeof(Movie))
        .SetString("actorName", actorName)
        .List<Movie>();
    }

    public Book GetBookByISBN(string isbn)
    {
      var sql = @"select b.* from Product b
        where b.ISBN = :isbn";
```

```
            return _session.CreateSQLQuery(sql)
                .AddEntity(typeof(Book))
                .SetString("isbn", isbn)
                .UniqueResult<Book>();
        }

        public IEnumerable<Product> GetProductsByPrice(
            decimal minPrice,
            decimal maxPrice)
        {
            var sql = @"select p.* from Product p
                where p.UnitPrice between :minPrice
                and :maxPrice
                order by p.UnitPrice asc";

            return _session.CreateSQLQuery(sql)
                .AddEntity(typeof(Product))
                .SetDecimal("minPrice", minPrice)
                .SetDecimal("maxPrice", maxPrice)
                .List<Product>();
        }

    }
}
```

3. Add a new class named `Recipe` to the folder:

```
using NH4CookbookHelpers;
using NHibernate;

namespace QueryRecipes.QueryBySql
{
  public class Recipe : QueryRecipe
  {
    protected override void Run(ISession session)
    {
      var queries=new SqlQueries(session);
      ShowQueryResults(queries);
    }
  }
}
```

4. Run the application and start the `QueryBySql` recipe.

How it works...

We won't get into the details of the SQL queries.

Eager loading with LINQ

Often, when we query for some set of entities, we also want to load some of the related entities. In this recipe, we'll show you how we can use LINQ extensions to eager load the child collections of our query results.

Getting ready

Complete the *Getting Ready* section at the beginning of this chapter.

How to do it...

1. Create a new folder named `EagerLoadingWithLinq` in the project.

2. Add a new class named `Recipe` to the folder:

```
using System.Linq;
using NH4CookbookHelpers.Queries;
using NH4CookbookHelpers.Queries.Model;
using NHibernate;
using NHibernate.Linq;

namespace QueryRecipes.EagerLoadingWithLinq
{
    public class Recipe : QueryRecipe
    {
        protected override void Run(ISession session)
        {
            var book = session.Query<Book>()
                .Fetch(x => x.Publisher)
                .FirstOrDefault();

            Show("Book:", book);

            var movies = session.Query<Movie>()
```

```
        .FetchMany(x => x.Actors)
        .ToList();

    Show("Movies:", movies);
    }
  }
}
```

3. Run the application and start the `EagerLoadingWithLinq` recipe.

4. Inspect the query log to see how the related entities have been included in the queries.

How it works...

In this recipe, we eagerly load the Publisher for our Book(s) and the `ActorRoles` for our Movies to avoid select N+1 problems. In a select N+1 situation, with one select statement, you can load a few entities from the database and begin to enumerate through them. As you enumerate through them, you access some lazy loaded property or collection. This triggers a separate database query for each entity in the original query. If we iterate through 1000 entities, we would have the original query plus 1000 nearly identical queries because we triggered lazy loading, hence the name select N+1. This creates N+1 round trips to the database, which will quickly kill performance, overwork the database, and even crash it.

Here, we iterate through each movie in the database. For each instance, we display the name of the actor in the starring role. This would normally trigger a separate database query for each movie, a potential select N+1 problem.

By specifying that we want to load the related `ActorRoles` in the same query, we can avoid this problem:

```
session.Query<Movie>()
  .FetchMany(x=>x.Actors)
```

This returns all movies and their actor roles, including the movies without actor roles. As can be seen in the query log, the `ActorRoles` are included using a LEFT JOIN.

The book and its publisher is fetched in a similar way, but since the `Publisher` property is a relation to one entity, as opposed to the `Actors` property which is a collection, we used `Fetch` instead of `FetchMany`. Why the difference? Well, we could actually have used Fetch for both types, but the eager loading doesn't have to stop at the first level. Consider if the `ActorRole` entity had an (admittedly weird) property called `BookAboutTheRole`. If we wanted to load that too, the query would look similar to this:

```
session.Query<Movie>()
    .FetchMany(x=>x.Actors)
  .ThenFetch(a=>a.BookAboutTheRole)
```

Had we used `Fetch(x=>x.Actors)`, the `ThenFetch` method would not know that it should act on a single `ActorRole`, rather than the `ISet<ActorRole>`.

There's more...

The `Then` prefixed methods have a very important distinction. They act upon the preceding fetched type, allowing us to dig down into the object structure. Using the standard `Fetch` or `FetchMany` immediately brings us back to the root. This is useful, since we can add more fetch instructions, for example if `ActorRole` had yet another property that we wanted to include:

```
session.Query<Movie>()
        .FetchMany(x=>x.Actors)
                .ThenFetch(a=>a.BookAboutTheRole)
        .FetchMany(x=>x.Actors)
                .ThenFetch(a=>a.DocumentaryAboutTheActor)
```

We have to use the same `FetchMany` twice, but that's just a syntactic inconvenience. It doesn't actually include the actors twice.

It would seem then that eager loading is something that can be used frequently, and it can. However, there are a few drawbacks and pitfalls. Extending the query with several *fetch requests* increases the complexity of the queries and the amount of data retrieved. It may be worth considering different strategies, such as projecting only the data that's really needed.

Another important issue is that these eager fetches causes tables to be joined into the query. When the fetched property is a collection, it means two things:

Limiting the result set doesn't work

Consider we want to fetch only two movies, but want their `Actors` collection to be eager loaded. It seems we want this query:

```
session.Query<Movie>()
    .FetchMany(x => x.Actors)
    .OrderBy(x=>x.Name)
    .Take(2)
```

Unfortunately, that could go horribly wrong. The limit will be applied to the entire query, including the joins, meaning that we will end up with only one movie, unless the first movie has only one actor. It also means that the `Actors` collection won't be properly initialized with all the included entities.

Eager loading multiple collections should be avoided

If our Movie class also had a collection property for `MakeUpArtists`, we might be tempted and eager to load them in the same query. We certainly can:

```
session.Query<Movie>()
    .FetchMany(x => x.Actors)
    .FetchMany(x => x.MakeUpArtists)
```

While it may work, in limited scenarios, this causes two unrelated joins to be added to the query. The result becomes what's called a Cartesian product. If a movie has 100 actors and 10 make-up artists, 1000 rows would be returned for that single movie. Adding more collections will multiply the result even further. Not only does that impact the performance, it also means that collections that allow duplicates (bags) may be filled with more duplicates than intended.

Fortunately, there are solutions to both these issues, which will be discussed in *Chapter 5, Improving Performance*.

Use batching as an alternative solution

An alternative for greatly reducing the impact of a select N+1 problem is to use the batch-size property in the mapping. Suppose we had added batch-size to our movies mapping, as shown in the following code:

```xml
<?xml version="1.0" encoding="utf-8" ?>
<hibernate-mapping xmlns="urn:nhibernate-mapping-2.2"
    assembly="Eg.Core"
    namespace="Eg.Core">
  <subclass name="Movie" extends="Product">
    <property name="Director" />
    <list name="Actors" cascade="all-delete-orphan"
          batch-size="10">
      <key column="MovieId" />
      <index column="ActorIndex" />
      <one-to-many class="ActorRole"/>
    </list>
  </subclass>
</hibernate-mapping>
```

With a typical select N+1 bug, we would trigger a query on each movie. This behavior changes when we set the batch-size to 10. NHibernate needs to query for the contents of an `Actors` collection to initialize it, but it notices the batch-size setting. It finds nine other uninitialized Actors collections in the session and loads all of them at once with a single query.

If we have 10 movies, we only need two queries instead of 11, for 20 movies, we need three instead of 21, and so on. This cuts out about 90 percent of our queries.

▶ *Eager loading multiple collections*

Eager loading with Criteria

In this recipe, we'll show you how to use `CriteriaQueries` to eager load the child collections of our query results.

Getting ready

Complete the *Getting Ready* instructions at the beginning of this chapter.

How to do it...

1. Create a new folder named `EagerLoadingWithCriteria` in the project.

2. Add a new `class` named `Recipe` to the folder:

```
using NH4CookbookHelpers.Queries;
using NH4CookbookHelpers.Queries.Model;
using NHibernate;
using NHibernate.Transform;

namespace QueryRecipes.EagerLoadingWithCriteria
{
    public class Recipe : QueryRecipe
    {
        protected override void Run(ISession session)
        {
            var book = session.CreateCriteria<Book>()
                .SetFetchMode("Publisher", FetchMode.Join)
                .UniqueResult<Book>();

            Show("Book:", book);

            var movies = session.CreateCriteria<Movie>()
                .SetFetchMode("Actors", FetchMode.Join)
                .SetResultTransformer(
                Transformers.DistinctRootEntity)
```

```
                        .List<Movie>();

                    Show("Movies:", movies);
            }
        }
    }
```

3. Run the application and start the `EagerLoadingWithCriteria` recipe.

4. Inspect the query log to see how the related entities have been included in the queries.

How it works...

For a detailed explanation of the eager loading mechanism, see the *Eager loading with LINQ* recipe. Take special note of the caveats mentioned in the *There's more...* section.

In this recipe, we use two criteria queries and both load related data eagerly. The first one loads one book and its related Publisher in one single query. The call to SetFetchMode specifies the "path" to the property we want to be included, and importantly sets the FetchMode to Join.

The second query is very similar, but this time we're fetching a collection property. Since the joined table will cause more rows to be returned, we need to tell NHibernate that we only want one of each movie and not as many movies as there are actors. This is done with a result transformer (discussed further in *Chapter 5, Improving performance*), called DistinctRootEntityTransformer, which reduces the result set to the list we want.

What if we also wanted to eager load a property of one of our related entities? That can be done too, as long as the entire path to said property is also eagerly loaded.

```
session.CreateCriteria<Movie>()
    .SetFetchMode("Actors", FetchMode.Join)
    .SetFetchMode("Actors.BookAboutTheRole", FetchMode.Join)
```

In other words, we need to specify that both Actors and Actors.BookAboutTheRole should be eagerly loaded.

Eager loading with QueryOver

In this recipe, we'll show you how to use QueryOver queries to eager load the child collections of our query results.

Getting ready

Complete the *Getting Ready* instructions at the beginning of this chapter.

How to do it...

1. Create a new folder named `EagerLoadingWithQueryOver` in the project.

2. Add a new class named `Recipe` in the folder:

```
using NH4CookbookHelpers.Queries;
using NH4CookbookHelpers.Queries.Model;
using NHibernate;
using NHibernate.Transform;

namespace QueryRecipes.EagerLoadingWithQueryOver
{
    public class Recipe : QueryRecipe
    {
        protected override void Run(ISession session)
        {
            var book = session.QueryOver<Book>()
                .Fetch(x => x.Publisher).Eager
                .SingleOrDefault();

            Show("Book:", book);

            var movies = session.QueryOver<Movie>()
                .Fetch(x => x.Actors).Eager
                .OrderBy(x => x.Name).Asc
                .TransformUsing(
                Transformers.DistinctRootEntity)
                .List();
            Show("Movies:", movies);
        }
    }
}
```

3. Run the application and start the `EagerLoadingWithQueryOver` recipe.

4. Inspect the query log to see how the related entities have been included in the queries.

How it works...

For a detailed explanation of the eager loading mechanism, see the recipe *Eager loading with LINQ*. Take special note of the caveats mentioned in the *There's more...* section.

Also read the *How it works...* section of the previous recipe. Since `QueryOver` is based on criteria queries, the same logic applies.

`QueryOver` replaces the `SetFetchMode` method of criteria queries with the convenient Fetch method, which expects a lambda expression pointing to the property we want to eager load. This method call must be followed by the "fluent" property `Eager`, which specifies that we indeed want this fetch to be an eager load.

Just as with the criteria queries, an eager load of a collection property effectively requires that we also specify a result transformer. This is done by adding `TransformUsing(Transformers.DistinctRootEntity)` to the call chain.

Should we want to include yet another level to the eager loading, as we did with `.SetFetchMode("Actors.BookAboutTheRole")` in the preceding recipe, we need to twist the lambda expression a bit:

```
.Fetch(x => x.Actors).Eager
.Fetch(x => x.Actors.First().BookAboutTheRole).Eager
```

It may look a bit strange, but the call to `First()` is needed to allow the lambda to point to a property of `ActorRole`. If the `Actors` collection type exposes indexed accessing `x.Actors[0].BookAboutTheRole` works just as well.

Eager loading with HQL

In this recipe, we'll show you how to use HQL queries to eager load the child collections of our query results.

Getting ready

Complete the *Getting Ready* section at the beginning of this chapter.

How to do it...

1. Create a new folder named `EagerLoadingWithHql` in the project.

2. Add a new class named `Recipe` to the folder:

   ```
   using NH4CookbookHelpers.Queries;
   using NH4CookbookHelpers.Queries.Model;
   ```

```
using NHibernate;

namespace QueryRecipes.EagerLoadingWithHql
{
    public class Recipe : QueryRecipe
    {
        protected override void Run(ISession session)
        {
            var book = session.CreateQuery(@"
                from Book b
                left join fetch b.Publisher")
                .UniqueResult<Book>();

            Show("Book:", book);

            var movies = session.CreateQuery(@"
                from Movie m
                left join fetch m.Actors")
                .SetResultTransformer(
Transformers.DistinctRootEntity)
                .List<Movie>();

            Show("Movies:", movies);
        }
    }
}
```

3. Run the application and start the EagerLoadingWithHql recipe.

4. Inspect the query log to see how the related entities have been included in the queries.

How it works...

For a detailed explanation of the eager loading mechanism, see the *Eager loading with LINQ* recipe. Take special note of the caveats mentioned in the *There's more...* section.

Eager loading in HQL is accomplished by adding the fetch qualifier to a join. In the recipe, we have used a left join, since we want the root entity, even when there are no child entities; however, fetch works equally well with standard (inner) joins.

It might be tempting to add an alias to the fetched join and perhaps use it in a `where` clause:

```
left join fetch m.Actors a
where a.Actor=:name
```

That is strongly discouraged though, since the where clause now acts on the same join as the fetch. Not only does that limit the fetched collection itself, so that we end up with `Movie` instances having invalid `Actors` collections. It also effectively turns the `left join` into an `inner join`. If the query requires a filter on an `ActorRole` property, use an extra separate `join` or a subquery instead.

There is one scenario where an alias on the fetch join is needed, and that is if we want to eager load even deeper:

```
left join fetch m.Actors a
left join fetch a.BookAboutTheRole
```

Just as with the `Criteria` and `QueryOver` queries, we need to process the results using the call to `SetResultTransformer(Transformers.DistinctRootEntity)`. If we don't, we may end up with more movies in the list than we expected.

Eager loading with SQL

As a final step in our walk-through of eager loading techniques, we've come to the native SQL queries. SQL should always be a last resort, but if it's necessary it certainly supports eager loading.

Getting ready

Complete the *Getting Ready* instructions at the beginning of this chapter.

How to do it...

1. Create a new folder named `EagerLoadingWithSql` in the project.
2. Add a new `class` named `Recipe` to the folder:

```
using NH4CookbookHelpers.Queries;
using NH4CookbookHelpers.Queries.Model;
using NHibernate;
using NHibernate.Transform;

namespace QueryRecipes.EagerLoadingWithSql
{
    public class Recipe : QueryRecipe
    {
```

```
protected override void Run(ISession session)
{
    var book = session.CreateSQLQuery(@"
        select {b.*}, {p.*} from Product b
        left join Publisher p
    ON b.PublisherId=p.Id
        where b.ProductType = 'Book'")
    .AddEntity("b", typeof(Book))
    .AddJoin("p", "b.Publisher")
    .UniqueResult<Book>();

    Show("Book:", book);

    var movies = session.CreateSQLQuery(@"
        select {m.*}, {ar.*} from Product m
        left join ActorRole ar ON ar.MovieId=m.Id
        where m.ProductType = 'Movie'
      ")
    .AddEntity("m", typeof(Movie))
    .AddJoin("ar", "m.Actors")
    .AddEntity("m", typeof(Movie))
    .SetResultTransformer(
        Transformers.DistinctRootEntity)
    .List<Movie>();

    Show("Movies:", movies);
    }
  }
}
```

3. Run the application and start the `EagerLoadingWithSql` recipe.

4. Inspect the query log to make sure that the related entities included in the queries did not cause any extra, lazy loading.

How it works...

For a detailed explanation of the eager loading mechanism, see the recipe *Eager loading with LINQ*.

In native SQL there are no special keywords to use, such as `fetch` in HQL. But here there is one addition to the SQL, which doesn't look quite native. Instead of just writing select * to get all the columns, we specify that we want each *mapped* column from each specified table/ alias, using the special syntax `{alias.*}`. NHibernate will parse the SQL query and replace these parts with fully qualified column references.

We also need to specify the alias that is the root entity, by calling `AddEntity` and then `AddJoin` to further define that the second alias represents a subproperty of the root entity.

The double call to `AddEntity` in the second query is necessary, since the result transformer will use the entry added last (through `AddEntity` or `AddJoin`) to deduce what it should perform its "distincting" operation on. Had we not added the extra `AddEntity`, we would end up with a list of `ActorRoles`.

Using named queries

Just as with SQL, mixing inline HQL with business logic is often a losing battle. The code becomes unreadable and the queries are nearly impossible to unit test properly. In this recipe, we'll show you how to move these HQL queries out of our code, improve readability and testability, and even improve performance by parsing and pre-compiling queries.

Getting ready

Complete the *Getting Ready* section at the beginning of this chapter.

How to do it...

1. Add a new folder named `NamedQueries` to the project.

2. Add a new mapping document named `Queries.hbm.xml` with the following `xml` code. Don't forget to set the **Build action** to **Embedded Resource**:

   ```xml
   <?xml version="1.0" encoding="utf-8" ?>
   <hibernate-mapping xmlns="urn:nhibernate-mapping-2.2">
     <query name="GetBookByISBN">
       <![CDATA[
       from Book b where b.ISBN = :isbn
       ]]>
     </query>
   </hibernate-mapping>
   ```

3. Add a new class named `NamedQueries` to the folder containing the following code:

   ```csharp
   using NH4CookbookHelpers.Queries.Model;
   using NHibernate;

   namespace QueryRecipes.NamedQueries
   {
       public class NamedQueries
       {
   ```

```
        private readonly ISession _session;

        public NamedQueries(ISession session)
        {
            _session = session;
        }

        public Book GetBookByISBN(string isbn)
        {
            return _session.GetNamedQuery("GetBookByISBN")
                    .SetString("isbn", isbn)
                    .UniqueResult<Book>();
        }
    }
}
```

4. Add a new class named `Recipe` to the folder:

```
using NH4CookbookHelpers.Queries;
using NHibernate;
using NHibernate.Cfg;

namespace QueryRecipes.NamedQueries
{
    public class Recipe : QueryRecipe
    {
        protected override void Configure(Configuration nhConfig)
        {
            nhConfig.AddResource(
"QueryRecipes.NamedQueries.Queries.hbm.xml",
GetType().Assembly);
        }

        protected override void Run(ISession session)
        {
            var queries = new NamedQueries(session);
            Show("This book:",
                queries.GetBookByISBN(
                "Steven Spielberg"));
        }
    }
}
```

5. Run the application and start the `NamedQueries` recipe.

How it works...

In this recipe, we use the familiar `GetBookByISBN` query. We use `GetNamedQuery` to build a standard HQL `IQuery` object. This time, we've defined the query in a mapping document rather than in code. For that reason, we used an override in the recipe class, which allows us to inject additional mapping:

```
nhConfig.AddResource(
"QueryRecipes.NamedQueries.Queries.hbm.xml",
GetType().Assembly);
```

This adds the named resource from the specified assembly to the existing mapping. The resource's name is derived from the assembly name and the location of the file.

As with any HQL query, NHibernate will parse, compile, and verify this query against our entity mappings and model. Since it's in a mapping document, this work is done upfront when we build the session factory. If NHibernate finds any errors, it will throw an exception when we build our session factory, instead of when we execute the query. This is preferable for the same reasons that compiler errors are preferable to runtime exceptions. It provides an obvious, upfront check. In addition, this upfront parsing and compilation is cached for later use. NHibernate only has to build the necessary SQL once.

Named SQL queries

In addition to HQL, NHibernate also allows us to create named queries in SQL. This is only appropriate in advanced cases where HQL simply won't work or where a query has been hand-optimized. The C# code for working with a SQL named query is identical to an HQL named query. This allows you to create queries in HQL and swap in a faster SQL query later without changing your application code. Only the mapping document is different. It looks similar to the following code:

```xml
<?xml version="1.0" encoding="utf-8" ?>
<hibernate-mapping xmlns="urn:nhibernate-mapping-2.2">
  <sql-query name="GetBookByISBN_SQL">
    <return alias="b" class="Eg.Core.Book, Eg.Core" />
    <![CDATA[
    SELECT
      b.Id AS [b.Id],
      b.Name AS [b.Name],
      b.Description AS [b.Description],
      b.UnitPrice AS [b.UnitPrice],
      b.Author AS [b.Author],
      b.ISBN as [b.ISBN]
    FROM Product b
    WHERE b.ProductType = 'Eg.Core.Book'
```

```
      AND b.ISBN = :isbn
      ]]>
      <query-param name="isbn" type="string"/>
    </sql-query>
</hibernate-mapping>
```

The return element defines the alias we use in our query results, as well as the entity to build from that data.

There's more...

MultiQuery (described in *Chapter 5, Improving Performance*) provides a shortcut for including named queries. It looks similar to the following code:

```
var multiQuery = session.CreateMultiQuery()
    .AddNamedQuery<int>("count", "CountAllProducts")
    .Add<Product>("page", pageQuery);
```

In this case, we use the shortcut to add our count query. In order to set the first result and maximum result count, we need to build our page query separately.

See also

- ▸ *Using the Hibernate Query Language*
- ▸ *Using detached queries*

Using detached queries

In some cases, it may be preferable to build an HQL or criteria query object in parts of your application without access to the NHibernate session and then execute them elsewhere with a session available. In this recipe, we'll show you how to use detached queries and criteria.

Getting ready

Complete the *Getting Ready* section at the beginning of this chapter.

How to do it...

1. Add a new folder named DetachedQueries to the project.
2. Add a new class named Recipe to the folder:

   ```
   using NH4CookbookHelpers.Queries;
   using NH4CookbookHelpers.Queries.Model;
   ```

```
using NHibernate;
using NHibernate.Criterion;

namespace QueryRecipes.DetachedQueries
{
    public class Recipe : QueryRecipe
    {
        protected override void Run(ISession session)
        {
            var isbn = "3043";

            var query = DetachedCriteria.For<Book>()
                .Add(Restrictions.Eq("ISBN", isbn));

            var book = query.GetExecutableCriteria(session)
                .UniqueResult<Book>();

            Show("Book with ISBN=3043",book);
        }
    }
}
```

3. Run the application and start the `DetachedQueries` recipe.

How it works...

In this recipe, we've used a `DetachedCriteria` object from the `NHibernate.Criterion` namespace. This allows us to set up our query without an active session. Later, inside a transaction, we call `GetExecutableCriteria` to return an `ICriteria` associated with the session. Finally, we call `UniqueResult` to return the book.

There's more...

NHibernate also provides `DetachedQuery` and `DetachedNamedQuery` in the `NHibernate.Impl` namespace for detached HQL queries. The code is given as follows:

```
var query = new DetachedNamedQuery("GetBookByISBN")
    .SetString("isbn", isbn);

var query = new DetachedQuery(hql)
    .SetString("isbn", isbn);
```

Detached criteria and queries implement the query objects pattern shown on *Martin Fowler's* website at `http://martinfowler.com/eaaCatalog/queryObject.html`

See also

- ▸ *Using CriteriaQueries*
- ▸ *Using the Hibernate Query Language*
- ▸ *Using named queries*

Using HQL for bulk data changes

In the previous chapter, we learned how to use NHibernate to insert, update, and delete individual entities using ISession methods. NHibernate also allows us to perform some bulk data changes with executable HQL. In this recipe, we'll show you how to use HQL to update all of our books with a single statement.

Getting ready

Complete the *Getting Ready* section at the beginning of this chapter.

How to do it...

1. Add a new folder named HqlBulkChanges to the project.

2. Add a new class named Recipe to the folder:

```
using System;
using NH4CookbookHelpers.Queries;
using NHibernate;

namespace QueryRecipes.HqlBulkChanges
{
    public class Recipe : QueryRecipe
    {
        protected override void Run(ISession session)
        {
            var hql = @"update Book b
                        set b.UnitPrice = :minPrice
                        where b.UnitPrice < :minPrice";

            var updated=session.CreateQuery(hql)
              .SetDecimal("minPrice", 55M)
```

```
                              .ExecuteUpdate();

                    Console.WriteLine("Number of books updated:" +
                     updated);

                         hql = @"delete from Book
                                 where UnitPrice=:minPrice";
                     var deleted = session.CreateQuery(hql)
                       .SetDecimal("minPrice", 55M)
                       .ExecuteUpdate();

                     Console.WriteLine("Number of books deleted:" +
                       deleted);

                         hql = @"insert into Book (Name,Description)
                                 select concat(Name,' - the book'),
                                 Description
                                 from Movie";
                     var inserted = session.CreateQuery(hql)
                       .ExecuteUpdate();

                     Console.WriteLine(@"Number of movies recreated
                       as books:" + inserted);

                 }
             }
         }
```

3. Run the application and start the `HqlBulkChanges` recipe.

How it works...

We have the following executable HQL query:

```
update Book b
set b.UnitPrice = :minPrice
where b.UnitPrice < :minPrice
```

We call `ExecuteUpdate` method of `IQuery` to run this statement. This results in the following SQL statement:

```
update Product
set    UnitPrice = 55
where  ProductType = 'Book'
       and UnitPrice < 55
```

The next query performs a deletion, with exactly the same logic. We delete the book we recently updated. The following SQL statement is executed:

```
delete
from
    Product
where
    ProductType = 'Book'
    and UnitPrice = 55
```

Now that we are all out of books, let's see if we can't create a couple of new ones by inserting "recreations" of all the movies. We execute the following HQL:

```
insert into Book (Name,Description)
select concat(Name,' - the book'),Description
from Movie
```

The HQL function `concat` is used to form a new product name from the concatenation of the movie name and the " – the book" String. SQL Server receives the following statement:

```
insert
into
    Product
    ( Name, Description, ProductType ) select
        (movie0_.Name+' - the book') as col_0_0_,
        movie0_.Description as col_1_0_,
        'Book'
    from
        Product movie0_
    where
        movie0_.ProductType='Movie'
```

Two things are worth noting here. First, the `concat` function is automatically translated to the correct statement for the target database, in this case using the plus operator. Also, NHibernate is clever enough to add the necessary `ProductType` column to the insert, so that the newly created entities will indeed be books.

These statements will only affect the database. The changes will not be reflected in the state of in-memory objects, the second-level cache or anywhere else outside the database.

There's more...

We could also define these queries in the mapping and load queries like any other named queries.

Bulk inserts

As we saw in the last query, NHibernate supports bulk inserts in the following form:

```
insert into destinationEntity (id, prop1, prop2) select b.id, b.prop1,
b.prop2 from sourceEntity b where...
```

There are a few things to keep in mind when considering this solution. First, property types must match exactly. While the database may be perfectly able to convert between types, such as `int` and `long`, NHibernate requires them to be the same type.

The `id` values are particularly limited. There are two options:

> ► The first option is to copy the id from a property of the source entity. This can be the source entity or any other property. Depending on your existing data, this is not always appropriate.

> ► The second option uses the entity's POID generator to create an identity for each newly inserted object. However, this only works when the `id` is database-generated. This excludes nearly all of the preferred identity generators, such as `guid.comb` and `hilo`. To use the entity's `id` generator, simply omit the `id` column from the list of properties to be set.

See also

> ► *Using named queries*

Filtering collections

In our model with Movies and `ActorRoles`, we may eventually have movies with hundreds of actors. If we want to display a movie and show all the roles played by Harrison Ford, we certainly can:

```
foreach (var actorRole in movie.Actors
            .Where(x=>x.Actor=="Harrison Ford"))
{
    Console.WriteLine("Harrison Ford played {0} in {1}",
        actorRole.Role,
        movie.Name);
}
```

While that would work fine in small data sets, there's a risk that we will load a lot more data than necessary, just to show a couple of roles. What happens is that as soon as we're using the Actors property on each `Movie` instance, we trigger the lazy loading mechanism and a query will be executed to fetch **all** `ActorRoles` of that movie. The `Where` expression specified doesn't affect this behavior, since it's effectively executed in memory.

For scenarios like this, NHibernate offers a function where an uninitialized (not yet loaded from database) collection can be filtered and ordered, so that only the relevant rows are retrieved.

Getting ready

Complete the *Getting Ready* section at the beginning of this chapter.

How to do it...

1. Add a folder named `CollectionFilters` to the project.

2. Add a class named `Recipe` to the folder having the following code:

```
using System;
using NH4CookbookHelpers.Queries;
using NH4CookbookHelpers.Queries.Model;
using NHibernate;

namespace QueryRecipes.CollectionFilters
{
    public class Recipe : QueryRecipe
    {
        protected override void Run(ISession session)
        {
            var movie = session.Get<Movie>(1);
            var actorFilter=session
                        .CreateFilter(movie.Actors,
                "WHERE Actor=:actor");
            actorFilter.SetString("actor",
              "Harrison Ford");
            var actors = actorFilter.List<ActorRole>();
            foreach (var actorRole in actors)
            {
                Console.WriteLine(
                    "Harrison Ford played {0} in {1}",
                    actorRole.Role,
                    movie.Name);
            }
        }
    }
}
```

3. Run the application and start the `CollectionFilters` recipe.

How it works...

When you run the recipe you will see in the query log that one query is executed to fetch the movie, and after that a query which only fetches ActorRoles where Actor='Harrison Ford'. That's exactly what we wanted!

The filter instance created by the CreateFilter method is actually an IQuery, just as the ones created by CreateQuery. This IQuery is automatically configured with a FROM clause to only fetch objects of the collection's element type (in this case ActorRole) and a WHERE restriction to get the items belonging to this particular relation. The extra criteria specified in the query string are added to the query.

A standard query performing the same task could look similar to this:

```
var actorQuery = session.CreateQuery(
    @"SELECT m.Actors FROM Movie m
      INNER JOIN m.Actors ar
      WHERE m=:movie
      AND ar.Actor=:actor");
actorQuery.SetEntity("movie", movie);
actorQuery.SetString("actor", "Harrison Ford");
```

Using CreateFilter is usually more convenient, since all we need to specify is which collection instance we want to filter.

There's more...

Filtering collections this way only makes sense when the entities we want to filter have not been loaded yet. This includes scenarios where the filter is applied to properties or sub collections, which themselves would trigger one or several lazy loads.

In the recipe, had we already loaded the Actors collection, either by lazy loading or using one of the eager loading mechanisms, it would have been better to just stick with the in memory Where implementation. NHibernate provides ways to check whether an entity has been initialized or not and we can use that to decide which querying technique to use at runtime:

```
if (NHibernateUtil.IsInitialized(movie.Actors))
{
    actors = movie.Actors.Where(x => x.Actor == "Harrison Ford");
}
else
{
```

```
actors = session
    .CreateFilter(movie.Actors,"WHERE Actor=:actor")
    .SetString("actor", "Harrison Ford")
    .List<ActorRole>();
}
```

Now, that may look a bit convoluted, and it is. Thankfully, several extensions have been developed, which makes this process transparent. One of those comes from Ricardo Peres, and the necessary code can be copied from his blog post at `http://weblogs.asp.net/ricardoperes/querying-an-uninitialized-collection-with-nhibernate`.

Using that code, we can not only rest assured that the best querying technique is used, but also specify the filter as a convenient lambda expression:

```
var actors = movie.Actors.Query()
                .Where(x => x.Actor == "Harrison Ford");
```

Using result transformers

In normal query scenarios we can rely on NHibernate's mechanisms to convert the query results into entities and objects that we can use. Sometimes, however, the queries may not map to classes we have defined in the mappings or maybe we want to customize what is returned. NHibernate provides many extension points and one of those is a result transformer, which can be injected into the flow of a query. It transforms the results of a query into the results that we need.

In the following recipe, we will try out two of the most commonly used built-in transformers.

How to do it...

1. Complete the steps in the *Getting Started* section at the beginning of this chapter.
2. Add a new folder named `ResultTransformers` to the project.
3. Add a new `class` named `Recipe` to the folder:

```
using System;
using NH4CookbookHelpers;
using NH4CookbookHelpers.Queries.Model;
using NHibernate;
using NHibernate.Transform;

namespace QueryRecipes.ResultTransformers
{
  public class Recipe : QueryRecipe
  {
```

```
protected override void Run(ISession session)
{
    var movieQuery = session.QueryOver<Movie>()
        .Inner.JoinQueryOver(x => x.Actors);

    Console.WriteLine(
        "Result count without transformer:{0}",
        movieQuery.List<Movie>().Count);

    movieQuery = movieQuery.
        TransformUsing(Transformers.DistinctRootEntity);

    Console.WriteLine(
        "Result count with transformer:{0}",
        movieQuery.List<Movie>().Count);

    var bookResults = session.CreateSQLQuery(@"
        select b.Name, b.Author,p.Name as PublisherName
        from Product b
        left join Publisher p ON b.PublisherId=p.Id
        where b.ProductType = 'Book'")

        .SetResultTransformer(Transformers.
AliasToBean<BookInfo>())
        .List<BookInfo>();

    Console.WriteLine("BookInfo objects:");
    foreach (var result in bookResults)
    {
        Console.WriteLine("{0}, by {1}, published by {2}",
            result.Name,
            result.Author,
            result.PublisherName);
    }
}
```

4. Run the application and start the ResultTransformers recipe.

How it works...

Result transformers don't act on the raw query results from the database. They come in the second phase, after the query results have been *hydrated* into objects.

In the first query of the recipe, the `DistinctRootEntityResultTransformer` (accessed by the shorthand `Transformers.DistinctRootEntity`) is fed a list of `Movies`, which due to the joined `Actors` property may contain several duplicates. It can remove all the redundant rows by feeding the entities' IDs through a `HashSet`, which doesn't allow duplicates.

The second query is a native SQL query, but could just as well have been an HQL query or a `Criteria` or `QueryOver` query with a special projection. We want to project just a few columns in a query and map those columns to properties of a class that we haven't even mapped. The class is completely unknown to NHibernate.

For that purpose we need to use a transformer that maps the results into `BookInfo` instances (which the transformer creates using the default constructor), based on property names and result column names. The `AliasToBeanResultTransformer` does just that. Note that the result column (alias) names must exactly match the property names and that all the returned columns must have a corresponding property, otherwise an exception will be thrown.

The `AliasToBeanResultTransformer` is very useful for custom queries, such as aggregates for reports, when very specific results should be mapped into convenient *Data Transfer Objects*.

There's more...

NHibernate has a range of result transformers that can be used in specific scenarios. Here's a short walk-through:

DistinctRootEntity

As mentioned previously, this transformer takes a list of results and reduces it so that all duplicates of the root entity are removed. Very useful for queries that joins other entities, possibly causing extra rows in the result set.

AliasToEntityMap

This transformer produces a list of `IDictionary` instances (`Hashtable`), where the keys are the column aliases and the values the corresponding entities or scalar values. The usefulness may seem limited, but it can be used when a single query returns multiple entity types, separated into columns.

PassThrough

As the name implies, results just pass through this transformer. It's potentially useful when architecture requires a specified result transformer for each query.

RootEntity

This performs the same function as `DistinctRootEntity`, in that it outputs the root entity. It does not remove duplicates though.

ToList

Transforms each result row from the usual `object[]` into a `List<object>`, which can be slightly more convenient to work with. The end result is an `IList<List<object>>`.

AliasToBean

Also used in the recipe. Creates new instances of the specified type and populates its properties, mapping column aliases to property names; it's very useful for custom projections.

AliasToBeanConstructor

Works similar to `AliasToBean`, but instead of populating the instances using properties, it injects the result *tuples* directly into the target class' constructor. This is useful when we want to create instances of a type where the values only can be set in the constructor. However, this requires that the results are projected in the same order as the constructor arguments.

Creating your own transformer

There may be occasions when the built-in transformers are not enough. Perhaps you want something that works similar to `AliasToBean`, but also needs to feed some of the values to the constructor. If so, you can design your own result transformer, by creating a class that implements the interface `IResultTransformer`:

```
public interface IResultTransformer
{
    object TransformTuple(object[] tuple, string[] aliases);
    IList TransformList(IList collection);
}
```

There are only two methods needed. The first one to be called is `TransformList`, which accepts an `IList` with all result rows. This is the stage where actions, such as sorting and duplicate removal should happen. Each item in the returned list is then fed into `TransformTuple`, where the array of tuples (entities or values, depending on the query), together with an array of aliases (in corresponding order), can be used to produce the actual output.

Extra lazy collections

Sometimes we only need to know the number of items in a collection. It may be for displaying purposes or some behavioral logic. Either way, it seems a bit resource intensive that we should have to load all of the entities from the database, just to count them. With extra lazy collections we can improve this situation a bit.

Getting ready

Refer to the *Getting Ready* section of this chapter instructions at the beginning of this chapter.

How to do it...

1. Add a new folder named `ExtraLazy` to the project.

2. Add a new class named `Accessory` to the folder, having the code:

```
using NH4CookbookHelpers.Queries.Model;

namespace QueryRecipes.ExtraLazy
{
    public class Accessory : Entity
    {
        public virtual string Name { get; set; }
    }
}
```

3. Add a new `class` named `Car` to the folder:

```
using System;
using System.Collections.Generic;

namespace QueryRecipes.ExtraLazy
{
    public class Car
    {
        public Car()
        {
            Accessories=new HashSet<Accessory>();
        }

        public virtual Guid Id { get; protected set; }
        public virtual string Make { get; set; }
        public virtual string Model { get; set; }
        public virtual ISet<Accessory> Accessories { get; set; }
    }
}
```

4. Add a new embedded resource named `Car.hbm.xml` to the folder:

```xml
<?xml version="1.0" encoding="utf-8" ?>
<hibernate-mapping xmlns="urn:nhibernate-mapping-2.2"
    assembly="QueryRecipes"
    namespace="QueryRecipes.ExtraLazy">
  <class name="Car">
    <id name="Id">
      <generator class="guid.comb" />
    </id>
    <property name="Make" />
    <property name="Model" />
    <set name="Accessories" table="CarAccessories" lazy="extra"
cascade="all">
      <key column="CarId" foreign-key=""/>
      <composite-element class="Accessory">
        <property name="Name"/>
      </composite-element>
    </set>
  </class>
</hibernate-mapping>
```

5. Add a new `class` named `Recipe` to the folder, having the code:

```csharp
using System;
using NH4CookbookHelpers.Queries;
using NHibernate;
using NHibernate.Cfg;

namespace QueryRecipes.ExtraLazy
{
    public class Recipe : QueryRecipe
    {
        private Guid _carId;
        private int _firstAccessoryId;

        protected override void Configure(
          Configuration nhConfig)
        {
            nhConfig.AddResource(
"QueryRecipes.ExtraLazy.Car.hbm.xml", GetType().Assembly);
        }
    }
}
```

6. Add a new method to the class, to add some data:

```
protected override void AddData(
  ISessionFactory sessionFactory)
{
  using (var session = sessionFactory.OpenSession())
  {
    using (var tx = session.BeginTransaction())
    {
      var car = new Car { Make = "SAAB", Model = "9-5" };
      for (var i = 0; i < 100; i++)
      {
        var accessory = new Accessory {
          Name = "Accessory" + i };
        car.Accessories.Add(accessory);
      }
      session.Save(car);
      _carId = car.Id;
      _firstAccessoryId = car.Accessories.First().Id;
      tx.Commit();
    }
  }
}
```

7. Add a new method to the class, to test the configuration:

```
protected override void Run(ISession session)
{
  //Get the car
  var car = session.Get<Car>(_carId);
  //And one of the accessories
  var accessory =
    session.Get<Accessory>(_firstAccessoryId);
  Console.WriteLine("Accessory count: {0}",
    car.Accessories.Count);
  Console.WriteLine("Car has accessory {0}: {1}",
    accessory.Name, car.Accessories.Contains(accessory));
}
```

8. Run the application and start the ExtraLazy recipe.

How it works...

In this mapping, the special addition is that we have specified the accessories collections laziness to be extra. This means that the accessory data isn't loaded from the database unless it's really, *really* needed. Just asking for the number of accessories on the car with `car.Accessories.Count` is not such an occasion. All that's really needed is to execute a `COUNT` query, and that's exactly what happens. The query log shows:

```
SELECT count(AccessoryId)
FROM CarAccessories
WHERE CarId=1
```

The next query is triggered by the `Contains` method, which can also be easily translated to a SQL query:

```
SELECT 1 FROM
CarAccessories
WHERE CarId=1
AND AccessoryId=1
```

There's more...

The extra lazy collections added functionality is limited to `Count` and `Contains`. Any other call to the collection, such as `Accessories.Any()` will trigger a full load of the related data.

So, shouldn't we then always use `lazy="extra"`, since it seems to be fool proof? No, the risk is that we need both the `Count` and all the items. If `Count` is executed before enumerating the data, we will have executed the COUNT query unnecessarily. Extra laziness is a convenient feature in certain scenarios, but it's usually better to code more explicit functions. If you only need to count, create a query that does just that.

5

Improving Performance

In this chapter, we will cover the following recipes:

- ▶ Reducing application startup time
- ▶ Using MultiCriteria
- ▶ Using MultiQuery
- ▶ Using Futures
- ▶ Eager loading child collections
- ▶ Using stateless sessions
- ▶ Using read-only entities
- ▶ Use the second-level cache
- ▶ Configuring the second-level cache with code
- ▶ Sharing databases for performance

Reducing application startup time

The process of configuring NHibernate is fairly intensive and takes time. NHibernate has to load, parse, and compile all our mappings and reflect the model. In this recipe, we'll show you how to reduce the start up time of your NHibernate application.

Getting ready

Complete the Configuring NHibernate with App.config recipe discussed in the *Chapter 1, The Configuration and Schema*.

How to do it...

1. Add a reference to `System.Configuration.dll`.

2. Add a new class named `ConfigurationBuilder`:

```
using System;
using System.Configuration;
using System.IO;
using System.Reflection;
using System.Runtime.Serialization.Formatters.Binary;
using Configuration = NHibernate.Cfg.Configuration;
namespace ConfigByAppConfig
{
    public class ConfigurationBuilder
    {
        private const string SERIALIZED_CFG = "configuration.bin";
    }
}
```

3. Add a method named `Build` with the following code:

```
public Configuration Build()
{
    Configuration cfg = LoadConfigurationFromFile();
    if (cfg == null)
    {
        cfg = new Configuration().Configure();
        SaveConfigurationToFile(cfg);
    }
    return cfg;
}
```

4. Add a method named `LoadConfigurationFromFile` with the following code:

```
private Configuration LoadConfigurationFromFile()
{
    if (!IsConfigurationFileValid())
    return null;
    try
    {
        using (var file = File.Open(SERIALIZED_CFG, FileMode.
Open))
        {
            var bf = new BinaryFormatter();
```

```
            return bf.Deserialize(file) as Configuration;
        }
    }
    catch (Exception)
    {
        // Something went wrong
        // Just build a new one
         return null;
    }
}
```

5. Add a method named `IsConfigurationFileValid` with the following code:

```
private bool IsConfigurationFileValid()
{
    // If we don't have a cached config,
    // force a new one to be built
    if (!File.Exists(SERIALIZED_CFG))
    return false;
    var configInfo = new FileInfo(SERIALIZED_CFG);
    var asm = Assembly.GetExecutingAssembly();
    if (asm.Location == null)
    return false;
      // If the assembly is newer,
      // the serialized config is stale
      var asmInfo = new FileInfo(asm.Location);
    if (asmInfo.LastWriteTime > configInfo.LastWriteTime)
    return false;
      // If the app.config is newer,
      // the serialized config is stale
    var appDomain = AppDomain.CurrentDomain;
    var appConfigPath = appDomain.SetupInformation.
ConfigurationFile;
    var appConfigInfo = new FileInfo(appConfigPath);
    if (appConfigInfo.LastWriteTime > configInfo.LastWriteTime)
    return false;
    // It's still fresh
    return true;
}
```

6. Add a method named `SaveConfigurationToFile` with this code:

```
private void SaveConfigurationToFile(Configuration cfg)
{
    using (var file = File.Open(SERIALIZED_CFG, FileMode.
Create))
```

```
    {
      var bf = new BinaryFormatter();
      Improving Performance
      bf.Serialize(file, cfg);
    }
  }
```

7. In `Program.cs`, replace the NHibernate configuration code with the following code:

    ```
    var nhConfig = new ConfigurationBuilder().Build();
    ```

How it works...

Validating the mappings and settings thoroughly takes time and effort. We can't escape this when our application runs for the very first time; however, if we serialize our `Configuration` object to disk, we can deserialize it the next time we run it, thus saving us all the work.

The `IsConfigurationFileValid` method ensures that the configuration we've serialized is still fresh. We need to rebuild our `Configuration` object from scratch once the executable or the `App.config` has been updated.

We compare the last write-time of the various files to check whether the serialized configuration is stale. We use a `BinaryFormatter` to serialize and deserialize the configuration.

Actual configuration may vary and batteries are not included. In this recipe, we only check the assembly containing our `ConfigurationBuilder` class and the `App.config`. If you store your configuration and mappings elsewhere, you will need to adjust this code accordingly.

There's more...

This technique is especially suited for development and test suites, where we frequently change code, but may not change our mappings or configuration. We can skip all the extra parsing and get running quickly and test our changes.

It also works well for desktop NHibernate applications. Since a user is waiting for your application to launch, every second counts. It's not just as useful for web applications in production because they basically launch once and stay running.

Using MultiCriteria

We need to run several queries to display forms and web pages. For example, it's common to display search results one page at a time. This typically requires two queries. The first counts all the available results and the second fetches the data for only 10 or 20 results. MultiCriteria allows us to combine these two queries into a single database round trip, potentially speeding up our application. In this recipe, we'll show you how to use MultiCriteria to fetch a paged-result set of products.

Getting ready

Complete the *Getting Ready* instructions at the beginning of *Chapter 4, Queries*.

How to do it...

1. Add a new folder named `MultiCriteria` to the `QueryRecipes` project.

2. Add a new `struct` named `PageOf` to the folder:

```
public struct PageOf<T>
    {
        public int PageCount;
        public int PageNumber;
        public IEnumerable<T> PageOfResults;
    }
```

3. Add a new class named `Queries` to the folder:

```
using System;
using System.Collections.Generic;
using System.Linq;
using NH4CookbookHelpers.Queries.Model;
using NHibernate;

namespace QueryRecipes.MultiCriteria
{
  public class Queries
  {
    private readonly ISession _session;

    public Queries(ISession session)
    {
```

```
        _session = session;
    }


    public PageOf<Product> GetPageOfProducts(
int pageNumber,
int pageSize)
    {
    var skip = (pageNumber - 1) * pageSize;

    var countQuery = GetCountQuery();
    var resultQuery = GetPageQuery(skip, pageSize);

    var multiCrit = _session.CreateMultiCriteria()
    .Add<int>("count", countQuery)
    .Add<Product>("page", resultQuery);

    var productCount = ((IList<int>)multiCrit
    .GetResult("count")).Single();

    var products = (IList<Product>)multiCrit
    .GetResult("page");

    var pageCount = (int)Math.Ceiling(
    productCount / (double)pageSize);

    return new PageOf<Product>()
    {
      PageCount = pageCount,
      PageOfResults = products,
      PageNumber = pageNumber
    };
    }

    private ICriteria GetCountQuery()
    {
      return _session.QueryOver<Product>()
      .SelectList(list => list
      .SelectCount(m => m.Id))
      .UnderlyingCriteria;
    }

    private ICriteria GetPageQuery(int skip, int take)
    {
```

```
        return _session.QueryOver<Product>()
        .OrderBy(m => m.UnitPrice).Asc
        .Skip(skip)
        .Take(take)
        .UnderlyingCriteria;
      }
    }
  }
```

4. Add a new class named `Recipe` to the folder:

```
using NH4CookbookHelpers.Queries;
using NHibernate;

namespace QueryRecipes.MultiCriteria
{
  public class Recipe : QueryRecipe
  {
    protected override void Run(ISession session)
    {
      var queries = new Queries(session);
      var result = queries.GetPageOfProducts(1, 2);
      var heading = string.Format("Page {0} of {1}",
      result.PageNumber,
      result.PageCount);
      Show(heading, result.PageOfResults);
    }
  }
}
```

5. Run the application and start the `MultiCriteria` recipe.

How it works...

The `MultiCriteria` API can be used with any NHibernate-supported RDBMS. However, currently only Microsoft SQL Server and Oracle can combine these queries into a single round trip to the database. For all other RDBMS, this functionality is simulated. In either case, your application doesn't need to be concerned. It just works.

In this recipe, we combine two criteria queries in a single round trip to the database. Our first query counts all the products in the database. Our second query returns a page with the first two of our three products, sorted by unit price. We use `QueryOver` instance `skip` and `Take` to accomplish this.

There are a couple of interesting things to point out with the `MultiCriteria` syntax:

```
var multiCrit = session.CreateMultiCriteria()
    .Add<int>("count", countQuery)
    .Add<Movie>("page", resultQuery);
```

First, you'll see that we've labeled our queries with `count` and `page`. This is not required. Instead, we could use the index of each criteria object in the `MultiCriteria` to fetch the results. It's a little more difficult to mess up names than list indices, so we'll use names.

We use generic arguments to specify the element type for our results. That is, our first query returns a list of integers and the second returns a list of movies. The MultiCriteria doesn't provide a method for directly returning a single entity or scalar value. Instead, we use LINQ to object's single method to fetch the first and only value from the list.

When we get the product count, both queries are immediately executed, and the results are stored in memory. When we get the page of products, the `MultiCriteria` simply returns the results of the already-executed query.

See also

▶ *Using QueryOver*

▶ *Using MultiQuery*

▶ *Using Futures*

Using MultiQuery

Similar to how we can combine several `ICriteria` and `QueryOver` queries into a single database round trip with `MultiCriteria`, we can combine several HQL and/or SQL queries with `MultiQuery`. Particularly in a production setting, where the database and application are on separate machines, each round trip to the database is very expensive. Combining work in this way can greatly improve application performance. In this recipe, we'll show you how to fetch a product count and page of product results using a `MultiQuery`.

Getting ready

Complete the *Getting Ready* instructions at the beginning of *Chapter 4, Queries*.

How to do it...

1. Add a new folder named `MultiQueries` to the `QueryRecipes` project.

2. Add a new `struct` named `PageOf` to the folder:

```
public struct PageOf<T>
  {
        public int PageCount;
        public int PageNumber;
        public IEnumerable<T> PageOfResults;
  }
```

3. Add a new class named `Queries` to the folder:

```
using System;
using System.Collections.Generic;
using System.Linq;
using NH4CookbookHelpers.Queries.Model;
using NHibernate;

namespace QueryRecipes.MultiQueries
{
  public class Queries
  {
    private readonly ISession _session;

    public Queries(ISession session)
    {
      _session = session;
    }

    public PageOf<Product> GetPageOfProducts(
int pageNumber,
int pageSize)
    {
      var skip = (pageNumber - 1) * pageSize;

      var countQuery = GetCountQuery();
      var resultQuery = GetPageQuery(skip, pageSize);

      var multiQuery = _session.CreateMultiQuery()
      .Add<long>("count", countQuery)
      .Add<Product>("page", resultQuery);

      var productCount = ((IList<long>)multiQuery
```

```
              .GetResult("count")).Single();

        var products = (IList<Product>)multiQuery
          .GetResult("page");

        var pageCount = (int)Math.Ceiling(
        productCount / (double)pageSize);

        return new PageOf<Product>()
        {
          PageCount = pageCount,
          PageOfResults = products,
          PageNumber = pageNumber
        };
      }

      private IQuery GetCountQuery()
      {
        var hql = @"select count(p.Id) from Product p";
        return _session.CreateQuery(hql);
      }

      private IQuery GetPageQuery(int skip, int take)
      {
        var hql = @"from Product p order by p.UnitPrice asc";
        return _session.CreateQuery(hql)
        .SetFirstResult(skip)
        .SetMaxResults(take);
      }

    }
  }
```

4. Add a new class named Recipe to the folder:

```
using NH4CookbookHelpers.Queries;
using NHibernate;

namespace QueryRecipes.MultiQueries
{
  public class Recipe : QueryRecipe
  {
    protected override void Run(ISession session)
    {
      var queries = new Queries(session);
```

```
        var result = queries.GetPageOfProducts(1, 2);
        var heading = string.Format("Page {0} of {1}",
        result.PageNumber,
        result.PageCount);
        Show(heading, result.PageOfResults);
      }
    }
  }
```

5. Run the application and start the `MultiQueries` recipe.

How it works...

In this recipe, we build two HQL queries. The first returns a count of all our products. It's important to note that HQL's count returns an Int64 or longer.

The second query returns a single page of products. We use `SetFirstResult` to determine where our results begin. For example, passing zero to `SetFirstResult` will return all the results. Passing 10 will skip the first 10 results, returning the 11th product and beyond. We combine this with `SetMaxResults` to return a single page of results. `SetFirstResult(10).SetMaxResults(10)` will return the 11th through 20th product.

We add our queries to our `MultiQuery` object, specifying a label or name, and the type of list to return with the generic argument. Just as with `MultiCriteria`, there's no way to return a single entity or scalar value directly. In this example, our count query will return a list of Int64s containing an item and our page query will return a list of `Products`. We'll use LINQ to objects's `Single()` method to extract the actual count value.

We again use the label in our call to `GetResults` to return a specific result set. The first call to `GetResults` executes all the queries in a single batch. Every subsequent call only returns the results of an already executed query.

See also

► *Using MultiCritieria*
► *Using named queries*

Using Futures

We've learned to use MultiCriteria and MultiQuery to batch our queries together. NHibernate's Futures feature provides a simpler API for batching criteria and queries. In this recipe, we'll show you how to use NHibernate's new Futures feature to return a paged product result. Both LINQ and HQL are used in the same method, to show the syntactic difference but also that they can work together.

Getting ready

Complete the *Getting Ready* instructions at the beginning of *Chapter 4, Queries*.

How to do it...

1. Add a new folder named `Futures` to the `QueryRecipes` project.
2. Add a new `struct` named `PageOf` to the folder:

```
using System.Collections.Generic;

namespace QueryRecipes.Futures
{
    public struct PageOf<T>
    {
        public int PageCount;
        public int PageNumber;
        public IEnumerable<T> PageOfResults;
    }
}
```

3. Add a new class named `Queries` to the folder:

```
using System;
using System.Linq;
using NH4CookbookHelpers.Queries.Model;
using NHibernate;
using NHibernate.Linq;

namespace QueryRecipes.Futures
{
  public class Queries
  {
```

```csharp
    private readonly ISession _session;

    public Queries(ISession session)
    {
      _session = session;
    }

    public PageOf<Product> GetPageOfProducts(
int pageNumber,
int pageSize)
    {
      var skip = (pageNumber - 1) * pageSize;

var productCount = _session.Query<Product>()
.ToFutureValue(x=>x.Count());

      var products = GetPageQuery(skip, pageSize)
.Future<Product>();


      var pageCount = (int)Math.Ceiling(
      productCount.Value / (double)pageSize);

      return new PageOf<Product>()
      {
        PageCount = pageCount,
        PageOfResults = products,
        PageNumber = pageNumber
      };
    }

    private IQuery GetPageQuery(int skip, int take)
    {
      var hql = @"from Product p order by p.UnitPrice asc";
      return _session.CreateQuery(hql)
      .SetFirstResult(skip)
      .SetMaxResults(take);
    }
  }
}
```

4. Add a new class named `Recipe` to the folder:

```
using NH4CookbookHelpers.Queries;
using NHibernate;

namespace QueryRecipes.Futures
{
  public class Recipe : QueryRecipe
  {
    protected override void Run(ISession session)
    {
      var queries = new Queries(session);
      var result = queries.GetPageOfProducts(1, 2);
      var heading = string.Format("Page {0} of {1}",
      result.PageNumber,
      result.PageCount);
      Show(heading, result.PageOfResults);
    }
  }
}
```

5. Run the application and start the `Futures` recipe.

How it works...

In this recipe, we will use the `Futures` syntax to retrieve a count of all the products, along with a page of products for display.

When we call `IQuery`, `ICriteria` instance `Future`, or `FutureValue`, NHibernate returns an object representing the potential results of that query. It also queues up the query in a hidden `MultiCriteria` or `MultiQuery` inside the session. The same thing happens for a LINQ query when `ToFuture` or `ToFutureValue` is used. The naming difference is purely a matter of following LINQ's naming conventions.

When we call `FutureValue`, it returns an `IFutureValue<>`, representing a single entity or scalar value. For Future, it returns an `IEnumerable<>`. NHibernate waits until we access the `Value` property of `IFutureValue<>` or enumerate the `IEnumerable`. When we do, NHibernate executes all the postponed `Futures` for this session.

In this specific example, both queries are executed when we use `productCount.Value` to calculate the page count. As you can see, this deferred loading is mostly transparent to the application.

There's more...

The two minor caveats while using Futures are as follows:

> ▸ An attempt to load the results of a Future query after the session has been closed and it will throw an exception.

> ▸ While the syntax is identical, `ICriteria` and `IQuery` objects are handled separately in the session. If you have an `ICriteria` and an `IQuery` based Future, evaluating one will not execute the other.

See also

> ▸ *Using Criteria Queries*

> ▸ *Using QueryOver*

> ▸ *Using MultiCriteria*

> ▸ *Using the Hibernate Query Language*

> ▸ *Using MultiQuery*

Eager loading child collections

Often, when we query for some set of entities, we also need to load a few children of those entities. In the *Eager loading with...* recipe, in the previous chapter, we learned how to use different `fetch` syntaxes to eager load referenced entities and collection. We concluded that there are a few scenarios where the standard methods don't work as desired. In this recipe, we'll show you how to use subqueries and/or NHibernate's Futures, together with the session cache, to overcome these issues.

Getting ready

Complete the *Getting Ready* instructions at the beginning of *Chapter 4, Queries*.

How to do it...

1. Add a new folder named `AdvancedEagerLoading` to the `QueryRecipes` project.

2. Add a new class named `Recipe` to the folder:
   ```
   using System.Linq;
   using NH4CookbookHelpers.Queries;
   using NH4CookbookHelpers.Queries.Model;
   using NHibernate;
   ```

```
using NHibernate.Linq;

namespace QueryRecipes.AdvancedEagerLoading
{
  public class Recipe : QueryRecipe
  {
  }
}
```

3. Add a new method to `Recipe` to fill the database with test data:

```
protected override void AddData(ISessionFactory sessionFactory)
{
  using (var session = sessionFactory.OpenSession())
  {
    using (var tx = session.BeginTransaction())
    {
      for (var i = 1; i <= 20; i++)
      {
        var movie = new Movie
        {
          Name = "Movie" + i,
          UnitPrice = i
        };
        movie.AddActor("Actor" + i, "Role" + i);
        movie.AddActor("Second Actor" + 1, "Second Role" + i);
        session.Save(movie);
      }
      tx.Commit();
    }
  }
}
```

4. Add a new method to test the queries:

```
protected override void Run(ISession session)
{
  var baseQuery = session.Query<Movie>()
    .Where(x => x.Name.StartsWith("Movie"))
    .OrderBy(x => x.Name)
    .Skip(5)
    .Take(5);

  var movies = session.Query<Movie>()
    .Where(x => baseQuery.Contains(x))
```

```
        .OrderBy(x => x.Name)
        .FetchMany(x => x.Actors)
        .ToList();

    Show("A page of movies", movies);

    var allProducts = session.Query<Product>()
        .OrderBy(x => x.UnitPrice)
        .ToFuture();

    session.Query<Movie>()
        .FetchMany(x => x.Actors)
        .ToFuture();

    session.Query<Book>()
        .Fetch(x => x.Publisher)
        .ToFuture();

    Show("All products",allProducts);
}
```

5. Run the application and start the `AdvancedEagerLoading` recipe.

6. Check the query log.

How it works...

In this recipe, we will try to solve the problems that we described at the end of the *Eager loading with LINQ* recipe. There were three problems:

Problem 1 – limiting the result set doesn't work

We saw that eager loading a collection would render limiting functions, such as `Skip`, `Take`, `SetFirstResult`, and `SetMaxResults` useless. The limits would be applied to the entire query, which is not what we want. To solve that, we have to change the query into something slightly more advanced. Our base query, with the criteria `and` limits all set, looks similar to the following example:

```
var baseQuery = session.Query<Movie>()
    .Where(x => x.Name.StartsWith("Movie"))
    .OrderBy(x => x.Name)
    .Skip(5)
    .Take(5);
```

We can use this as a subquery in the following query:

```
var movies = session.Query<Movie>()
    .Where(x => baseQuery.Contains(x))
    .OrderBy(x => x.Name)
    .FetchMany(x => x.Actors)
    .ToList();
```

The result is a SQL query that looks similar to the following example SQL Server:

```
select     movie0_.id              as id0_0_,
    actors1_.id                     as id2_1_,
    movie0_.NAME                    as name0_0_,
    movie0_.description             as descript4_0_0_,
    movie0_.unitprice               as unitprice0_0_,
    movie0_.director                as director0_0_,
    actors1_.actor                  as actor2_1_,
    actors1_.role                   as role2_1_,
    actors1_.movieid                as movieid2_1_,
    actors1_.movieid               as movieid0__,
    actors1_.id                    as id0__
from     product movie0_
left outer join actorrole actors1_ on movie0_.id=actors1_.movieid
where     movie0_.producttype='Movie'
and       movie0_.id IN
    (
        select   movie2_.id
     from       product movie2_
     where      movie2_.producttype='Movie'
     and        movie2_.name like (@p0+'%')
     order by movie2_.name asc
     offset @p1 rows
     fetch first @p2 rows only
    )
order by          movie0_.name asc
```

What's interesting here is that the `Contains` call, `Where(x => baseQuery.Contains(x))`, has been rendered as an `IN` subquery. The subquery performs the actual limiting function, in this case, using SQL Server's `OFFSET/FETCH` without being affected by any joins. Instead, the `FetchMany` on the outer query gives us the eager loading that we want.

The performance of a query similar to this depends on how well the DBMS manages to optimize the execution, but generally it should work well.

Problem 2 – only the queried class' properties can be eager loaded

In our recipe, we want to load all the `Products` and present them in a list format. For movies, we show the names of the `Actors` and for books we include the name of the `Publisher`. However, since the query is on the base type, `Product`, we have no way to specify the eager loading of those properties. This is where the `Future` queries come in handy.

Our recipe uses three Futures queries. The first simply returns all products, sorted by unit price. The second Futures query, shown next, has the secret sauce:

```
session.Query<Movie>()
    .FetchMany(x=>x.Actors)
      .ToFuture();
```

You have probably observed that we don't actually assign the resulting `IEnumerable<Movie>` to a variable and use it anywhere. That's because we don't actually care about the results of this query. Its only purpose is to sneak into the session's hidden `MultiQuery` for Futures and get executed.

We do the same for the books:

```
session.Query<Book>()
      .Fetch(x => x.Publisher)
      .ToFuture();
```

When we enumerate the result of the first query, all three queries get executed. First, NHibernate loads up all the products, including movies and book, and then puts them in the session cache. At this point, every movie's `Actors` collection is uninitialized. When NHibernate executes the second query, it initializes the collections as it loads the query results. Finally, when the last query is executed, all books get their `Publisher` set and get initialized.

The end result is that we can output the name of a movie's `Actors` or a book's `Publisher`, without causing another query. That data has already been loaded.

The following are the resulting SQL queries:

```
select
  product0_.Id as Id0_,
  product0_.Name as Name0_,
  product0_.Description as Descript4_0_,
  product0_.UnitPrice as UnitPrice0_,
  product0_.ISBN as ISBN0_,
  product0_.Author as Author0_,
  product0_.PublisherId as Publishe8_0_,
  product0_.Director as Director0_,
  product0_.ProductType as ProductT2_0_
from
  Product product0_
order by
  product0_.UnitPrice asc


select
  movie0_.Id as Id0_0_,
  actors1_.Id as Id2_1_,
  movie0_.Name as Name0_0_,
  movie0_.Description as Descript4_0_0_,
  movie0_.UnitPrice as UnitPrice0_0_,
  movie0_.Director as Director0_0_,
  actors1_.Actor as Actor2_1_,
  actors1_.Role as Role2_1_,
  actors1_.MovieId as MovieId2_1_,
  actors1_.MovieId as MovieId0__,
  actors1_.Id as Id0__
from
  Product movie0_
left outer join
```

```
    ActorRole actors1_
    on movie0_.Id=actors1_.MovieId
where
    movie0_.ProductType='Movie'


select
    book0_.Id as Id0_0_,
    publisher1_.Id as Id1_1_,
    book0_.Name as Name0_0_,
    book0_.Description as Descript4_0_0_,
    book0_.UnitPrice as UnitPrice0_0_,
    book0_.ISBN as ISBN0_0_,
    book0_.Author as Author0_0_,
    book0_.PublisherId as Publishe8_0_0_,
    publisher1_.Name as Name1_1_
from
    Product book0_
left outer join
    Publisher publisher1_
    on book0_.PublisherId=publisher1_.Id
where
    book0_.ProductType='Book'
```

Problem 3 – eager loading multiple collections should be avoided

As we mentioned in the previous chapter, eager loading more than one collection in a query will give us a result, which in SQL terms is called a CROSS JOIN, a Cartesian product. Eager loading three different collections, with 100 items in each, will result in 100*100*100 (one million) rows and maybe that's just for one of the items in our output. Cleary, this should be avoided and again the Futures make it possible.

While we don't actually show it in the recipe, we could use the same strategy as we did for the `Actors` property. Just add more Future queries, one per collection that we want to eager load:

```
session.Query<Movie>()
    .FetchMany(x=>x.Actors)
    .ToFuture();

session.Query<Movie>()
    .FetchMany(x=>x.MakeUpArtists)
    .ToFuture();

session.Query<Movie>()
    .FetchMany(x=>x.StageBuilders)
    .ToFuture();
```

There's more...

In this recipe we only used LINQ, but the Future strategy can be used with all the querying techniques. Just combine what you learned in the corresponding *Eager loading with...* recipe with the correct Future syntax. The paging subquery might be a bit trickier and currently, it can't be solved in HQL but works fine with `Criteria` and `QueryOver`.

Criteria

Refer the following code for `Criteria`:

```
var baseCrit = DetachedCriteria.For<Movie>()
    .Add(Restrictions.Like("Name", "Movie", MatchMode.Start))
    .AddOrder(new Order("Name", true))
    .SetProjection(Property.ForName("Id"))
    .SetFirstResult(5)
    .SetMaxResults(5);

var movies = session.CreateCriteria<Movie>()
    .Add(Subqueries.PropertyIn("Id", baseCrit))
    .AddOrder(new Order("Name", true))
    .SetFetchMode("Actors", FetchMode.Join)
    .List<Movie>();
```

QueryOver

Refer the following code for `QueryOver`:

```
var baseQuery = QueryOver.Of<Movie>()
    .Where(
        Restrictions.On<Movie>(x => x.Name)
```

```
        .IsLike("Movie", MatchMode.Start)
    )
    .OrderBy(x => x.Name).Asc
    .Select(x=>x.Id)
    .Skip(5)
    .Take(5);

var movies = session.QueryOver<Movie>()
    .WithSubquery
    .WhereProperty(m => m.Id)
    .In(baseQuery)
    .Fetch(x => x.Actors).Eager
    .List();
```

See also

- ▸ *Eager loading with LINQ*
- ▸ *Eager loading with Criteria*
- ▸ *Eager loading with QueryOver*
- ▸ *Eager loading with HQL*
- ▸ *Using Futures*

Using stateless sessions

When processing large amounts of data, you can usually improve performance by using an API that's closer to the bare metal, often times trading off some higher-level features in the process. In NHibernate, this high performance, low-level API is the stateless session.

Here we'll use a stateless session to update our movie prices.

Getting ready

Complete the *Getting Ready* instructions at the beginning of *Chapter 4, Queries*.

How to do it...

1. Add a new folder named Stateless to the QueryRecipes project.

2. Create a class named Recipe in the folder:

```
using NH4CookbookHelpers.Queries;
using NH4CookbookHelpers.Queries.Model;
using NHibernate;
using NHibernate.Linq;
using System;
using System.Linq;

namespace QueryRecipes.Stateless
{
  public class Recipe : QueryRecipe
  {


  }
}
```

3. To create some data with which to work, add the following method to your Recipe class:

```
protected override void AddData(ISessionFactory sessionFactory)
{
  using (var session = sessionFactory.OpenStatelessSession())
  {
    using (var tx = session.BeginTransaction())
    {
      for (int i = 0; i < 1000; i++)
        session.Insert(new Movie()
        {
          Name = "Movie " + i,
          Description = "A great movie!",
          UnitPrice = 14.95M,
          Director = "Johnny Smith"
        });
      tx.Commit();
    }
  }
}
```

4. Next, let's update our movie prices and add the following method to the `Recipe` class:

```
protected override void Run(ISessionFactory sessionFactory)
{
  using (var session = sessionFactory.OpenStatelessSession())
  {
    using (var tx = session.BeginTransaction())
    {
      var movies = session.Query<Movie>().ToList();
      foreach (var movie in movies)
      {
        UpdateMoviePrice(movie);
        session.Update(movie);
      }
      tx.Commit();
    }
  }
}
```

5. Finally, add our `UpdateMoviePrice` method:

```
static Random rnd = new Random();

static void UpdateMoviePrice(Movie movie)
{
  // Random price between $9.95 and $24.95
  movie.UnitPrice = (decimal) rnd.Next(10, 26) - 0.05M;
}
```

6. Run the application and start the `Stateless` recipe.

How it works...

Using a stateless session, we create 1000 movies. Stateless sessions don't implement transactional write-behind, meaning that the SQL statements are not delayed until we commit the transaction. However, if we have turned on batching, they don't happen immediately either. Instead the insert statements are queued up and sent all together. If batching is turned off, these would be sent one at a time immediately with each call to `session.Insert`.

Next, we fetch all of our movies from the database with the help of a query. These movies are detached; they are not associated with a session; entities can't be associated with stateless sessions. In this case, we load our entities with a query or the `Get` method.

Since stateless sessions don't implement automatic dirty checking, we have to call `session. Update` to save our changes to each movie.

There's more...

A stateless session is essentially a stripped-down version of a standard NHibernate session. It doesn't use a first-level cache or perform automatic dirty checking and it doesn't support lazy loading. In fact, it doesn't even keep references to entities, which helps avoid memory leaks when processing thousands of entities. Cascading is ignored and you must explicitly insert, update, or delete each entity, one at a time. Stateless sessions also bypass the second-level cache, event listeners, and interceptors.

Despite these limitations, stateless sessions are very useful in high-performance batch processing situations where you need to work with real objects. When you can work with the raw data, there are usually even better alternatives, such as plain old SQL, HQL bulk actions, SqlBulkCopy, or ETL tools. For the plain old SQL route, simply access the ADO.NET connection object from `session.Connection` and write your ADO.NET code as you normally would.

Using read-only entities

By treating entities as read-only, we allow NHibernate to skip the memory and resource intensive dirty checking, which determines how and if an entity should be updated in the database. In *Chapter 2, Models and Mappings*, we learned how to configure the read-only behavior in a mapping. Here we'll see how the same thing can be accomplished programmatically, at runtime.

Getting ready

Complete the *Getting Ready* instructions at the beginning of *Chapter 4, Queries*.

How to do it...

1. Add a new folder named `ReadOnly` to the `QueryRecipes` project.
2. Create a class named `Recipe` in the folder:

```
using NH4CookbookHelpers.Queries;
using NH4CookbookHelpers.Queries.Model;
using NHibernate;

namespace QueryRecipes.ReadOnly
{
  public class Recipe : QueryRecipe
  {
    private bool _readOnly=true;

    protected override void Run(ISessionFactory sessionFactory)
```

```
      {
        RunWithReadOnlySession(sessionFactory);
        RunWithQuery(sessionFactory);
        RunWithSetReadOnly(sessionFactory);
      }

    private void RunWithReadOnlySession(ISessionFactory
  sessionFactory)
      {
        using (var session = sessionFactory.OpenSession())
        {
          session.DefaultReadOnly = _readOnly;
          using (var tx = session.BeginTransaction())
          {
            var movie = session.Get<Movie>(1);
            movie.Director = "Updated in session";
            tx.Commit();
          }
        }
      }

    private void RunWithQuery(ISessionFactory sessionFactory)
      {
        using (var session = sessionFactory.OpenSession())
        {
          using (var tx = session.BeginTransaction())
          {
            var query = session.QueryOver<Movie>()
              .Where(x => x.Id == 1);

            if (_readOnly)
            {
              query.ReadOnly();
            }
            var movie=query.SingleOrDefault();

            movie.Director = "Updated in query";
            tx.Commit();
          }
        }
      }

    private void RunWithSetReadOnly(ISessionFactory
  sessionFactory)
```

```
        {
          using (var session = sessionFactory.OpenSession())
          {
            using (var tx = session.BeginTransaction())
            {
              var movie = session.Get<Movie>(1);
              session.SetReadOnly(movie, _readOnly);
              movie.Director = "Updated with SetReadOnly";
              tx.Commit();
            }
          }
        }
      }
```

3. Run the application and start the ReadOnly recipe.

How the movie is never updated, despite being modified several times. Set the _readOnly variable to false and run the recipe again. This time the entity will be updated thrice.

How it works...

We have already covered how to set a specific class as read-only in the mapping. In this recipe, we used three different techniques to configure the same thing at runtime.

Setting the session to be read-only

In the RunWithReadOnlySession method, we configure the session using the DefaultReadOnly property. This means that any entity that is loaded from the database into the session, after the property and set to true, will be marked as read-only. Toggling the value will never affect any entities already loaded.

Setting a query to load entities as read-only

We can also configure a specific query to load the entities with the read-only flag set. For an HQL query or a native SQL query, in other words a query implementing IQuery, this is done using the SetReadOnly(bool) method. The same method is also available on CriteriaQueries.

SetReadOnly will only affect the entities that are directly loaded by the query. Lazy loaded entities are not affected, but will respect the session's DefaultReadOnly setting. It's therefore sometimes better to just set DefaultReadOnly to true before a query is run and reset it to false once all the entities have been loaded.

It's also worth noting that specifying SetReadOnly on a query will override the DefaultReadOnly setting, making it possible to force query loaded entities to be writable (non read-only) even if DefaultReadOnly is true.

Our recipe uses the QueryOver syntax, which instead of SetReadOnly has a ReadOnly method, which can only set the value to true. Currently, the LINQ provider doesn't support ReadOnly, although such a feature is scheduled for a future release.

Making a specific entity read-only

The most granular way to use read-only entities is to specify it on a specific entity. By calling session.SetReadOnly(entity, bool), we can cause a writable entity to become read-only or a read-only entity to become writable. In the latter case, NHibernate consider the current state of the entity to be the baseline. Any changes performed before setting the entity the writable will be ignored in the updates.

There's more...

A read-only entity may not be quite as read-only as expected. For further details, read the *How it works...* section in *Chapter 2, Models and Mappings*.

One more way to avoid dirty checks and update is by setting session.FlushMode = FlushMode.Never. We tell NHibernate that we never want any changes flushed to the database. Saving a new entity, with a database generated POID, will still call the database, but other than that no updates, deletes, or inserts will be performed, unless session.Flush() is explicitly called.

Use the second-level cache

Caching is used frequently; rarely updated data can greatly improve the performance of websites and other high traffic applications. In this recipe, we'll configure NHibernate's cache, just as we would for a typical public facing website.

Getting ready

Complete the *Getting Ready* instructions at the beginning of *Chapter 4, Queries*.

How to do it...

1. Add a reference to NHibernate.Caches.SysCache using NuGet Package manager console.

2. Open or create a new App.config file in the project.

3. In the `configSections` element, declare a section for the cache configuration:

```
<section name="syscache"
type="NHibernate.Caches.SysCache.SysCacheSectionHandler,
NHibernate.Caches.SysCache" />
```

4. Add the `syscache` section:

```
<syscache>
<cache region="hourly" expiration="60" priority="3" />
</syscache>
```

5. Add a new folder named `Caching` to the `QueryRecipes` project.

6. Add a new XML file named `hibernate.cfg.xml` to the folder. Set its **Copy to Output directory** property to **Copy always**:

```
<?xml version="1.0" encoding="utf-8"?>
<hibernate-configuration xmlns="urn:nhibernate-configuration-2.2">
  <session-factory>
    <property name="cache.provider_class">
      NHibernate.Caches.SysCache.SysCacheProvider,
      NHibernate.Caches.SysCache
    </property>
    <property name="cache.use_second_level_cache">
      true
    </property>
    <property name="cache.use_query_cache">
      true
    </property>
    <class-cache class="NH4CookbookHelpers.Queries.Model.
Product,NH4CookbookHelpers"
    region="hourly" usage="read-write"/>
    <class-cache class="NH4CookbookHelpers.Queries.Model.
ActorRole,NH4CookbookHelpers"
    region="hourly" usage="read-write"/>
    <collection-cache collection="NH4CookbookHelpers.Queries.
Model.Movie.Actors"
    region="hourly" usage="read-write"/>
  </session-factory>
</hibernate-configuration>
```

7. Add a new class named `Recipe` to the folder:

```
using NH4CookbookHelpers.Queries;
using NH4CookbookHelpers.Queries.Model;
using NHibernate;
```

```
using NHibernate.Cfg;

namespace QueryRecipes.Caching
{
  public class Recipe : QueryRecipe
  {
    protected override void Configure(Configuration nhConfig)
    {
      nhConfig.Configure("Caching/hibernate.cfg.xml");
    }
  }
}
```

8. In `Recipe`, add the following methods:

```
protected override void Run(ISessionFactory sessionFactory)
{
  ShowMoviesBy(sessionFactory, "Steven Spielberg");
  ShowMoviesBy(sessionFactory, "Steven Spielberg");
  UpdateMoviesBy(sessionFactory, "Steven Spielberg");
  ShowMoviesBy(sessionFactory, "Steven Spielberg");
}

private void ShowMoviesBy(ISessionFactory sessionFactory,
   string director)
{
  using (var session = sessionFactory.OpenSession())
  {
    using (var tx = session.BeginTransaction())
    {
      var movies = session.QueryOver<Movie>()
        .Where(x => x.Director == director)
        .Cacheable()
        .List();
      Show("Movies found:", movies);
      tx.Commit();
    }
  }
}

private void UpdateMoviesBy(ISessionFactory sessionFactory,
   string director)
{
```

```
using (var session = sessionFactory.OpenSession())
{
  using (var tx = session.BeginTransaction())
  {
    session.CreateQuery(@"update Movie
            set Description='Good'
            where Director=:director")
      .SetString("director", director)
      .ExecuteUpdate();
    tx.Commit();
  }
}
```

9. Run the application and start the `Caching` recipe.

In the query log, you will see how the `SELECT` query, which is used to find the movies, is only executed the first and third time we call `ShowMoviesBy`. The second time, the query results are found in the query cache and the returned entities are loaded from the entity cache.

How it works...

What happened after the second query? Why weren't the cached results used? The `UpdateMoviesBy` method was called and while it didn't actually affect the movies included in the query, NHibernate has no way of knowing that. Such deduction logic would be extremely complex. Instead, a defensive but safe approach is taken, which sees that the `Product` table was affected by the update and as a result all cached query results involving that table are invalidated. Consistency is much more important than performance.

We deliberately used separate sessions for each call to `ShowMoviesBy`, so that the first level cache would not be involved.

The `cache.provider_class` configuration property defines the cache provider to use. In this case, we're using `syscache`, NHibernate's wrapper for ASP.NET's `System.Web. Caching.Cache`.

The `cache.use_second_level_cache` setting enables the second-level cache. If the second-level cache is enabled, setting `cache.use_query_cache` will also allow query results to be cached.

Caching must be set up on a per-class hierarchy, per-collection, and per-query basis. That is, you must also set up caching for each specific item to be cached. In this recipe, we've set up caching for the product entity class, which, because they're in the same class hierarchy, implicitly sets up caching for book and movie with the same settings. In addition, we've set up caching for our `ActorRole` entity class. Finally, because caching for collections is configured separately from entities, we set up caching for the movie's `Actors` collection.

Each of these caches use a region named hourly. A cache region partitions the cached data and defines a set of rules governing when that data will expire. In this case, our hourly region is set to remove an item from the cache after 60 minutes or under stress, such as low memory. The priority can be set to a value from 1 to 5, with 1 being the lowest priority and thus the first to be removed from the cache.

The cache concurrency strategy for each item, set with the `usage` attribute, defines how an object's cache entry may be updated. In this recipe, where we are both storing and retrieving entities, we've set all of our strategies to read-write. In other scenarios, such as a public-facing website, which never updates the data, it may be appropriate to use read-only.

It should be added that the class level caching configuration can be specified in the mapping files:

```
<class name="Product">
    <cache region="hourly" usage="read-write"/>
    . . .
</class>
```

Using that approach tidies things up a bit, but it's worth considering whether caching should be a mapping concern (often embedded in the code) or a configuration setting.

Caching is only meant to improve the performance of a properly designed NHibernate application. Your application shouldn't depend on the cache to function properly. Before adding caching, you should correct poorly performing queries and issues, such as `SELECT N+1`. This will usually give a significant performance boost, reducing the need for caching and its added complexity.

There's more...

NHibernate allows us to configure a cache with the same scope as the session factory. Logically, this cache is divided into three parts.

Entity cache

The entity cache doesn't store the actual entities. Instead the objects are stored as a dictionary of POIDs to arrays of values.

The `Movie.Actors` collection has a cache entry of its own. Also notice that in this entry, we're storing the POIDs of the `ActorRole` objects, not the `ActorRole` data. There is no data duplication in the cache. From the cached data shown in the diagram, we can easily rehydrate the entire object graph for the movie without the chance of any inconsistent results.

Query cache

In addition to caching entities, NHibernate can also cache query results. In the cache, each query is associated with an array of POIDs for the entities of the query returns, similar to the way our movie actor collection is stored in the previous image. The entity data should already be stored in the entity cache. Again, this eliminates the chance of inconsistent results. However, it's very important that the return types of the queries are configured to be cacheable. If not, each returned entity will be fetched from the database, probably causing the cached query to be slower and more resource consuming than a non-cached query.

Update timestamp cache

The third part of the cache stores a last-updated timestamp for each table. When data is first placed in the cache, the timestamp is set to a value in the `Future`, ensuring that the cache will never return uncommitted data from a pending transaction. Once the transaction is committed, the timestamp is set back to the present, thus allowing that data to be read from the cache.

The rules

There are some basic requirements when using the cache:

- Always begin a transaction before any database interaction, even when reading data from the database. This is a recommended practice with NHibernate in general, but it is especially important for interacting with the cache. Without an explicit transaction, caching is bypassed.

- When opening a session, don't provide your own database connection. This also affects caching. If you need to use different connections, implement your own `IConnectionProvider` and set the `connection.provider` configuration property as shown in the *Using dynamic connection strings* recipe in *Chapter 7, Data Access Layer*.

See also

- *Configuring NHibernate with App.config*
- *Using dynamic connection strings*
- *Configuring the cache with code*

Configuring the second-level cache with code

NHibernate also provides an option for cache configuration with the `NHibernate.Cfg.Loquacious` namespace. In this recipe, we'll show you how to configure the second-level cache with code.

Getting ready

Complete the *Getting Ready* instructions at the beginning of. *Chapter 4, Queries*.

How to do it...

1. Add a reference to `NHibernate.Caches.SysCache` using NuGet Package Manager Console.
2. Add a new folder named `CachingWithCode` to the project.
3. Add a new class named `Recipe` to the folder:

```
using NH4CookbookHelpers.Queries;
using NH4CookbookHelpers.Queries.Model;
using NHibernate;
using NHibernate.Caches.SysCache;
using NHibernate.Cfg;

namespace QueryRecipes.CachingWithCode
{
  public class Recipe : QueryRecipe
  {
  }
}
```

4. In `Recipe`, add the following method:

```
protected override void Configure(Configuration nhConfig)
{
  nhConfig
    .Cache(x =>
    {
      x.Provider<SysCacheProvider>();
      x.UseQueryCache = true;
    })
    .EntityCache<Product>(c =>
    {
```

```
            c.Strategy = EntityCacheUsage.ReadWrite;
            c.RegionName = "hourly";
        })
        .EntityCache<ActorRole>(c =>
        {
            c.Strategy = EntityCacheUsage.ReadWrite;
            c.RegionName = "hourly";
        })
        .EntityCache<Movie>(c => c.Collection(
        movie => movie.Actors,
        coll =>
        {
            coll.Strategy = EntityCacheUsage.ReadWrite;
            coll.RegionName = "hourly";
        }));
}
```

5. In `Recipe`, add the two following methods:

```
protected override void Run(ISessionFactory sessionFactory)
{
    ShowMoviesBy(sessionFactory, "Steven Spielberg");
    ShowMoviesBy(sessionFactory, "Steven Spielberg");
}

private void ShowMoviesBy(ISessionFactory sessionFactory, string
director)
{
    using (var session = sessionFactory.OpenSession())
    {
        using (var tx = session.BeginTransaction())
        {
            var movies = session.QueryOver<Movie>()
                .Where(x => x.Director == director)
                .Cacheable()
                .List();
            Show("Movies found:", movies);
            tx.Commit();
        }
    }
}
```

6. Run the application and start the `CachingWithCode` recipe.

How it works...

1. For details on how the caching behaves, see the preceding recipe, *Use the second-level cache.*

2. By calling the following code, we not only specify the provider we want to use (`cache.provider_class`) but also specify that the query cache should be enabled (`cache.use_query_cache`):

```
.Cache(x =>
        {
            x.Provider<SysCacheProvider>();
            x.UseQueryCache = true;
        })
```

3. We also implicitly enable the second-level cache (`cache.use_second_level_cache`).

4. We configure the class cache for our `Product` hierarchy and `ActorRole` entities with the following code:

```
.EntityCache<Product>(c =>
{
  c.Strategy = EntityCacheUsage.ReadWrite;
  c.RegionName = "hourly";
})
.EntityCache<ActorRole>(c =>
{
  c.Strategy = EntityCacheUsage.ReadWrite;
  c.RegionName = "hourly";
})
```

5. Finally, we configure the collection cache for our `Actors` collection with the following code:

```
nhConfig
    .EntityCache<Movie>(c => c.Collection(
    movie => movie.Actors,
    coll =>
    {
      coll.Strategy = EntityCacheUsage.ReadWrite;
      coll.RegionName = "hourly";
    }));
```

Note how we call `Collection()`, passing an expression for our `Actors` collection, as well as the settings for our collection cache.

There's more...

Just as with XML mappings, it's perfectly possible to specify the class-level cache configuration in coded mappings.

- For NHibernate's built in class mappings it looks similar to this:

```csharp
public class ProductMapping : ClassMapping<Product>
{
  public ProductMapping()
  {
    ...
    Cache(c =>
    {
      c.Usage(CacheUsage.ReadWrite);
      c.Region("hourly");
    });
  }
}


public class MovieMapping : SubclassMapping<Movie>
{
  public MovieMapping()
  {
    ...
    Set(x => x.Actors, x =>
      {
        x.Cache(c =>
        {
          c.Usage(CacheUsage.ReadWrite);
          c.Region("hourly");
        });
        ...
      }
    , x => x.OneToMany());
  }
}
```

- For Fluent NHibernate:

```csharp
public class ProductMap : ClassMap<Product>
{
  public ProductMap()
  {
    ...
```

```
        Cache.ReadWrite().Region("hourly");
    }
}
public class MovieMap : SubclassMap<Movie>
{
    public MovieMap()
    {
        ...
        HasMany(x => x.Actors)
          .AsSet()
          .Cache.ReadWrite().Region("hourly");
    }
}
```

See also

▶ *Use the second-level cache*

Sharding databases for performance

There are a few scenarios where it may be appropriate to partition data horizontally across several servers, with performance being the most obvious reason. The concept itself is known as sharding and is used in many large scale applications, such as Facebook.

In this recipe, we'll show you how to use NHibernate.Shards to split our data set across three databases.

Getting ready

In SQL Server, create three new, blank databases named Shard1, Shard2, and Shard3. Complete the *Getting Ready* instructions at the beginning of *Chapter 4, Queries*.

How to do it...

1. Add a reference to NHibernate.Shards using NuGet Package Manager Console:

   Install-Package NHibernate.Shards -Project QueryRecipes

2. Add a new folder named Sharding to the project:

3. Add a new embedded resource named ShardedProduct.hbm.xml:

   ```xml
   <?xml version="1.0" encoding="utf-8" ?>
   <hibernate-mapping xmlns="urn:nhibernate-mapping-2.2"
     assembly="QueryRecipes"
   ```

```xml
         namespace="QueryRecipes.Sharding">
         <class name="ShardedProduct">
           <id name="Id">
             <generator class="NHibernate.Shards.Id.ShardedUUIDGenerator,
NHibernate.Shards" />
           </id>
           <property name="Name" />
         </class>
       </hibernate-mapping>
```

4. Add an `App.config` file with the following connection strings (or add to your existing file):

```xml
<?xml version="1.0" encoding="utf-8" ?>
<configuration>
  <connectionStrings>
  <add name="Shard1" connectionString="Server=.\SQLExpress;
Database=Shard1; Trusted_Connection=SSPI"/>
  <add name="Shard2" connectionString="Server=.\SQLExpress;
Database=Shard2; Trusted_Connection=SSPI"/>
  <add name="Shard3" connectionString="Server=.\SQLExpress;
Database=Shard3; Trusted_Connection=SSPI"/>
  </connectionStrings>
</configuration>
```

5. Add a new class named `ShardedProduct`:

```csharp
namespace QueryRecipes.Sharding
{
  public class ShardedProduct
  {
    public virtual string Id { get; protected set; }
    public virtual string Name { get; set; }
  }
}
```

6. Add a new class named `ShardStrategyFactory` with the following code:

```csharp
using System.Collections.Generic;
using NHibernate.Shards;
using NHibernate.Shards.LoadBalance;
using NHibernate.Shards.Strategy;
using NHibernate.Shards.Strategy.Access;
using NHibernate.Shards.Strategy.Resolution;
using NHibernate.Shards.Strategy.Selection;

namespace QueryRecipes.Sharding
{
```

```
      public class ShardStrategyFactory : IShardStrategyFactory
      {
        public IShardStrategy NewShardStrategy(
          IEnumerable<ShardId> shardIds)
        {
          var loadBalancer =
    new RoundRobinShardLoadBalancer(shardIds);
          return new ShardStrategyImpl(
            new RoundRobinShardSelectionStrategy(loadBalancer),
            new AllShardsShardResolutionStrategy(shardIds),
            new SequentialShardAccessStrategy());
        }
      }
    }
```

7. Add a new class named `Recipe`:

```
using System;
using System.Collections.Generic;
using System.Linq;
using NH4CookbookHelpers;
using NHibernate.Cfg;
using NHibernate.Dialect;
using NHibernate.Driver;
using NHibernate.Shards;
using NHibernate.Shards.Cfg;
using NHibernate.Shards.Session;
using NHibernate.Shards.Tool;

namespace QueryRecipes.Sharding
{
    public class Recipe : BaseRecipe
    {
        private IShardedSessionFactory _sessionFactory;
    }
}
```

8. Add a new method `Initialize` to the class:

```
public override void Initialize()
{
    var connStrNames = new List<string> {
"Shard1", "Shard2", "Shard3"
    };

    var shardConfigs = connStrNames.Select((x, index) =>
```

```
            new ShardConfiguration
            {
                ShardId = (short)index,
                ConnectionStringName = x
            }
        );

        var protoConfig = new Configuration()
            .DataBaseIntegration(
                x =>
                {
                    x.Dialect<MsSql2012Dialect>();
                    x.Driver<Sql2008ClientDriver>();
                })
            .AddResource("QueryRecipes.Sharding.ShardedProduct.hbm.xml",
                GetType().Assembly);

        var shardedConfig = new ShardedConfiguration(
            protoConfig,
            shardConfigs,
            new ShardStrategyFactory()
        );

        CreateSchema(shardedConfig);

        try
        {
            _sessionFactory =
                shardedConfig.
                BuildShardedSessionFactory();
        }
        catch
        {
            DropSchema(shardedConfig);
            throw;
        }
    }
```

9. Add two methods for creating and dropping the schema:

```
private void CreateSchema(ShardedConfiguration
shardedConfiguration)
{
    new ShardedSchemaExport(shardedConfiguration)
```

```
            .Create(false, true);
    }

    private void DropSchema(ShardedConfiguration shardedConfiguration)
    {
        new ShardedSchemaExport(shardedConfiguration)
            .Drop(false, true);
    }
```

10. Finally, add a new Run method, which inserts data and queries it:

```
public override void Run()
{
    using (var session = _sessionFactory.OpenSession())
    {
        using (var tx = session.BeginTransaction())
        {
            for (var i = 0; i < 100; i++)
            {
                var product=new ShardedProduct()
                {
                    Name = "Product" + i,
                };
                session.Save(product);
            }
            tx.Commit();
        }
    }

    using (var session = _sessionFactory.OpenSession())
    {
        using (var tx = session.BeginTransaction())
        {
            var query = @"from ShardedProduct p
                            where upper(p.Name)
                            like '%1%'";
            var products = session.CreateQuery(query)
                .List<ShardedProduct>();

            foreach (var p in products)
            {
                Console.WriteLine(
"Product Id: {0}, Name: {1}",p.Id,p.Name);
            }
```

```
                        tx.Commit();
                }
                session.Close();
            }
        }
```

11. Run the application and start the `Sharding` recipe.

12. Inspect the product table in each of the three databases. You should find one third of the products in each.

How it works...

NHibernate Shards allows you to split your data across several databases, named shards, while hiding this additional complexity behind the familiar NHibernate APIs. In this recipe, we use the sharded UUID POID generator, which generates UUIDs with a four-digit shard ID, followed by a 28 hexadecimal digit unique ID. A typical ID looks similar to 0001000069334c47a07afd3f6f46d587. You can provide your own POID generator, provided the shard ID is somehow encoded in the persistent object's IDs.

The `ShardConfiguration` class configures a session factory for each shard. These session factories are grouped together with an implementation of `IShardStrategyFactory` to build an `IShardedSessionFactory`. A sharded session factory implements the familiar `ISessionFactory` interface, so the impact on larger applications is minimal.

An implementation of `IShardStrategyFactory` must return three strategies to control the operation of NHibernate shards.

First, the `IShardSelectionStrategy` assigns each new entity to a shard. In this recipe, we use a simple round-robin technique that spreads the data across each shard equally. The first entity is assigned to shard 1, the second to shard 2, the third to shard 3, the fourth to shard 1, and so on.

Next, the `IShardResolutionStrategy` is used to determine the correct shard, given an entity name and entity ID. In this example, we use the `AllShardsShardResolutionStrategy`, which doesn't attempt to determine the correct shard. Instead, all shards are queried for an entity. We could provide our own implementation to get the shard ID from the first four characters of the entity ID. This would allow us to determine which shard contains the entity we want and query only that shard, reducing the load on each database. In this recipe though, we used an ID generator implementing `IShardEncodingIdentifierGenerator` and that is enough to solve the resolution issue.

Finally, the `IShardAccessStrategy` determines how the shards will be accessed. In this example, we use the `SequentialShardAccessStrategy`, so the first shard will be queried, then the next, and so on. NHibernate Shards also includes a parallel strategy.

Once we've built a sharded session factory, the application code looks similar to any other NHibernate application. However, there are a few caveats. The major one possibly being that currently, LINQ or QueryOver are not supported. Also, many of the lesser used features of NHibernate cannot be used. For example, `session.Delete("from Products")` throws a `NotImplementedException`. Additionally, sharded sessions expect to be explicitly closed before being disposed.

NHibernate Shards doesn't support object graphs spread across shard boundaries. The idea of well-defined boundaries between object graphs fits well with the domain-driven design pattern of aggregate roots and is generally considered a good NHibernate practice, even without sharding.

6
Testing

In this chapter, we will cover the following recipes:

- ► Using NHibernate Profiler
- ► Profiling NHibernate with Glimpse
- ► Fast testing with the SQLite in-memory database
- ► Preloading data with SQLite
- ► Using Fluent NHibernate persistence testing
- ► Using the Ghostbusters test

Introduction

Testing is a critical step in the development of any application. The recipes in this chapter are designed to ease the testing process and expose common issues.

Using NHibernate Profiler

NHibernate Profiler from Hibernating Rhinos is a powerful tool for analyzing, visualizing what is happening inside your NHibernate application, and for discovering issues you may have. In this recipe, we will show you how to get up and running with NHibernate Profiler.

Getting ready

Download NHibernate Profiler from `http://nhprof.com` and unzip it. As it is a commercial product, you will also need a license file. You can request a 30-day trial license from the NHProf website.

Using our `Eg.Core` model from *Chapter 2, Models and Mapping*, set up a new NHibernate console application with `log4net`, just as we did in *Chapter 1, The Configuration and Schema*.

How to do it...

1. Install `NHibernateProfiler.Appender` using the NuGet Package Manager Console by executing the following command:

    `Install-Package NHibernateProfiler.Appender`

2. In the `session-factory` element of `App.config`, set the `generate_statistics` property to `true`.

3. Add the following code to your `Main` method:

    ```
    HibernatingRhinos.Profiler.Appender.
    NHibernate.NHibernateProfiler.Initialize();

    var nhConfig = new Configuration().Configure();
    var sessionFactory = nhConfig.BuildSessionFactory();

    using (var session = sessionFactory.OpenSession())
    {
      var books = from b in session.Query<Book>()
                  where b.Author == "Jason Dentler"
                  select b;

      foreach (var book in books)
        Console.WriteLine(book.Name);
    }
    ```

4. Run `NHProf.exe` from the NH Profiler download and activate the license.

5. Build and run your console application.

6. Check the NH Profiler. It should look similar to the next screenshot. Note the gray dots, which indicate alerts, next to **Session #1** and **Recent Statements**:

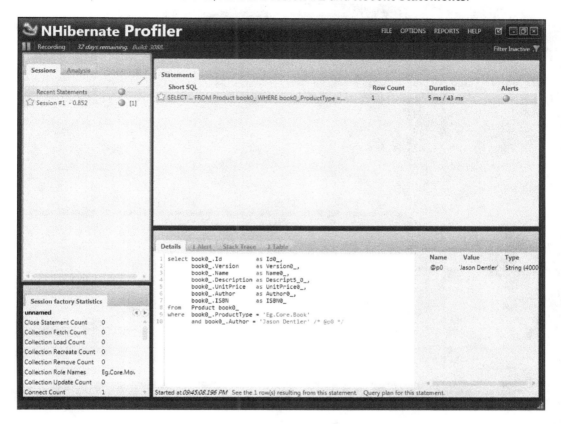

7. Select **Session #1** from the **Sessions** list in the top-left pane.

8. Select a statement from the top-right pane.

9. Note the SQL statement in the following screenshot:

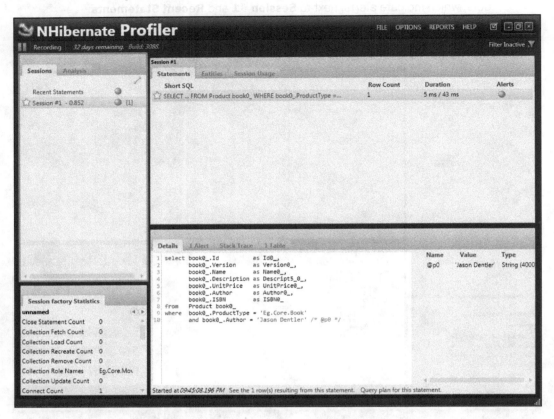

10. Click on **See the 1 row(s) resulting from this statement**.

11. Enter your database connection string in the field provided and click on **OK**.

12. Close the query results window.

13. Switch to the **Alerts** tab and note the alert message, which reads **Use of implicit transaction is discouraged**.

14. Click on the **Read more** link for more information and suggested solutions to this particular issue.

15. Switch to the **Stack Trace** tab, as shown in the next screenshot:

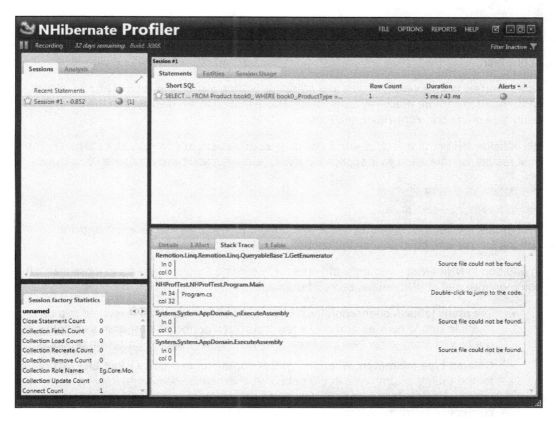

16. Double-click on the **NHProfTest.NHProfTest.Program.Main** stack frame to jump to that location inside Visual Studio.

17. Using the following code, wrap the `foreach` loop in a transaction and commit the transaction:

```
using (var tx = session.BeginTransaction())
{
  foreach (var book in books)
    Console.WriteLine(book.Name);
  tx.Commit();
}
```

18. In NHibernate Profiler, right-click on **Sessions** in the top-left pane and select **Clear All Sessions**.

19. Build and run your application.

20. Check NHibernate Profiler for alerts.

How it works...

NHibernate Profiler uses a custom log4net appender to capture data about NHibernate activities inside your application and transmits that data to the NHibernate Profiler application.

As we learned in *Chapter 2, Models and Mapping*, setting `generate_statistics` allows NHibernate to capture many key data points. These statistics are displayed in the lower left-hand side of the pane of NHibernate Profiler.

We initialize NHibernate Profiler with a call to `NHibernateProfiler.Initialize()`. For best results, do this when your application starts, just after you have configured `log4net`.

There's more...

NHibernate Profiler also supports offline and remote profiling, as well as command-line options for use with build scripts and continuous integration systems.

In addition to NHibernate warnings and errors, NHibernate Profiler alerts us to more than 12 common misuses of NHibernate. Some of them are:

▶ **Too many joins**: A query contains a large number of joins. When executed in a batch, multiple simple queries with only a few joins often perform better than a complex query with many joins. This alert can also indicate unexpected Cartesian products.

▶ **Column type mismatch**: When the type of parameter in a query is not an exact match for the table's column type in the database, this can cause several implicit conversion issues, which in turn lead to performance issues (for example, ignored indexes) and conversion overflow issues.

▶ **Different parameter sizes result in inefficient query plan cache usage**: NHibernate detected two-identical queries with different parameter sizes. Each of these queries will create a query plan. This problem grows exponentially with the size and number of parameters used. Setting `prepare_sql` to `true` allows NHibernate to generate queries with consistent parameter sizes.

▶ **Don't query from the view**: This alert is raised when the profiler detects that a query was executed inside a view in an MVC application. Issuing queries in an MVC view is a bad practice for several reasons.

▶ **Ends with queries (`like '%...'`) will force the database to scan the full table**: The database cannot use an index for this kind of query and it is, hence, forced to perform a full table scan, inspecting each of the values in the database for a match.

▶ **Excessive number of rows**: In nearly all cases, this indicates a poorly designed query or a bug.

- **Large number of individual writes**: This indicates a failure to batch writes, either because `adonet.batch_size` is not set or possibly because an Identity-type POID generator is used, which effectively disables batching.

- **More than one session-per-request**: It is usually recommended to use one session-per-request.

- **Queries and data bindings should not mix**: This alert is raised whenever the profiler detects that a query has been generated because of a data binding operation.

- **Query on unindexed column**: A query on an unindexed column forces the database to perform a table scan.

- **Select N+1**: This alert indicates a particular type of anti-pattern where, typically, we load and enumerate a list of parent objects and lazy-load their children as we move through the list. Instead, we should eagerly fetch those children before enumerating the list.

- **Superfluous updates use** `inverse="true"`: NHibernate Profiler detected an unnecessary update statement from a bi-directional one-to-many relationship. Use `inverse="true"` on the many side (list, bag, set, and so on) of the relationship to avoid this.

- **Too many cache calls per session**: This alert is targeted particularly at applications using a distributed (remote) second-level cache. By design, NHibernate does not batch calls to the cache, which can easily lead to hundreds of slow remote calls. It can also indicate an over reliance on the second-level cache, whether remote or local.

- **Too many database calls per session**: This usually indicates a misuse of the database, such as querying inside a loop, a select N+1 bug, or an excessive number of writes.

- **Too many expressions per where clause**: Having too many expressions inside the where statement can lead to poor performance, especially when the application grows and has a big data set.

- **Too many nested select statements**: The query has many nested SELECT statements, which makes the SQL hard to follow and more resource-intensive for the database to parse and execute.

- **Too many tables in selected statement**: The more tables there are in a query, the more work the database has to do, irrespective of whether this is achieved via sub selects, joins, or nested queries.

- **Too many where clauses in statement**: Having too many where statements can lead to poor performance, especially when the application grows and has a big data set.

- **Transaction disposed without explicit rollback or commit**: If no action is taken, transactions will rollback when disposed. However, this often indicates a missing commit rather than a desire to rollback the transaction.

- ▶ **Unbounded result set**: NHibernate Profiler detected a query without a row limit. When the application is moved to production, these queries may return very large result sets, thus leading to catastrophic performance issues. You should limit the maximum number of rows returned by each query as an insurance against these issues.

- ▶ **Use of implicit transactions is discouraged**: Nearly all session activity should happen inside an NHibernate transaction.

- ▶ **Using a single session on multiple threads is likely a bug**: A session should only be used by one thread at a time. Sharing a session across threads is usually a bug, not an explicit design choice, which will require proper locking.

See also

- ▶ *Configuring NHibernate with App.config*
- ▶ *Configure log4net logging*
- ▶ *Profiling NHibernate with Glimpse*

Profiling NHibernate with Glimpse

Glimpse is a popular diagnostics and profiling framework, built especially for .NET web applications. In this recipe, we will show you how to use Glimpse and the Glimpse.NHibernate add-on, in order to profile NHibernate requests.

Getting ready

Open an existing ASP.NET web application project that uses NHibernate or complete the *Setting up session-per-web request* recipe from *Chapter 3, Sessions and Transactions*.

How to do it...

1. Install Glimpse for MVC using the NuGet Package Manager Console by executing the following command:

   ```
   Install-Package Glimpse.MVC5
   ```

2. Install the `NHibernate.Glimpse` package using the NuGet Package Manager Console by executing the following command:

   ```
   Install-Package NHibernate.Glimpse
   ```

3. Run the web application.

4. Navigate to `/glimpse.axd`.

5. Click the button labeled **Turn Glimpse On**.

6. Navigate to any URL which executes NHibernate queries, such as the /books page in the example application.

7. Click on the Glimpse logo in the bottom-right corner of the page.

8. Investigate the query log in the **NHibernate** tab, as shown in this screenshot:

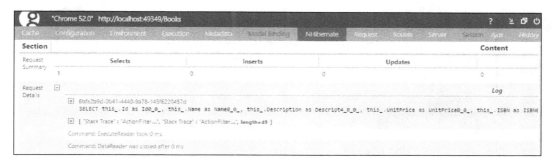

How does it work...

Once enabled, Glimpse uses an ASP.NET HttpModule, which injects markup and script into your page, in order to display its user interface. Normally, this is activated only when the application is running locally.

Additionally, the NHibernate add-on configures a custom logger, which intercepts NHibernate's log messages and parses them into data points for Glimpse.

All necessary configurations will be added by the NuGet package installer, but if you want to see detailed data about the executed commands, you can edit an appSetting in web.config.

```
<add key="NHibernate.Glimpse.Loggers" value="command,connection,flush,load,transaction"/>
```

More information about Glimpse can be found at http://getglimpse.com.

See also

▶ *Setting up a session-per-web request*

▶ *Configure log4net logging*

▶ *Using NHibernate Profiler*

Fast testing with the SQLite in-memory database

Running a full range of tests for a large NHibernate application can take some time. In this recipe, we will show you how to use SQLite's in-memory database to speed up this process.

 This is not meant to replace running integration tests against the real RDBMS before moving to production. Rather, it is a smoke test to provide feedback to developers quickly before running the slower integration tests.

Getting ready

Download and install NUnit from `http://nunit.org`.

 This recipe will work with other test frameworks such as MSTest, MbUnit, and xUnit. Just replace the NUnit-specific attributes with those for your preferred framework.

How to do it...

1. Create a new empty class library project.
2. Add references to our `Eg.Core` model from *Chapter 2, Models and Mapping*
3. Install the `NUnit` package using the NuGet Package Manager Console by executing the following command:

   ```
   Install-Package NUnit
   ```

4. Install SQLite using the NuGet Package Manager Console by executing the following command:

   ```
   Install-Package System.Data.SQLite.Core
   ```

   Further information about SQLite can be found at `https://system.data.sqlite.org`.

    `System.Data.SQLite` has 32-bit and 64-bit versions. Use the appropriate file for your operating system and target platform.

5. Install the `log4net` package using NuGet Package Manager Console by executing the following command:

   Install-Package log4net

6. Add an application configuration file with `NHibernate` and `log4net` configuration sections just as we did in *Chapter 1*, The Configuration and Schema.

7. Change the `log4net` configuration to use a `ConsoleAppender`.

8. Add a new class named `TestConnectionProvider` with the following code:

```
public class TestConnectionProvider :
    DriverConnectionProvider
{

  [ThreadStatic]
  private static IDbConnection _connection;

  public static void CloseDatabase()
  {
    if (_connection != null)
      _connection.Dispose();
    _connection = null;
  }

  public override IDbConnection GetConnection()
  {
    if (_connection == null)
    {
      _connection = Driver.CreateConnection();
      _connection.ConnectionString = ConnectionString;
      _connection.Open();
    }
    return _connection;
  }

  public override void CloseConnection(IDbConnection conn)
  {
  }
}
```

9. Add a new, static class named `NHibernateSessionFactoryProvider` with the following code:

```
private const string CONN_STR =
  "Data Source=:memory:;Version=3;New=True;";

private static readonly Configuration _configuration;
private static readonly ISessionFactory _sessionFactory;

static NHibernateSessionFactoryProvider()
{

  _configuration = new Configuration().Configure()
    .DataBaseIntegration(db =>
    {
      db.Dialect<SQLiteDialect>();
      db.Driver<SQLite20Driver>();
      db.ConnectionProvider<TestConnectionProvider>();
      db.ConnectionString = CONN_STR;
    })
    .SetProperty(Environment.CurrentSessionContextClass,
      "thread_static");

  var props = _configuration.Properties;
  if (props.ContainsKey(Environment.ConnectionStringName))
    props.Remove(Environment.ConnectionStringName);

  _sessionFactory = _configuration.BuildSessionFactory();
}
public static Configuration Configuration
{
  get { return _configuration; }
}

public static ISessionFactory SessionFactory
{
  get { return _sessionFactory; }
}
```

10. Add a new, abstract class named `BaseFixture` with the following code:

```
protected static ILog log = new Func<ILog>(() =>
{
  log4net.Config.XmlConfigurator.Configure();
  return LogManager.GetLogger(typeof(BaseFixture));
```

```
}).Invoke();

protected virtual void OnFixtureSetup() { }
protected virtual void OnFixtureTeardown() { }
protected virtual void OnSetup() { }
protected virtual void OnTeardown() { }

[TestFixtureSetUp]
public void FixtureSetup()
{
  OnFixtureSetup();
}

[TestFixtureTearDown]
public void FixtureTeardown(){
  OnFixtureTeardown();
}

[SetUp]
public void Setup(){
  OnSetup();
}

[TearDown]
public void Teardown(){
  OnTeardown();
}
```

11. Add a new, abstract class named `NHibernateFixture`, inheriting `BaseFixture`, with the following code:

```
protected ISessionFactory SessionFactory
{
  get { return NHibernateSessionFactoryProvider.SessionFactory; }
}

protected ISession Session
{
  get { return SessionFactory.GetCurrentSession(); }
}

protected override void OnSetup()
{
  SetupNHibernateSession();
```

```csharp
      base.OnSetup();
    }

    protected override void OnTeardown()
    {
      TearDownNHibernateSession();
      base.OnTeardown();
    }

    protected void SetupNHibernateSession()
    {
      TestConnectionProvider.CloseDatabase();
      SetupContextualSession();
      BuildSchema();
    }

    protected void TearDownNHibernateSession()
    {
      TearDownContextualSession();
      TestConnectionProvider.CloseDatabase();
    }

    private void SetupContextualSession()
    {
      var session = SessionFactory.OpenSession();
      CurrentSessionContext.Bind(session);
    }

    private void TearDownContextualSession()
    {
      var sessionFactory = NHibernateSessionFactoryProvider.
SessionFactory;
      var session = CurrentSessionContext.Unbind(sessionFactory);
      session.Close();
    }

    private void BuildSchema()
    {
      var cfg = NHibernateSessionFactoryProvider.Configuration;
      var schemaExport = new SchemaExport(cfg);
      schemaExport.Create(false, true);
    }
```

12. Add a new class named `PersistenceTests`, inheriting `NHibernateFixture`.

13. Decorate the `PersistenceTests` class with NUnit's `TestFixture` attribute.

14. Add the following test method to `PersistenceTests`:

```
[Test]
public void Movie_cascades_save_to_ActorRole()
{

  Guid movieId;
  Movie movie = new Movie()
  {
    Name = "Mars Attacks",
    Description = "Sci-Fi Parody",
    Director = "Tim Burton",
    UnitPrice = 12M,
    Actors = new List<ActorRole>
      {
        new ActorRole()
        {
          Actor = "Jack Nicholson",
          Role = "President James Dale"
        }
      }
  };

  using (var session = SessionFactory.OpenSession())
  using (var tx = session.BeginTransaction())
  {
    movieId = (Guid)session.Save(movie);
    tx.Commit();
  }

using (var session = SessionFactory.OpenSession())
  using (var tx = session.BeginTransaction())
  {
    movie = session.Get<Movie>(movieId);
    tx.Commit();
  }

  Assert.That(movie.Actors.Count == 1);
}
```

15. Build the project.

16. Start NUnit.

17. Select **File | Open Project**.

18. Select the project's compiled assembly from the `bin\Debug` folder.

19. Click on **Run**.

How it works...

`NHibernateSessionFactoryProvider` loads a NHibernate configuration from the `App.config` and then overwrites the dialect, driver, connection provider, and connection string properties to use SQLite instead. It also uses the thread static session context to provide sessions to code that might rely on NHibernate contextual sessions. Finally, we remove the `connection.connection_string_name` property, as we have provided a connection string value.

The magic of SQLite happens in our custom `TestConnectionProvider` class. Typically, a connection provider will return a new connection from each call to `GetConnection()` and close the connection when `CloseConnection()` is called. However, normally SQLite's in-memory databases only support a single connection. That is, each new connection creates and connects to its own in-memory database. When the connection is closed, the database is lost.

At the start of each test, we close any lingering connections. This ensures we get a fresh and empty database. When NHibernate first calls `GetConnection()`, we open a new connection. We then return the same connection for each subsequent call, ignoring any calls to `CloseConnection()`. Finally, when the test is completed, we dispose the database connection, thus effectively disposing the in-memory database with it.

This provides a perfectly clean database for each test, ensuring that remnants of a previous test cannot contaminate the current test, possibly altering the results.

In `BaseFixture`, we configure log4net and set up some virtual methods that can be overridden in inherited classes.

In `NHibernateFixture`, we override `OnSetup`, which runs just before each test. For code that may use contextual sessions, we open a session and bind it to the context. We also create our database tables with NHibernate's schema export. This, of course, opens a database connection, establishing our in-memory database.

We override `OnTeardown`, which runs after each test, to unbind the session from the session context, close the session, and finally close the database connection. When the connection is closed, the database is erased from the memory.

The test uses the session from `NHibernateFixture` to save a movie with an associated `ActorRole`. We use two separate sessions to save and then fetch the movie to ensure that when we fetch it, we load it from the database rather than just returning the instance from the first level cache. This gives us a true test of what we have persisted in the database. Once we have fetched the movie from the database, we make sure it still has an `ActorRole`. This test ensures that when we save a movie, the save cascades down to `ActorRoles` in the `Actors` list as well.

There's more...

Since SQLite version 3.3, in-memory databases can actually handle multiple connections, which means that the special connection handling used in this recipe isn't strictly needed. Instead, we could just use a connection string, with the `cache=shared` setting, for example:

```
FullUri=file:mydatabase.db?mode=memory&cache=shared
```

However, there is one caveat with this approach, which is the fact that SQLite doesn't allow simultaneous write access for multiple connections. A test method that opens multiple sessions may therefore fail in a way that the production code wouldn't. In many ways, the "singleton connection" approach better resembles a production scenario.

SQLite's speed and small memory footprint makes it great for providing quick test feedback. However, since it's in some ways a bit limited, it is best to run all tests against the production database engine (but not the production database!) before deploying the application. There are a few approaches to testing with a real RDBMS, each with its share of issues:

- ▶ Drop and recreate the database between each test. This is extremely slow for enterprise-level databases. A full set of integration tests may take hours to run, but this is the least intrusive option.

- ▶ Roll back every transaction to prevent changes to the database. This is very limiting. For instance, even our simple Persistence test would require some significant changes to work in this way. This may require you to change business logic to suit a testing limitation.

- ▶ Clean up on a test-by-test basis. For instance, after every test, use SQL to delete all rows in all tables. This is error-prone and potentially very slow.

See also

- ▶ *Preloading data with SQLite*
- ▶ *Using the Fluent NHibernate Persistence tester*
- ▶ *Using the Ghostbusters test*

Preloading data with SQLite

It is often desirable to preload the database with test data before running tests. In this recipe, we will show you how to load the in-memory database with data from a SQLite file database.

Getting ready

Complete the previous recipe, *Fast-testing with the SQLite in-memory database*.

Create a SQLite file database with the desired schema (tables and columns), containing test data. This can be accomplished in a number of ways. Perhaps the easiest is to export an in-memory database using `SQLiteLoader.ExportData` from this recipe.

How to do it...

1. Add a new class named `SQLiteLoader` using the following code:

```
private static ILog log =
    LogManager.GetLogger(typeof(SQLiteLoader));

private const string ATTACHED_DB = "asdfgaqwernb";

public void ImportData(
    SQLiteConnection conn,
    string sourceDataFile)
{

    var tables = GetTableNames(conn);
    AttachDatabase(conn, sourceDataFile);

    foreach (var table in tables)
    {
        var sourceTable = string.Format("{0}.{1}",
            ATTACHED_DB, table);

        CopyTableData(conn, sourceTable, table);
    }

    DetachDatabase(conn);
}

public void ExportData(
    SQLiteConnection conn,
```

```
    string destinationDataFile)
{
  var tables = GetTableNames(conn);
  AttachDatabase(conn, destinationDataFile);

  foreach (var table in tables)
  {
    var destTable = string.Format(
      "{0}.{1}",
      ATTACHED_DB, table);

    CopyTableData(conn, table, destTable);
  }
  DetachDatabase(conn);
}

private IEnumerable<string> GetTableNames(
  SQLiteConnection conn)
{
  string tables = SQLiteMetaDataCollectionNames.Tables;
  DataTable dt = conn.GetSchema(tables);
  return from DataRow R in dt.Rows
         select (string)R["TABLE_NAME"];
}

private void AttachDatabase(
  SQLiteConnection conn,
  string sourceDataFile)
{
  SQLiteCommand cmd = new SQLiteCommand(conn);
  cmd.CommandText = String.Format("ATTACH '{0}' AS {1}",
    sourceDataFile, ATTACHED_DB);
  log.Debug(cmd.CommandText);
  cmd.ExecuteNonQuery();
}

private void CopyTableData(
  SQLiteConnection conn,
  string source,
  string destination)
{
  SQLiteCommand cmd = new SQLiteCommand(conn);
  cmd.CommandText = string.Format(
```

```
          "INSERT INTO {0} SELECT * FROM {1}",
          destination, source);

          log.Debug(cmd.CommandText);
          cmd.ExecuteNonQuery();
}


    private void DetachDatabase(SQLiteConnection conn)
    {
        SQLiteCommand cmd = new SQLiteCommand(conn);
        cmd.CommandText = string.Format(«DETACH {0}», ATTACHED_DB);
        log.Debug(cmd.CommandText);
        cmd.ExecuteNonQuery();
    }
```

2. Add a new abstract class named `DataDependentFixture`, inherited from `NHibernateFixture`, using the following code:

```
protected abstract string GetSQLiteFilename();

protected override void OnSetup()
{
    base.OnSetup();
    var conn = (SQLiteConnection) Session.Connection;
    new SQLiteLoader().ImportData(conn, GetSQLiteFilename());
}
```

3. Add a new class named `QueryTests`, inherited from `DataDependentFixture`.

4. In `QueryTests`, override `GetSQLiteFilename()` to return the path to your SQLite file.

5. Add the following test to `QueryTests`:

```
[Test]
public void Director_query_should_return_one_movie()
{
    var query = Session.QueryOver<Movie>()
        .Where(m => m.Director == "Tim Burton");

    using (var tx = Session.BeginTransaction())
    {
        var movies = query.List<Movie>();
        Assert.That(movies.Count == 1);
        tx.Commit();
    }
}
```

6. Decorate `QueryTests` with NUnit's `TestFixture` attribute.

7. Build the project.

8. Run the NUnit tests.

How it works...

In the `QueryTests` fixture, `GetSQLiteFilename()` returns the path of the SQLite file containing our test data. `DataDependentFixture` passes this file path and our connection to the SQLite in-memory database over to `SQLiteLoader.ImportData()`.

We call `SQLiteConnection.GetSchema()` to create a list of table names in the database.

Next, we attach the file database to the in-memory database using the `ATTACH 'filePath' AS schemaName` command, where `filePath` is the path to the file database and `schemaName` is a string constant. This allows us to reference the tables in the file database from the memory database. For example, if our file database has a table named `tblTestData` and we use the `asdf` string for `schemaName`, we can execute `SELECT * FROM asdf.tblTestData`.

We loop through each table executing the `INSERT INTO tableName SELECT * FROM schemaName.tableName` statement. This command quickly copies all the data from a table in the file database to an identical table in the memory database, because SQLite doesn't enforce foreign key constraints, we do not need to be concerned with the order we use to copy this data.

Finally, we detach the file database using the `DETACH schemaName` command.

There's more...

We can use `SQLiteLoader.ExportData` to move data from the SQLite in-memory database to a file database. In addition, each test fixture can use test data from a different file database.

See also

▸ *Fast testing with the SQLite in-memory database*

▸ *Using the Ghostbusters test*

Using Fluent NHibernate persistence testing

Mappings are a critical part of any NHibernate application. In this recipe, we'll show you how to use Fluent NHibernate's persistence testing, in order to make sure that your mappings work as expected. You don't have to use Fluent NHibernate mappings in order to take advantage of this recipe.

Getting ready

Complete the *Fast testing with the SQLite in-Memory database* recipe mentioned earlier in this chapter.

How to do it...

1. Install `FluentNHibernate` using the NuGet Package Manager Console by executing the following command:

    Install-Package FluentNHibernate

2. In `PersistenceTests.cs`, add the following `using` statement:

    ```
    using FluentNHibernate.Testing;
    ```

3. Add the following three tests to the `PersistenceTests` fixture:

    ```
    [Test]
    public void Product_persistence_test()
    {
      new PersistenceSpecification<Product>(Session)
        .CheckProperty(p => p.Name, "Product Name")
        .CheckProperty(p => p.Description, "Product Description")
        .CheckProperty(p => p.UnitPrice, 300.85M)
        .VerifyTheMappings();
    }
    [Test]
    public void ActorRole_persistence_test()

    {
      new PersistenceSpecification<ActorRole>(Session)
       .CheckProperty(p => p.Actor, "Actor Name")
       .CheckProperty(p => p.Role, "Role")
       .VerifyTheMappings();
    }

    [Test]
    ```

```
public void Movie_persistence_test()
{
  new PersistenceSpecification<Movie>(Session)
  .CheckProperty(p => p.Name, "Movie Name")
  .CheckProperty(p => p.Description, "Movie Description")
  .CheckProperty(p => p.UnitPrice, 25M)
  .CheckProperty(p => p.Director, "Director Name")
  .CheckList(p => p.Actors, new List<ActorRole>()
  {
    new ActorRole() { Actor = "Actor Name", Role = "Role" }
  })
  .VerifyTheMappings();
}
```

4. Run these tests with NUnit.

How it works...

The Persistence tester in Fluent NHibernate can be used with any mapping method. It performs the following four steps:

1. Create a new instance of the entity (Product, ActorRole, Movie) using the values provided.
2. Save the entity to the database.
3. Get the entity from the database.
4. Verify that the fetched instance matches the original.

At a minimum, each entity type should have a simple persistence test, such as the one shown previously. You can find more information about Fluent NHibernate persistence testing at https://github.com/jagregory/fluent-nhibernate/wiki/Persistence-specification-testing.

See also

▸ *Fast testing with the SQLite in-memory database*
▸ *Using the Ghostbusters test*

Using the Ghostbusters test

As a part of automatic dirty checking, NHibernate compares the original state of an entity to its current state. An otherwise unchanged entity may be updated unnecessarily because a type conversion caused this comparison to fail. In this recipe, we will show you how to detect these "ghost update" issues with the Ghostbusters test.

Getting ready

Complete the *Fast testing with the SQLite in-memory database* recipe in this chapter.

How to do it...

1. Add a new class named `Ghostbusters` using the following code:

```
private static readonly ILog log =
  LogManager.GetLogger(typeof(Ghostbusters));

private readonly Configuration _configuration;
private readonly ISessionFactory _sessionFactory;
private readonly Action<string> _failCallback;
private readonly Action<string> _inconclusiveCallback;

public Ghostbusters(Configuration configuration,
ISessionFactory sessionFactory,
Action<string> failCallback,
Action<string> inconclusiveCallback)
{
  _configuration = configuration;
  _sessionFactory = sessionFactory;
  _failCallback = failCallback;
  _inconclusiveCallback = inconclusiveCallback;
}

public void Test()
{
  var mappedEntityNames = _configuration.ClassMappings
  .Select(mapping => mapping.EntityName);

  foreach (string entityName in mappedEntityNames)
```

```csharp
    Test(entityName);
}

public void Test<TEntity>()
{
  Test(typeof(TEntity).FullName);
}

public void Test(string entityName)
{
  object id = FindEntityId(entityName);
  if (id == null)
  {
    var msg = string.Format(
     "No instances of {0} in database.",
      entityName);
    _inconclusiveCallback.Invoke(msg);
    return;
  }
  log.DebugFormat("Testing entity {0} with id {1}",
    entityName, id);
  Test(entityName, id);
}

public void Test(string entityName, object id)
{
  var ghosts = new List<String>();
  var interceptor = new GhostInterceptor(ghosts);

  using (var session = _sessionFactory.OpenSession(interceptor))
  using (var tx = session.BeginTransaction())
  {
    session.Get(entityName, id);
    session.Flush();
    tx.Rollback();
  }

  if (ghosts.Any())
    _failCallback.Invoke(string.Join("\n", ghosts.ToArray()));
}

private object FindEntityId(string entityName)
{
  object id;
```

```
using (var session = _sessionFactory.OpenSession())
{
  var idQueryString = string.Format(
    "SELECT e.id FROM {0} e",
    entityName);

  var idQuery = session.CreateQuery(idQueryString)
  .SetMaxResults(1);

  using (var tx = session.BeginTransaction())
  {
    id = idQuery.UniqueResult();
    tx.Commit();
  }
}
return id;
}
```

2. Add another class named `GhostInterceptor` using the following code:

```
private static readonly ILog log =
  LogManager.GetLogger(typeof(GhostInterceptor));

private readonly IList<string> _ghosts;
private ISession _session;

public GhostInterceptor(IList<string> ghosts)
{
  _ghosts = ghosts;
}

public override void SetSession(ISession session)
{
  _session = session;
}

public override bool OnFlushDirty(
object entity, object id, object[] currentState,
object[] previousState, string[] propertyNames, IType[] types)
{
  var msg = string.Format("Flush Dirty {0}",
    entity.GetType().FullName);
  log.Error(msg);
  _ghosts.Add(msg);
  ListDirtyProperties(entity);
```

```
    return false;
}

public override bool OnSave(
object entity, object id, object[] state,
string[] propertyNames, IType[] types)
{
  var msg = string.Format("Save {0}",
    entity.GetType().FullName);
  log.Error(msg);
  _ghosts.Add(msg);
  return false;
}

public override void OnDelete(
object entity, object id, object[] state,
string[] propertyNames, IType[] types)
{
  var msg = string.Format("Delete {0}",
    entity.GetType().FullName);
  log.Error(msg);
  _ghosts.Add(msg);
}

private void ListDirtyProperties(object entity)
{
  string className =
    NHibernateProxyHelper.GuessClass(entity).FullName;

  var sessionImpl = _session.GetSessionImplementation();

  var persister =
    sessionImpl.Factory.GetEntityPersister(className);

  var oldEntry =
    sessionImpl.PersistenceContext.GetEntry(entity);

  if ((oldEntry == null) && (entity is INHibernateProxy))
  {
    var proxy = entity as INHibernateProxy;
    object obj =
      sessionImpl.PersistenceContext.Unproxy(proxy);

    oldEntry = sessionImpl.PersistenceContext.GetEntry(obj);
```

```
    }

    object[] oldState = oldEntry.LoadedState;

    object[] currentState = persister.GetPropertyValues(entity,
      sessionImpl.EntityMode);

    int[] dirtyProperties = persister.FindDirty(currentState,
      oldState, entity, sessionImpl);

    foreach (int index in dirtyProperties)
    {
      var msg = string.Format(
        "Dirty property {0}.{1} was {2}, is {3}.",
        className,
        persister.PropertyNames[index],
        oldState[index] ?? "null",
        currentState[index] ?? "null");
      log.Error(msg);
      _ghosts.Add(msg);
    }

}
```

3. Add the following test to the `PersistenceTests` fixture:

```
[Test]
public void GhostbustersTest()
{

  using (var tx = Session.BeginTransaction())
  {

    Session.Save(new Movie()
    {
      Name = "Ghostbusters",
      Description = "Science Fiction Comedy",
      Director = "Ivan Reitman",
      UnitPrice = 7.97M,
      Actors = new List<ActorRole>()
      {
        new ActorRole()
        {
          Actor = "Bill Murray",
```

```
                Role = "Dr. Peter Venkman"
            }
        }
    });

    Session.Save(new Book()
    {
        Name = "Who You Gonna Call?",
        Description = "The Real Ghostbusters comic series",
        UnitPrice = 30.00M,
        Author = "Dan Abnett",
        ISBN = "1-84576-141-3"
    });

    tx.Commit();
}

new Ghostbusters(
    NHibernateSessionFactoryProvider.Configuration,
    NHibernateSessionFactoryProvider.SessionFactory,
    new Action<string>(msg => Assert.Fail(msg)),
    new Action<string>(msg => Assert.Inconclusive(msg))
).Test();


}
```

4. Run the tests with NUnit.

How it works...

The Ghostbusters test finds issues where a session's automatic dirty checking determines that an entity is dirty (has unsaved changes) when, in fact, no changes were made. This can happen for a few reasons, but it commonly occurs when a database field that allows nulls is mapped to a non-nullable property, such as `integer` or `DateTime`, or when an `enum` property is mapped with `type="int"`. For example, when a null value is loaded into an integer property, the value is automatically converted to the integer's default value, zero. When the session is flushed, automatic dirty checking will see that the value is no longer null and update the database value to zero. This is referred to as a "ghost" update.

At the heart of our Ghostbusters test, we have the `GhostInterceptor`. An interceptor allows an application to intercept session events before any database action occurs. This interceptor can be set globally on the NHibernate configuration or passed as a parameter to `sessionFactory.OpenSession`, as we've done in this recipe.

When we flush a session containing a dirty entity, the interceptor's `OnFlushDirty` method is called. `GhostInterceptor` compares the current values of the dirty entity's properties to their original values and reports these back to our `Ghostbusters` class. Similarly, we also intercept `Save` and `Delete` events, though these are much less common.

Our `Ghostbusters` class coordinates the testing. For example, we can call `Test(entityName, id)` to test using a particular instance of an entity. If we strip this test down to its core, we end up with the following code:

```
session.Get(entityName, id);
session.Flush();
tx.Rollback();
```

Note that we simply get an entity from the database and immediately flush the session. This runs automatic dirty checking on a single unchanged entity. Any database changes resulting from this `Flush()` are ghosts.

If we call `Test(entityName)` or `Test<Entity>()`, `Ghostbusters` will first query the database for an ID for the entity, then run the test. For a test on our `Movie` entity, this ID query would be:

SELECT e.id FROM Eg.Core.Movie e

This lowercase `id` property has special meaning in HQL. In HQL, lowercase `id` always refers to the entity's POID. In our model, it happens to be named `Id`, but we could have just as easily named it "*Bob*."

Finally, if we simply call the `Test()` method, `Ghostbusters` will test one instance of each mapped entity. We used this method in our tests.

This Ghostbusters test has somewhat limited value in the automated tests as we've done here. It really shines when testing migrated or updated production data.

See also

▸ *Using the Hibernate Query Language*

7

Data Access Layer

In this chapter, we will cover the following topics:

- ▶ Transaction auto-wrapping for the data access layer
- ▶ Setting up an NHibernate repository
- ▶ Using named queries in the data access layer
- ▶ Using ICriteria in the data access layer
- ▶ Using paged queries in the data access layer
- ▶ Using LINQ specifications in the data access layer

Introduction

There are two types of data access layers that are common in today's applications: **Repositories** and **Data Access Objects** (**DAO**). In reality, the distinction between these two has become quite blurred; however, in theory, it's as follows:

- ▶ A repository should act like an in-memory collection. Entities are added to and removed from the collection and its contents can be enumerated. Queries are typically handled by sending query specifications to the repository.
- ▶ A DAO is simply an abstraction of an application's data access. Its purpose is to hide the implementation details of the database access from the consuming code.

The first recipe shows the beginning of a typical data access object. The remaining recipes show how to set up a repository-based data access layer with NHibernate's various APIs.

Transaction auto-wrapping for the data access layer

In this recipe, we'll show you how to set up the data access layer to wrap all data access in NHibernate transactions automatically.

Getting ready

Complete the Eg.Core model and mappings from *Chapter 2, Models and Mappings*.

How to do it...

1. Create a new class library named Eg.Core.Data.
2. Install NHibernate to Eg.Core.Data using the NuGet Package Manager Console.
3. Add the following two DataAccessObject classes:

```
public class DataAccessObject<T, TId>
  where T : Entity<TId>
{

  private readonly ISessionFactory _sessionFactory;

  private ISession session
  {
    get
    {
      return _sessionFactory.GetCurrentSession();
    }
  }

  public DataAccessObject(ISessionFactory sessionFactory)
  {
    _sessionFactory = sessionFactory;
  }

  public T Get(TId id)
  {
    return WithinTransaction(() => session.Get<T>(id));
  }

  public T Load(TId id)
  {
```

```
      return WithinTransaction(() => session.Load<T>(id));
    }

    public void Save(T entity)
    {
      WithinTransaction(() => session.SaveOrUpdate(entity));
    }

    public void Delete(T entity)
    {
      WithinTransaction(() => session.Delete(entity));
    }

    private TResult WithinTransaction<TResult>(Func<TResult> func)
    {
      if (!session.Transaction.IsActive)
      {
        // Wrap in transaction
        TResult result;
        using (var tx = session.BeginTransaction())
        {
          result = func.Invoke();
          tx.Commit();
        }
        return result;
      }

      // Don't wrap;
      return func.Invoke();
    }

    private void WithinTransaction(Action action)
    {
      WithinTransaction<bool>(() =>
      {
        action.Invoke();
        return false;
      });
    }

  }

  public class DataAccessObject<T>
```

```
       : DataAccessObject<T, Guid>
       where T : Entity
{
}
```

How it works...

NHibernate requires every data access to occur inside a NHibernate transaction. As we saw with the *Transaction action filter* recipe in *Chapter 3, Sessions and Transactions*, this can, in some environments, be accomplished with non-intrusive code elements, such as .NET attributes. This technique is sometimes called **Aspect Oriented Programming (AOP)**.

 The ambient transaction created by a transaction scope is not a substitute for an NHibernate transaction.

This recipe, however, shows a more explicit approach. To ensure that at least all our data access layers are wrapped in transactions, we create a private `WithinTransaction` method that accepts a delegate and consists of some data access methods, such as `session.Save` or `session.Get`. The `WithinTransaction` method first checks whether the session has an active transaction. If it does, the delegate is invoked immediately. If it does not, a new NHibernate transaction is created, the delegate is invoked and finally the transaction is carried out. If the data access method throws an exception, the transaction will be rolled back automatically, as the exception bubbles up to the `using` block.

There's more...

This transactional auto-wrapping can also be set using `SessionWrapper` from the unofficial NHibernate AddIns project at `https://bitbucket.org/fabiomaulo/unhaddins`. This class wraps a standard NHibernate session. By default, it will throw an exception when the session is used without an NHibernate transaction. However, it can be configured to check for and create a transaction automatically, much in the same way as I have shown you here.

See also

▶ *Setting up an NHibernate repository*

Setting up an NHibernate repository

Many developers prefer the repository pattern to data access objects. In this recipe, we will show you how to set up the repository pattern with NHibernate.

Getting ready

Set up the `Eg.Core` project with the model and mappings from *Chapter 2, Models and Mappings*.

How to do it...

1. Create a new and empty class library project named `Eg.Core.Data`.

2. Add a reference to `Eg.Core` project in *Chapter 2, Models and Mappings*.

3. Add the following `IRepository` interface:

```
public interface IRepository<T>: IEnumerable<T>
  where T : Entity
{
  void Add(T item);
  bool Contains(T item);
  int Count { get; }
  bool Remove(T item);
}
```

4. Create a new and empty class library project named `Eg.Core.Data.Impl`.

5. Add references to the `Eg.Core` and `Eg.Core.Data` projects.

6. Add a new abstract class named `NHibernateBase` using the following code:

```
protected readonly ISessionFactory _sessionFactory;

protected virtual ISession session
{
  get
  {
    return _sessionFactory.GetCurrentSession();
  }
}

public NHibernateBase(ISessionFactory sessionFactory)
{
  _sessionFactory = sessionFactory;
}

protected virtual TResult WithinTransaction<TResult>(
Func<TResult> func)
{
  if (!session.Transaction.IsActive)
```

```
  {
    // Wrap in transaction
    TResult result;
    using (var tx = session.BeginTransaction())
    {
      result = func.Invoke();
      tx.Commit();
    }
    return result;
  }

  // Don't wrap;
  return func.Invoke();
}

protected virtual void WithinTransaction(Action action)
{
  WithinTransaction<bool>(() =>
  {
    action.Invoke();
    return false;
  });
}
```

7. Add a new class named NHibernateRepository using the following code:

```
public class NHibernateRepository<T> :
  NHibernateBase,
  IRepository<T> where T : Entity
{

  public NHibernateRepository(
    ISessionFactory sessionFactory)
    : base(sessionFactory)
  {
  }

  public void Add(T item)
  {
    WithinTransaction(() => session.Save(item));
  }

  public bool Contains(T item)
  {
    if (item.Id == default(Guid))
```

```
        return false;
      return WithinTransaction(() =>
        session.Get<T>(item.Id)) != null;
    }

    public int Count
    {
      get
      {
        return WithinTransaction(() =>
          session.Query<T>().Count());
      }
    }

    public bool Remove(T item)
    {
      WithinTransaction(() => session.Delete(item));
      return true;
    }

    public IEnumerator<T> GetEnumerator()
    {
      return WithinTransaction(() => session.Query<T>()
            .Take(1000).GetEnumerator());
    }

    IEnumerator IEnumerable.GetEnumerator()
    {
      return WithinTransaction(() => GetEnumerator());
    }

}
```

How it works...

The repository pattern, as explained in `https://martinfowler.com/eaaCatalog/repository.html`, has two key features:

- It behaves as an in-memory collection
- Query specifications are submitted to the repository for satisfaction

In this recipe, we are concerned with only the first feature: behaving as an in-memory collection. The remaining recipes in this chapter will build on this base and show various methods for satisfying the second point.

As our repository should act like an in-memory collection, it makes sense that our `IRepository<T>` interface should resemble `ICollection<T>`.

Our NHibernateBase class provides both contextual session management and automatic transaction wrapping, as explained in the previous recipe.

`NHibernateRepository` simply implements the members of `IRepository<T>`.

There's more...

The repository pattern reduces data access to its absolute simplest form, but this simplification comes with a price. We lose much of the power of NHibernate behind an abstraction layer. Our application must either do without even basic session methods such as `Merge`, `Refresh`, and `Load`, or allow them to leak through the abstraction.

See also

- ▸ *Transaction auto-wrapping for the data access layer*
- ▸ *Using named queries in the data access layer*
- ▸ *Using ICriteria in the data access layer*
- ▸ *Using paged queries in the data access layer*
- ▸ *Using LINQ specifications in the data access layer*

Using named queries in the data access layer

Named queries encapsulated in query objects are a powerful combination. In this recipe, we will show you how to use named queries with your data access layer.

Getting ready

To complete this recipe, you will need the common service locator from Microsoft patterns and practices. The documentation and source code can be found at `http://commonservicelocator.codeplex.com`.

Complete the previous recipe: *Setting up an NHibernate repository*.

Following *Fast testing with SQLite in-memory database recipe* in *Chapter 6, Testing*, create a new NHibernate test project named `Eg.Core.Data.Impl.Test`.

Include the `Eg.Core.Data.Impl` assembly as an additional mapping assembly in your test project's `App.Config` with the following xml:

```xml
<mapping assembly="Eg.Core.Data.Impl"/>
```

How to do it...

1. In the `Eg.Core.Data` project, add a folder for the `Queries` namespace.

2. Add the following `IQuery` interfaces:

```
public interface IQuery
{
}

public interface IQuery<TResult> : IQuery
{
   TResult Execute();
}
```

3. Add the following `IQueryFactory` interface:

```
public interface IQueryFactory
{
   TQuery CreateQuery<TQuery>() where TQuery :IQuery;
}
```

4. Change the `IRepository` interface to implement the `IQueryFactory` interface, as shown in the following code:

```
public interface IRepository<T>
   : IEnumerable<T>, IQueryFactory
   where T : Entity
{
   void Add(T item);
   bool Contains(T item);
   int Count { get; }
   bool Remove(T item);
}
```

5. In the `Eg.Core.Data.Impl` project, change the `NHibernateRepository` constructor and add the `_queryFactory` field, as shown in the following code:

```
private readonly IQueryFactory _queryFactory;

public NHibernateRepository(
   ISessionFactory sessionFactory,
   IQueryFactory queryFactory)
   : base(sessionFactory)
```

```
{
    _queryFactory = queryFactory;
}
```

6. Add the following method to `NHibernateRepository`:

```
public TQuery CreateQuery<TQuery>() where TQuery : IQuery
{
    return _queryFactory.CreateQuery<TQuery>();
}
```

7. In the `Eg.Core.Data.Impl` project, add a folder for the `Queries` namespace.

8. Install the common service locator using the NuGet Package Manager Console, using the following command:

    Install-Package CommonServiceLocator

9. To the `Queries` namespace, add this `QueryFactory` class:

```
public class QueryFactory : IQueryFactory
{
    private readonly IServiceLocator _serviceLocator;

    public QueryFactory(IServiceLocator serviceLocator)
    {
        _serviceLocator = serviceLocator;
    }

    public TQuery CreateQuery<TQuery>() where TQuery : IQuery
    {
        return _serviceLocator.GetInstance<TQuery>();
    }
}
```

10. Add the following `NHibernateQueryBase` class:

```
public abstract class NHibernateQueryBase<TResult>
    : NHibernateBase, IQuery<TResult>
{
    protected NHibernateQueryBase(
        ISessionFactory sessionFactory)
        : base(sessionFactory) { }

    public abstract TResult Execute();
}
```

11. Add an empty `INamedQuery` interface, as shown in the following code:

```
public interface INamedQuery
{
  string QueryName { get; }
}
```

12. Add a `NamedQueryBase` class, as shown in the following code:

```
public abstract class NamedQueryBase<TResult>
  : NHibernateQueryBase<TResult>, INamedQuery
{
  protected NamedQueryBase(ISessionFactory sessionFactory)
    : base(sessionFactory) { }

  public override TResult Execute()
  {
    var nhQuery = GetNamedQuery();
    return Transact(() => Execute(nhQuery));
  }

  protected abstract TResult Execute(IQuery query);

  protected virtual IQuery GetNamedQuery()
  {
    var nhQuery = session.GetNamedQuery(QueryName);
    SetParameters(nhQuery);
    return nhQuery;
  }

  protected abstract void SetParameters(IQuery nhQuery);

  public virtual string QueryName
  {
    get { return GetType().Name; }
  }
}
```

13. In `Eg.Core.Data.Impl.Test`, add a test fixture named `QueryTests` inherited from `NHibernateFixture`.

14. Add the following test and three helper methods:

```
[Test]
public void NamedQueryCheck()
{
```

```
    var errors = new StringBuilder();

    var queryObjectTypes = GetNamedQueryObjectTypes();
    var mappedQueries = GetNamedQueryNames();

    foreach (var queryType in queryObjectTypes)
    {
      var query = GetQuery(queryType);

      if (!mappedQueries.Contains(query.QueryName))
      {
        errors.AppendFormat(
          "Query object {0} references non-existent " +
          "named query {1}.",
          queryType, query.QueryName);
        errors.AppendLine();
      }

    }

    if (errors.Length != 0)
      Assert.Fail(errors.ToString());

}

private IEnumerable<Type> GetNamedQueryObjectTypes()
{
  var namedQueryType = typeof(INamedQuery);
  var queryImplAssembly = typeof(BookWithISBN).Assembly;

  var types = from t in queryImplAssembly.GetTypes()
              where namedQueryType.IsAssignableFrom(t)
              && t.IsClass
              && !t.IsAbstract
              select t;
  return types;
}

private IEnumerable<string> GetNamedQueryNames()
{
  var nhCfg = NHConfigurator.Configuration;

  var mappedQueries = nhCfg.NamedQueries.Keys
```

```
                .Union(nhCfg.NamedSQLQueries.Keys);

        return mappedQueries;
    }

    private INamedQuery GetQuery(Type queryType)
    {
        return (INamedQuery) Activator.CreateInstance(
            queryType,
            new object[] { SessionFactory });
    }
```

15. For our example query, in the `Queries` namespace of `Eg.Core.Data` add the following interface:

```
public interface IBookWithISBN : IQuery<Book>
{
    string ISBN { get; set; }
}
```

16. Add the implementation to the `Queries` namespace of `Eg.Core.Data.Impl` using the following code:

```
public class BookWithISBN :
    NamedQueryBase<Book>, IBookWithISBN
{

    public BookWithISBN(ISessionFactory sessionFactory)
        : base(sessionFactory) { }

    public string ISBN { get; set; }

    protected override void SetParameters(
        NHibernate.IQuery nhQuery)
    {
        nhQuery.SetParameter("isbn", ISBN);
    }

    protected override Book Execute(NHibernate.IQuery query)
    {
        return query.UniqueResult<Book>();
    }
}
```

17. Finally, add the embedded resource mapping, `BookWithISBN.hbm.xml`, to `Eg.Core.Data.Impl` with the following xml code:

```xml
<?xml version="1.0" encoding="utf-8" ?>
<hibernate-mapping xmlns="urn:nhibernate-mapping-2.2">
  <query name="BookWithISBN">
    <![CDATA[
    from Book b where b.ISBN = :isbn
    ]]>
  </query>
</hibernate-mapping>
```

How it works...

As we learned in the previous recipe, according to the repository pattern, the repository is responsible for fulfilling queries based on the specifications submitted to it. These specifications are limiting. They only concern themselves with whether a particular item matches the given criteria or not. They don't care about other necessary technical details, such as the eager loading of children, batching, query caching, and so on. We need something more powerful than simple `where` clauses. We in other words lose too much to the abstraction.

The query object pattern defines a query object as a group of criteria that can self-organize into a SQL query. The query object is not responsible for the execution of this SQL. This is handled elsewhere by some generic query runner, perhaps inside the repository. While a query object can better express the different technical requirements, such as eager loading, batching, and query caching, a generic query runner can't easily implement those concerns for every possible query, especially across the half-dozen query APIs provided by NHibernate.

These details about the execution are specific to each query and should be handled by the query object. This enhanced query object pattern, as Fabio Maulo has named it, not only self-organizes into SQL but also executes the query, returning the results. In this way, technical concerns in respect of a query's execution are defined and cared for with the query itself, rather than spreading into some highly complex, generic query runner.

According to the abstraction we've built, the repository represents the collection of entities that we are querying. Since the two are already logically linked, if we allow the repository to build the query objects, we can add some context to our code. For example, suppose we have an application service that runs product queries. When we inject dependencies, we could specify `IQueryFactory` directly. This doesn't give us much information beyond "This service runs queries." If, however, we inject `IRepository<Product>`, we will have a much better idea about what data the service is using.

The `IQuery` interface is simply a marker interface for our query objects. Besides advertising the purpose of our query objects, it allows us to easily identify them with reflection.

The IQuery<TResult> interface is implemented by each query object. It specifies only the return type and a single method to execute the query.

The IQueryFactory interface defines a service to create query objects. For the purpose of explanation, the implementation of this service, QueryFactory, is a simple service locator. IQueryFactory is used internally by the repository to instantiate query objects.

The NamedQueryBase class handles most of the plumbing for query objects, based on named HQL and SQL queries. As a convention, the name of the query is the name of the query object type. That is, the underlying named query for BookWithISBN is also named BookWithISBN. Each individual query object must simply implement SetParameters and Execute(NHibernate.IQuery query), which usually consists of a simple call to query.List<SomeEntity>() or query.UniqueResult<SomeEntity>().

The INamedQuery interface, both identifies query objects based on named queries and provides access to the query name. The NamedQueryCheck test uses this to verify that each INamedQuery query object has a matching named query.

Each query has an interface. This interface is used to request the query object from the repository. It also defines any parameter used in the query. In this example, IBookWithISBN has a single string parameter, ISBN. The implementation of this query object sets the :isbn parameter on the internal NHibernate query, executes it, and returns the matching Book object.

Finally, we also create a mapping containing the named query BookWithISBN, which is loaded into the configuration with the rest of our mappings.

The code used in the query object setup would look like the following:

```
var query = bookRepository.CreateQuery<IBookWithISBN>();
query.ISBN = "12345";
var book = query.Execute();
```

See also

► *Transaction auto-wrapping for the data access layer*

► *Setting up an NHibernate repository*

► *Using ICriteria in the data access layer*

► *Using paged queries in the data access layer*

► *Using LINQ specifications in the data access layer*

Using ICriteria in the data access layer

For queries where the criteria are not known in advance, such as a website's advanced product search, ICriteria queries are more appropriate than named HQL queries. In this recipe, we will show you how to use the same DAL infrastructure with ICriteria and QueryOver queries.

Getting ready

Complete the previous recipe, *Using named queries in the data access layer*.

How to do it...

1. In Eg.Core.Data.Impl.Queries, add a new, empty, public interface named ICriteriaQuery.

2. Add a class named CriteriaQueryBase with the following code:

```
public abstract class CriteriaQueryBase<TResult> :
  NHibernateQueryBase<TResult>, ICriteriaQuery
{

  public CriteriaQueryBase(ISessionFactory sessionFactory)
    : base(sessionFactory) { }

  public override TResult Execute()
  {
    var criteria = GetCriteria();
    return WithinTransaction(() => Execute(criteria));
  }

  protected abstract ICriteria GetCriteria();

  protected abstract TResult Execute(ICriteria criteria);

}
```

3. In Eg.Core.Data.Queries, add the following enum:

```
public enum AdvancedProductSearchOrderDirection
{
  Ascending,
  Descending
}
```

4. Add a new interface named `IAdvancedProductSearch` with the following code:

```
public interface IAdvancedProductSearch
    : IQuery<IEnumerable<Product>>
{

    string Name { get; set; }
    string Description { get; set; }
    decimal? MinimumPrice { get; set; }
    decimal? MaximumPrice { get; set; }
    string OrderBy { get; set; }
    AdvancedProductSearchOrderDirection OrderDirection
        { get; set; }
}
```

5. In `Eg.Core.Data.Impl.Queries`, add the following class:

```
public class AdvancedProductSearch
    : CriteriaQueryBase<IEnumerable<Product>>,
    IAdvancedProductSearch
{

    public AdvancedProductSearch(
        ISessionFactory sessionFactory)
        : base(sessionFactory) { }

    public string Name { get; set; }
    public string Description { get; set; }
    public decimal? MinimumPrice { get; set; }
    public decimal? MaximumPrice { get; set; }
    public string OrderBy { get; set; }
    public AdvancedProductSearchOrderDirection OrderDirection
        { get; set; }

    protected override ICriteria GetCriteria()
    {
        return GetProductQuery().UnderlyingCriteria;
    }

    protected override IEnumerable<Product> Execute(
        ICriteria criteria)
    {
        return criteria.List<Product>();
    }
```

```csharp
private IQueryOver GetProductQuery()
{
  var query = session.QueryOver<Product>();
  AddProductCriterion(query);
  return query;
}

private void AddProductCriterion(
  IQueryOver<Product, Product> query)
{

  if (!string.IsNullOrEmpty(Name))
    query = query.WhereRestrictionOn(p => p.Name)
      .IsInsensitiveLike(Name, MatchMode.Anywhere);

  if (!string.IsNullOrEmpty(Description))
    query.WhereRestrictionOn(p => p.Description)
      .IsInsensitiveLike(Description, MatchMode.Anywhere);

  if (MinimumPrice.HasValue)
    query.Where(p => p.UnitPrice >= MinimumPrice);

  if (MaximumPrice.HasValue)
    query.Where(p => p.UnitPrice <= MaximumPrice);

  if (!string.IsNullOrEmpty(OrderBy))
  {
    var order = Property.ForName(OrderBy));
    switch (OrderDirection)
    {
      case AdvanceProductSearchOrderDirection.Descending:
        query = query.OrderBy(order).Desc;
        break;
      case AdvanceProductSearchOrderDirection.Ascending:
        query = query.OrderBy(order).Asc;
        break;
    }
  }
  else
  {
    query = query.OrderBy(p => p.UnitPrice).Asc;
  }
}
}
```

How it works...

In this recipe, we reuse the repository and query infrastructure from the *Using named queries in the data access layer* recipe. Our simple base class for ICriteria-based query objects splits query creation from query execution and handles transactions for us automatically.

The example query we use is typical of an advanced product search use case. When a user fills in a particular field on the UI, the corresponding criterion is included in the query. When the user leaves the field blank, we ignore it.

We check each search parameter for data. If the parameter has data, we add the appropriate criterion to the query. Finally, we set the order by clause, based on the OrderBy parameter, and return the completed ICriteria query. The query is executed inside a transaction and the results are returned.

For this type of query, each query parameter would be set to the value of some field on your product search UI. On using this query, your code looks as shown:

```
var query = repository.CreateQuery<IAdvancedProductSearch>();
query.Name = searchData.PartialName;
query.Description = searchData.PartialDescription;
query.MinimumPrice = searchData.MinimumPrice;
query.MaximumPrice = searchData.MaximumPrice;
query.OrderBy = searchData.OrderBy;
query.OrderDirection = searchData.OrderDirection;
var results = query.Execute();
```

There's more...

You may have noticed that we used the same CreateQuery method in this recipe as we did in the previous named query recipe. This means that we have successfully hidden the querying technique used from the consuming code. If there's suddenly a need to switch from named queries to criteria queries, HQL, LINQ, or even plain SQL, it can be done without affecting the rest of the application code. All that's needed is a new class implementing the correct IQuery interface.

See also

- ▸ *Transaction auto-wrapping for the data access layer*
- ▸ *Setting up an NHibernate repository*
- ▸ *Using named queries in the data access layer*
- ▸ *Using paged queries in the data access layer*
- ▸ *Using LINQ specifications in the data access layer*

Using paged queries in the data access layer

In an effort to avoid overwhelming the user and increase application responsiveness, large result sets are commonly broken into smaller pages of results. In this recipe, we'll show you how to easily add paging to a `QueryOver` query object in our DAL.

Getting ready

Complete the recipe, *Using named queries in the data access layer*.

How to do it...

1. In `Eg.Core.Data.Queries`, add a class using the following code:

```
public class PagedResult<T>
{

    public int TotalCount { get; set; }
    public IEnumerable<T> Items { get; set; }

}
```

2. Add an interface using the following code:

```
public interface IPagedQuery<T>
    : IQuery<PagedResult<T>>
{

    int PageNumber { get; set; }
    int PageSize { get; set; }

}
```

3. In `Eg.Core.Data.Impl.Queries`, add the following class:

```
public abstract class PagedQueryOverBase<T>
    : NHibernateQueryBase<PagedResult<T>>,
      IPagedQuery<T>
{

    public PagedQueryOverBase(ISessionFactory sessionFactory)
        : base(sessionFactory) { }

    public int PageNumber { get; set; }
```

```csharp
    public int PageSize { get; set; }

    public override PagedResult<T> Execute()
    {
      var query = GetQuery();
      SetPaging(query);
      return WithinTransaction(() => Execute(query));
    }

    protected abstract IQueryOver<T, T> GetQuery();

    protected virtual void SetPaging(
      IQueryOver<T, T> query)
    {
      int maxResults = PageSize;
      int firstResult = (PageNumber - 1) * PageSize;
      query.Skip(firstResult).Take(maxResults);
    }

    protected virtual PagedResult<T> Execute(
      IQueryOver<T, T> query)
    {
      var results = query.Future<T>();
      var count = query.ToRowCountQuery().FutureValue<int>();
      return new PagedResult<T>()
      {
        Items = results,
        TotalCount = count.Value
      };
    }

}
```

4. In `Eg.Core.Data.Queries`, add an interface for the example query:

```csharp
public interface IPagedProductSearch
  : IPagedQuery<Product>
{

  string Name { get; set; }
  string Description { get; set; }
  decimal? MinimumPrice { get; set; }
  decimal? MaximumPrice { get; set; }
```

```
        string OrderBy { get; set; }
        SortOrderDirection SortOrder
          { get; set; }
    }
```

5. Add the following enumeration for choosing the sort option:

```
public enum SortOrderDirection
{
    Ascending,
    Descending
}
```

6. In `Eg.Core.Data.Impl.Queries`, implement the interface using the following class:

```
public class PagedProductSearch
    : PagedQueryOverBase<Product>,
      IPagedProductSearch
{
    public PagedProductSearch(ISessionFactory sessionFactory)
      : base(sessionFactory) { }

    public string Name { get; set; }
    public string Description { get; set; }
    public decimal? MinimumPrice { get; set; }
    public decimal? MaximumPrice { get; set; }
    public SortOrderDirection SortDirection { get; set; }

    protected override IQueryOver<Product, Product> GetQuery()
    {
        var query = session.QueryOver<Product>();
        if (!string.IsNullOrEmpty(Name))
          query = query.WhereRestrictionOn(p => p.Name)
            .IsInsensitiveLike(Name, MatchMode.Anywhere);

        if (!string.IsNullOrEmpty(Description))
          query.WhereRestrictionOn(p => p.Description)
            .IsInsensitiveLike(Description, MatchMode.Anywhere);

        if (MinimumPrice.HasValue)
          query.Where(p => p.UnitPrice >= MinimumPrice);

        if (MaximumPrice.HasValue)
```

```
        query.Where(p => p.UnitPrice <= MaximumPrice);

    if (!string.IsNullOrEmpty(OrderBy))
    {
      var order = Property.ForName(OrderBy));
      switch (SortDirection)
      {
        case SortOrderDirection.Descending:
          query = query.OrderBy(order).Desc;
          break;
        case SortOrderDirection.Ascending:
          query = query.OrderBy(order).Asc;
          break;
      }
    }
    else
    {
      query = query.OrderBy(p => p.UnitPrice).Asc;
    }
    return query;
  }
}
```

How it works...

In this recipe, we have defined a common `PagedResult<T>` return type for all paged queries. We have also defined the `IPagedQuery<T>` interface, which specifies the paging parameters and return type of `PagedResult<T>`.

As defined in `PagedQueryOverBase`, each subclassed query object must return a standard `IQueryOver<T, T>` query from `GetQuery()`. The `PagedQueryOverBase` class sets the appropriate `Skip` and `Take` values based on the specified page number and items per page. Then it uses Futures to get the results. The row count query is created from the result set query using the new `ToRowCountQuery()` method. Future queries are executed when the count query result is put into the `PagedResult<T>` object.

See also

- ▸ *Transaction auto-wrapping for the data access layer*
- ▸ *Setting up an NHibernate repository*
- ▸ *Using named queries in the data access layer*
- ▸ *Using ICriteria in the data access layer*
- ▸ *Using LINQ specifications in the data access layer*

Using LINQ specifications in the data access layer

The specification pattern is a way to encapsulate query criteria inside aptly named business rule objects, called specifications. A specification has a single purpose. It should answer whether an entity of some type satisfies the conditions or criteria for a specific business rule or not.

In this recipe, we'll show you how to set up and use the specification pattern with the NHibernate repository and LINQ expressions.

Getting ready

To complete this recipe we will need a `LinqSpecs` library. The documentation and source code can be found at `http://linqspecs.codeplex.com`.

Complete the *Setting up an NHibernate repository* recipe.

How to do it...

1. Install `LinqSpecs` using the NuGet Package Manager console by executing the following command:

   ```
   Install-Package LinqSpecs
   ```

2. Add the following two methods to the `IRepository` interface:

   ```
   IEnumerable<T> FindAll(Specification<T> specification);
   T FindOne(Specification<T> specification);
   ```

3. Add the following three methods to `NHibernateRepository`:

   ```
   public IEnumerable<T> FindAll(Specification<T> specification)
   {
     var query = GetQuery(specification);
     return WithinTransaction(() => query.ToList());
   }

   public T FindOne(Specification<T> specification)
   {
     var query = GetQuery(specification);
     return WithinTransaction(() => query.SingleOrDefault());
   }

   private IQueryable<T> GetQuery(
   ```

```
      Specification<T> specification)
{
    return session.Query<T>()
      .Where(specification.IsSatisfiedBy());
}
```

4. Add the following specification to `Eg.Core.Data.Queries`:

```
public class MoviesDirectedBy : Specification<Movie>
{
    private readonly string _director;

    public MoviesDirectedBy(string director)
    {
        _director = director;
    }

    public override
        Expression<Func<Movie, bool>> IsSatisfiedBy()
    {
        return m => m.Director == _director;
    }
}
```

5. Add another specification to `Eg.Core.Data.Queries`, using the following code:

```
public class MoviesStarring : Specification<Movie>
{
    private readonly string _actor;

    public MoviesStarring(string actor)
    {
        _actor = actor;
    }

    public override Expression<Func<Movie, bool>> IsSatisfiedBy()
    {
        return m => m.Actors.Any(a => a.Actor == _actor);
    }
}
```

How it works...

The specification pattern allows us to separate the process of selecting objects from the concern about which objects to select. The repository handles selecting objects, while the specification objects are concerned only with the objects that satisfy their requirements.

In our specification objects, the `IsSatisfiedBy` method of the specification object returns a LINQ expression to determine which objects to select.

In the repository, we get an `IQueryable` from the session, pass this LINQ expression to the `where` method, and execute the LINQ query. Only objects that satisfy the specification will be returned.

For a detailed explanation of the specification pattern, check out `http://martinfowler.com/apsupp/spec.pdf`.

There's more...

To use our new specifications with the `repository`, use the following code:

```
var movies = repository.FindAll(
    new MoviesDirectedBy("Stephen Spielberg"));
```

Specification composition

We can also combine specifications to build queries that are more complex. For example, the following code will find all movies directed by Steven Speilberg and starring Harrison Ford:

```
var movies = repository.FindAll(
    new MoviesDirectedBy("Steven Spielberg")
    && new MoviesStarring("Harrison Ford"));
```

`LinqSpecs` handles this rather intuitive syntax using operator overloading. When two specifications are combined, for example with an `&&` operator, the LINQ expressions will be combined accordingly.

See also

- ▶ *Transaction auto-wrapping for the data access layer*
- ▶ *Setting up an NHibernate repository*
- ▶ *Using named queries in the data access layer*
- ▶ *Using ICriteria in the data access layer*
- ▶ *Using paged queries in the data access layer*

8
Extending NHibernate

In this chapter, we will cover the following topics:

- ▶ Creating an encrypted string type
- ▶ Creating a money type
- ▶ Using well-known instance types
- ▶ Using dependency injection with entities
- ▶ Creating an audit-event listener
- ▶ Creation and change stamping of entities
- ▶ Generating trigger-based auditing
- ▶ Implementing a soft-delete pattern
- ▶ Setting Microsoft SQL's Context_Info
- ▶ Using dynamic connection strings
- ▶ Using custom dialect functions
- ▶ Using custom functions with LINQ
- ▶ Extending the LINQ provider

Introduction

NHibernate is incredibly extensible. The recipes in this chapter demonstrate ways to extend NHibernate to accomplish common tasks such as data encryption and auditing.

Creating an encrypted string type

In this age of identity theft, data security is more important than ever. Sensitive data such as credit card numbers should always be encrypted. In this recipe, we will show you how to use NHibernate to encrypt a single property.

How to do it...

1. Create a new class library project named `EncryptedStringExample`.

2. Install the `NHibernate` and `log4net` packages using the NuGet Package Manager Console by executing the following command:

```
Install-Package NHibernate
Install-Package log4net
```

3. Add a new public interface named `IEncryptor` with the following three method definitions:

```
public interface IEncryptor
{
  string Encrypt(string plainText);
  string Decrypt(string encryptedText);
  string EncryptionKey { get; set; }
}
```

4. Create an implementation of `IEncryptor` named `SymmetricEncryptorBase` using the following code:

```
public abstract class SymmetricEncryptorBase : IEncryptor
{

  private readonly SymmetricAlgorithm _cryptoProvider;
  private byte[] _myBytes;

  protected SymmetricEncryptorBase(
    SymmetricAlgorithm cryptoProvider)
  {
    _cryptoProvider = cryptoProvider;
  }

  public string EncryptionKey { get; set; }

  public string Encrypt(string plainText)
  {
    var bytes = GetEncryptionKeyBytes();
```

```csharp
using (var memoryStream = new MemoryStream())
{
  var encryptor = _cryptoProvider
    .CreateEncryptor(bytes, bytes);

  using (var cryptoStream = new CryptoStream(
    memoryStream, encryptor, CryptoStreamMode.Write))
  {
    using (var writer = new StreamWriter(cryptoStream))
    {
      writer.Write(plainText);
      writer.Flush();
      cryptoStream.FlushFinalBlock();
      return Convert.ToBase64String(
        memoryStream.GetBuffer(),
        0,
        (int) memoryStream.Length);
    }
  }
}

private byte[] GetEncryptionKeyBytes()
{
  if (_myBytes == null)
    _myBytes = Encoding.ASCII.GetBytes(EncryptionKey);

  return _myBytes;
}

public string Decrypt(string encryptedText)
{
  var bytes = GetEncryptionKeyBytes();
  using (var memoryStream = new MemoryStream(
    Convert.FromBase64String(encryptedText)))
  {
    var decryptor = _cryptoProvider
      .CreateDecryptor(bytes, bytes);
    using (var cryptoStream = new CryptoStream(
      memoryStream, decryptor, CryptoStreamMode.Read))
    {
```

```
            using (var reader = new StreamReader(cryptoStream))
            {
              return reader.ReadToEnd();
            }
          }
        }
      }
    }

  }
```

5. Create a concrete implementation named `DESEncryptor` with the following code:

```
public class DESEncryptor : SymmetricEncryptorBase
{

  public DESEncryptor()
    : base(new DESCryptoServiceProvider())
  { }

}
```

6. Add an implementation of `IUserType` named `EncryptedString` using the following code:

```
public class EncryptedString :
  IUserType,
  IParameterizedType
{

  private IEncryptor _encryptor;

  public object NullSafeGet(
    IDataReader rs,
    string[] names,
    object owner)
  {
    //treat for the posibility of null values
    object passwordString =
      NHibernateUtil.String.NullSafeGet(rs, names[0]);
    if (passwordString != null)
    {
      return _encryptor.Decrypt((string)passwordString);
    }
```

```
    return null;
  }

  public void NullSafeSet(
    IDbCommand cmd,
    object value,
    int index)
  {
    if (value == null)
    {
      NHibernateUtil.String.NullSafeSet(cmd, null, index);
      return;
    }

    string encryptedValue =
      _encryptor.Encrypt((string)value);
    NHibernateUtil.String.NullSafeSet(
      cmd,
      encryptedValue,
      index);
  }

  public object DeepCopy(object value)
  {
    return value == null
      ? null
      : string.Copy((string)value);
  }

  public object Replace(object original,
    object target, object owner)
  {
    return original;
  }

  public object Assemble(object cached, object owner)
  {
    return DeepCopy(cached);
  }
```

```csharp
public object Disassemble(object value)
{
  return DeepCopy(value);
}

public SqlType[] SqlTypes
{
  get { return new[] { new SqlType(DbType.String) }; }
}

public Type ReturnedType
{
  get { return typeof(string); }
}

public bool IsMutable
{
  get { return false; }
}

public new bool Equals(object x, object y)
{
  if (ReferenceEquals(x, y))
  {
    return true;
  }
  if (x == null || y == null)
  {
    return false;
  }
  return x.Equals(y);
}

public int GetHashCode(object x)
{
  if (x == null)
  {
    throw new ArgumentNullException("x");
  }
  return x.GetHashCode();
}


public void SetParameterValues(
```

```
        IDictionary<string, string> parameters)
    {
        if (parameters != null)
        {
            var encryptorTypeName = parameters["encryptor"];
            _encryptor = !string.IsNullOrEmpty(encryptorTypeName)
                    ? (IEncryptor) Instantiate(encryptorTypeName)
                    : new DESEncryptor();
            var encryptionKey = parameters["encryptionKey"];
            if (!string.IsNullOrEmpty(encryptionKey))
                _encryptor.EncryptionKey = encryptionKey;
        }
        else
        {
            _encryptor = new DESEncryptor();
        }
    }

    private static object Instantiate(string typeName)
    {
        var type = Type.GetType(typeName);
        return Activator.CreateInstance(type);
    }

}
```

7. Add an entity class named `Account` with the following properties:

```
public virtual Guid Id { get; set; }
public virtual string Name { get; set; }
public virtual Money Balance { get; set; }
```

8. Add a mapping document with the following XML. Don't forget to set **Build Action** to **Embedded Resource**:

```
<?xml version="1.0" encoding="utf-8" ?>
<hibernate-mapping xmlns="urn:nhibernate-mapping-2.2"
    assembly="EncryptedStringExample"
    namespace="EncryptedStringExample">
  <typedef
    name="encrypted"
    class="EncryptedStringExample.EncryptedString,
EncryptedStringExample">
    <param name="encryptor">
      EncryptedStringExample.DESEncryptor,
```

```
            EncryptedStringExample
        </param>
        <param name="encryptionKey">12345678</param>
      </typedef>
      <class name="Account">
        <id name="Id">
          <generator class="guid.comb" />
        </id>
        <property name="Name" not-null="true" />
        <property name="EMail" not-null="true" />
        <property name="CardNumber" not-null="true" type="encrypted"
/>
        <property name="ExpirationMonth" not-null="true" />
        <property name="ExpirationYear" not-null="true" />
        <property name="ZipCode" not-null="true" />
      </class>
    </hibernate-mapping>
```

How it works...

As we saw in the *Mapping enumerations* recipe in *Chapter 2, Models and Mappings*, we can set the type attribute on a property to specify a class used for converting data between our application and the database. We will use this to encrypt and decrypt our credit card number.

Our `Account` class mapping defined a type using the `<typedef>` element. The `name` attribute defines a nickname for our `encryption` type. This nickname matches the `type` attribute on our `CardNumber` property's mapping. The `class` attribute specifies the .NET class that will be used to convert our data in the standard `namespace.typeName`, `assemblyName` format.

Our `EncryptedString` type happens to use two parameters: `encryptor` and `encryptionKey`. These are set in the mapping as well.

`DESEncryptor`, our implementation of `IEncryptor`, uses `DESCryptoServiceProvider` to encrypt and decrypt our data. This is one of the symmetric encryption algorithms available in the .NET framework.

Our `EncryptedString` type implements `IUserType`, NHibernate's interface for defining custom types. When implementing `IUserType`, `NullSafeGet` is responsible for reading data from the ADO.NET data reader and returning an appropriate object, in this case, a string. In our `EncryptedString`, we read the encrypted data, use `IEncryptor` to decrypt it, and return the unencrypted string, which is used to set the `CardNumber` property. `NullSafeSet` takes some value, in this case, our unencrypted `CardNumber`, and sets a parameter on the ADO.NET `command`. In `EncryptedString`, we encrypt the card number before setting it on the `command`. The `SqlTypes` property returns an array representing the types of each database field used to store this user type. In our case, we have a single string field. The `ReturnedType` property returns the .NET type. Since our `CardNumber` is a string, we return the string type.

`EncryptedString` also implements `IParameterizedType`. The `SetParameterValues` method provides a dictionary of parameters from the mapping document. From that dictionary, we get the `IEncryptor` implementation to use, as well as the encryption key.

 The class mapping is not the best place to store encryption keys. This recipe can easily be adapted to read the encryption keys from a properly secured location.

There's more...

There are three categories of encryption algorithms. A symmetric algorithm uses the same key to encrypt and decrypt the data. Because our application is responsible for encryption and decryption, this type of algorithm makes the most sense.

An asymmetric algorithm encrypts data using a pair of keys: one public and one private. The key pairs are generated in such a way that the public key used to encrypt the data gives no hint as to the private key required to decrypt that data. It is not necessary to keep the public key a secret. This type of algorithm is typically used when the data is encrypted in one location and decrypted in another. System A generates the keys, holds onto the private key, and shares the public key with System B. System B encrypts data with the public key. Only System A has the private key necessary to decrypt the data.

Finally, a hash algorithm is used when the data does not need to be decrypted. With a hash algorithm, as the original data cannot be calculated from the hash value, the chance of finding different data with the same hash value is extremely small, and even a slight change in the data produces a wildly different hash value. This type of algorithm is typically used for passwords. We store the hash of the real password. When a user logs in, we do not need to know what the real password is, only that the attempted password matches the real password. We hash the attempted password. If the hash of the attempted password matches the previously stored hash of the real password, we know that the passwords match.

See also

 ▸ *Using well-known instance types*

 ▸ *Using dependency injection with entities*

Creating a money type

Sometimes you will need more complex types to be stored in the database, such as
currencies. In this recipe, we will show you how to implement a money type and the
corresponding composite user type.

How to do it...

1. Create a new class library project named `MoneyExample`.

2. Install the `NHibernate` package using the NuGet Package Manager Console by
   executing the following command:

   ```
   Install-Package NHibernate
   ```

3. Create the following `Money` class:

   ```
   public struct Money : IEquatable<Money>
   {
     public decimal Amount { get; }

     public string Currency { get; }

     public Money(decimal amount, string currency)
     {
       Amount = amount;
       Currency = currency;
     }

     public override bool Equals(object obj)
     {
       if (ReferenceEquals(null, obj)) return false;
       return obj is Money && Equals((Money) obj);
     }

     public bool Equals(Money other)
     {
   ```

```
    return Amount == other.Amount && string.Equals(Currency,
  other.Currency);
  }

  public override int GetHashCode()
  {
    unchecked
    {
      return (Amount.GetHashCode()*397) ^ Currency.GetHashCode();
    }
  }

  public static bool operator ==(Money left, Money right)
  {
    return left.Equals(right);
  }

  public static bool operator !=(Money left, Money right)
  {
    return !left.Equals(right);
  }
}
```

4. Add an implementation of ICompositeUserType named MoneyUserType using the following code:

```
public class MoneyUserType : ICompositeUserType
{
  public object GetPropertyValue(object component, int property)
  {
    var money = (Money) component;
    switch (property)
    {
      case 0:
        return money.Amount;
      case 1:
        return money.Currency;
      default:
        throw new NotSupportedException();
    }
  }

  public void SetPropertyValue(object component, int property,
  object value)
  {
```

```
            throw new InvalidOperationException("Money is an immutable
        object. SetPropertyValue isn't supported.");
            }

        public new bool Equals(object x, object y)
        {
            if (ReferenceEquals(x, y)) return true;
            if (ReferenceEquals(x, null)) return false;
            if (ReferenceEquals(y, null)) return false;
            return x.Equals(y);
        }

        public int GetHashCode(object x)
        {
            var moneyX = (Money) x;
            return moneyX.GetHashCode();
        }

        public object NullSafeGet(IDataReader dr, string[] names,
        ISessionImplementor session, object owner)
        {
            var val = (decimal) NHibernateUtil.Decimal.NullSafeGet(dr,
        names[0], session, owner);
            var currency = (string) NHibernateUtil.String.NullSafeGet(dr,
        names[1], session, owner);

            return new Money(val, currency);
        }

        public void NullSafeSet(IDbCommand cmd, object value, int index,
        bool[] settable, ISessionImplementor session)
        {
            if (value == null)
                return;
            var money = (Money) value;
            var amount = money.Amount;
            var currency = money.Currency;
            NHibernateUtil.Double.NullSafeSet(cmd, amount, index,
        session);
            NHibernateUtil.String.NullSafeSet(cmd, currency, index + 1,
        session);
        }

        public object DeepCopy(object value)
```

```
  {
    var money = (Money) value;
    return new Money(money.Amount, money.Currency);
  }

  public object Disassemble(object value, ISessionImplementor
session)
  {
    return DeepCopy(value);
  }

  public object Assemble(object cached, ISessionImplementor
session, object owner)
  {
    return DeepCopy(cached);
  }

  public object Replace(object original, object target,
ISessionImplementor session, object owner)
  {
    throw new NotImplementedException();
  }

  public string[] PropertyNames
  {
    get { return new[] {"Amount", "Currency"}; }
  }

  public IType[] PropertyTypes
  {
    get { return new IType[] {NHibernateUtil.Double,
NHibernateUtil.String}; }
  }

  public Type ReturnedClass
  {
    get { return typeof(Money); }
  }

  public bool IsMutable
  {
    get { return false; }
  }
}
```

5. Add a mapping document with the following XML. Don't forget to set the **Build Action** to **Embedded Resource**:

```xml
<?xml version="1.0" encoding="utf-8"?>

<hibernate-mapping xmlns="urn:nhibernate-mapping-2.2"
                   assembly="MoneyExample"
                   namespace="MoneyExample">
  <typedef
    name="money"
    class="MoneyExample.MoneyUserType, MoneyExample">
  </typedef>
  <class name="Account">
    <id name="Id">
      <generator class="guid.comb" />
    </id>
    <property name="Name" not-null="true" />
    <property name="Balance" not-null="true" type="money" >
      <column name="Balance_Amount" not-null="true" />
      <column name="Balance_Currency" length="3" not-null="true" />
    </property>
  </class>
</hibernate-mapping>
```

How it works...

As we saw in the *Creating an encrypted string type* recipe, we can set the type attribute on a property to specify a class used for converting data between our application and the database. We will use this to store our complex user type. The composite user type is a type that can have multiple columns in the database.

Our `MoneyUserType` type implements `ICompositeUserType`, NHibernate's interface for defining custom composite types. When implementing `ICompositeUserType`, `NullSafeGet` is responsible for reading data from the ADO.NET data reader and returning an appropriate object. `NullSafeSet` takes some value, in this case, our `Amount` and `Currency`, and sets a parameter on the ADO.NET command. The `PropertyTypes` property returns an array representing the types of each database field used to store this user type. In our case, we have two fields of decimal and string types. The `PropertyNames` property returns an array representing the names of each database field used to store this user type. The `GetPropertyValue` method returns the value of the property by its index. Indexes should match the indexes in the `PropertyTypes` and `PropertyNames` arrays. `SetPropertyValue` method throws `InvalidOperationException` because our user type is immutable as it is a value type (`struct`). The `ReturnedType` property returns our custom type.

There's more...

Instead of implementing your own money type, you can use the well-written and well-tested library, NMoneys, sources of which you can find at `https://github.com/dgg/nmoneys`.

See also

▸ *Creating an encrypted string type*

▸ *Mapping a component*

Using well-known instance types

Most applications contain a set of static relational data, such as a list of countries, states, credit card types, and others. The application does not need to waste time retrieving this static data from the database; it never changes. In this recipe, we will show you how you can use the well-known instance type from the unofficial NHibernate AddIns project to avoid this unnecessary work.

How to do it...

1. Create a new class library project named `WKITExample`.

2. Install the `NHibernate` package using the NuGet Package Manager Console by executing the following command:

   `Install-Package NHibernate`

3. Add the following `GenericWellKnownInstanceType` class:

   ```
   [Serializable]
   public abstract class GenericWellKnownInstanceType<T, TId>
     IUserType where T : class
   {

     private Func<T, TId, bool> findPredicate;
     private Func<T, TId> idGetter;
     private IEnumerable<T> repository;

     protected GenericWellKnownInstanceType(
       IEnumerable<T> repository,
       Func<T, TId, bool> findPredicate,
       Func<T, TId> idGetter)
     {
       this.repository = repository;
   ```

```
      this.findPredicate = findPredicate;
      this.idGetter = idGetter;
   }

   public Type ReturnedType
   {
      get { return typeof(T); }
   }

   public bool IsMutable
   {
      get { return false; }
   }

   public new bool Equals(object x, object y)
   {
      if (ReferenceEquals(x, y))
      {
         return true;
      }
      if (ReferenceEquals(null, x) ||
         ReferenceEquals(null, y))
      {
         return false;
      }

      return x.Equals(y);
   }

   public int GetHashCode(object x)
   {
      return (x == null) ? 0 : x.GetHashCode();
   }

   public object NullSafeGet(IDataReader rs,
      string[] names, object owner)
   {
      int index0 = rs.GetOrdinal(names[0]);
      if (rs.IsDBNull(index0))
      {
         return null;
      }

      var value = (TId)rs.GetValue(index0);
```

```
      return repository.FirstOrDefault(x =>
        findPredicate(x, value));
    }

    public void NullSafeSet(IDbCommand cmd,
      object value, int index)
    {
      if (value == null)
      {
        ((IDbDataParameter)cmd.Parameters[index])
          .Value = DBNull.Value;
      }
      else
      {
        ((IDbDataParameter)cmd.Parameters[index])
          .Value = idGetter((T)value);
      }
    }

    public object DeepCopy(object value)
    {
      return value;
    }

    public object Replace(object original,
      object target, object owner)
    {
      return original;
    }

    public object Assemble(object cached, object owner)
    {
      return cached;
    }

    public object Disassemble(object value)
    {
      return value;
    }

    /// <summary>
    /// The SQL types for the columns
    /// mapped by this type.
    /// </summary>
    public abstract SqlType[] SqlTypes { get; }

}
```

4. Add the following `StateType` class:

```
public class StateType
  : GenericWellKnownInstanceType<State, string>
{

  private static readonly SqlType[] sqlTypes =
    new[] { SqlTypeFactory.GetString(2) };

  public StateType()
    : base(new States(),
    (entity, id) => entity.PostalCode == id,
    entity => entity.PostalCode)
  { }

  public override SqlType[] SqlTypes
  {
    get { return sqlTypes; }
  }

}
```

5. Add the following `State` class:

```
[Serializable]
public class State
{

  public virtual string PostalCode { get; private set; }
  public virtual string Name { get; private set; }

  internal State(string postalCode, string name)
  {
    PostalCode = postalCode;
    Name = name;
  }

}
```

6. Add the following `States` collection class:

```
public class States : ReadOnlyCollection<State>
{

  public static State Arizona = new State("AZ", "Arizona");
  public static State California =
    new State("CA", "California");
```

```
public static State Colorado = new State("CO", "Colorado");
public static State Oklahoma = new State("OK", "Oklahoma");
public static State NewMexico =
  new State("NM", "New Mexico");
public static State Nevada = new State("NV", "Nevada");
public static State Texas = new State("TX", "Texas");
public static State Utah = new State("UT", "Utah");

public States()
  : base(new State[] { Arizona, California, Colorado,
     Oklahoma, NewMexico, Nevada, Texas, Utah })
{ }

}
```

7. Add an `Address` class using the following properties:

```
public virtual Guid Id { get; set; }
public virtual string Line1 { get; set; }
public virtual string Line2 { get; set; }
public virtual string City { get; set; }
public virtual State State { get; set; }
public virtual string Zip { get; set; }
```

8. Add the following mapping document:

```xml
<?xml version="1.0" encoding="utf-8" ?>
<hibernate-mapping xmlns="urn:nhibernate-mapping-2.2"
    assembly="WKITExample"
    namespace="WKITExample">
  <typedef
    class="WKITExample.StateType, WKITExample"
    name="State"/>
  <class name="Address">
    <id name="Id">
      <generator class="guid.comb" />
    </id>
    <property name="Line1" not-null="true" />
    <property name="Line2" />
    <property name="City" not-null="true" />
    <property name="State" type="State" not-null="true" />
    <property name ="Zip" not-null="true" />
  </class>
</hibernate-mapping>
```

How it works...

In this recipe, we have an `Address` entity with a `State` property. Suppose we have a requirement to print the state's postal abbreviation on shipping labels, but we need to display the full state name when the user completes an order. It would be a waste of resources to fetch these `State` entities from the database each time.

`GenericWellKnownInstanceType` allows us to create a static list of `States` in our application, and use them with our `Address` entity. We use the `PostalCode` property to uniquely identify it in the list. In the database, this postal code value is stored in the `State` field of `Address`. When NHibernate loads an `Address` from the database, it attaches the appropriate `State` instance to the `State` property. In this way, `State` works just like an entity. This is handled by the `StateType` class, which implements `IUserType`. When loading an `Address`, the `StateType` class is responsible for reading the abbreviation from the raw data and returning the correct `State` instance. Similarly, when we save an address, it translates the `State` instance to the abbreviation stored in the `Address` table.

When inheriting from `GenericWellKnownInstanceType`, we must provide the following four items:

- A collection of all the well-known instances; this is our `states` collection
- A predicate to locate the correct well-known instance given a database value
- A delegate that returns the database value from a well-known instance
- The type of database field used to store this database value: in this case, a two-character string field

The unofficial NHibernate AddIns project also includes a `WellKnownInstanceType`, which specifies a 32-bit integer database value.

See also

- *Creating an encrypted string type*
- *Mapping enumerations*

Using dependency injection with entities

In this recipe, we will show you how you can inject services into your entities to separate implementation details from your real business logic.

Getting ready

- ▶ Download uNHAddIns.CommonServiceLocatorAdapters.dll from the unofficial NHibernate AddIns project at https://bitbucket.org/fabiomaulo/unhaddins

- ▶ Download Ninject.dll and CommonServiceLocator.NinjectAdapter.dll from the Ninject project at http://ninject.org

- ▶ Download Microsoft.Practices.ServiceLocation.dll from the Microsoft patterns and practices team and available at http://commonservicelocator.codeplex.com/

- ▶ Put these three assemblies in your solution's Lib folder

How to do it...

1. Create a new console application project named IoCByteCode.

2. Add a reference to NHibernate.dll, Ninject.dll, CommonServiceLocator.NinjectAdapter.dll, uNHAddIns.CommonServiceLocatorAdapters.dll, and Microsoft.Practices.ServiceLocation.dll.

3. Add an interface named IPasswordHasher with the following method definition:

```
string HashPassword(string email, string password);
```

4. Add an implementation named PasswordHasher using the following code:

```
public class PasswordHasher : IPasswordHasher
{

    private readonly HashAlgorithm _algorithm;

    public PasswordHasher(HashAlgorithm algorithm)
    {
      _algorithm = algorithm;
    }

    public string HashPassword(string email, string password)
    {
      var plainText = email + password;
      var plainTextData = Encoding.Default.GetBytes(plainText);
      var hash = _algorithm.ComputeHash(plainTextData);
      return Convert.ToBase64String(hash);
    }

}
```

5. Add a `UserAccount` entity class using the following code:

```
public class UserAccount
{

  private readonly IPasswordHasher _passwordHasher;

  public UserAccount(IPasswordHasher passwordHasher)
  {
    _passwordHasher = passwordHasher;
  }

  public virtual Guid Id { get; protected set; }
  public virtual string EMail { get; protected set; }
  public virtual string HashedPassword { get; protected set; }

  public virtual void SetCredentials(
    string email, string plainTextPassword)
  {
    EMail = email;
    SetPassword(plainTextPassword);
  }

  public virtual void SetPassword(string plainTextPassword)
  {
    HashedPassword = _passwordHasher.HashPassword(
      EMail, plainTextPassword);
  }

}
```

6. Add the following mapping document:

```xml
<?xml version="1.0" encoding="utf-8" ?>
<hibernate-mapping xmlns="urn:nhibernate-mapping-2.2"
    assembly="IoCByteCode"
    namespace="IoCByteCode">
  <class name="UserAccount">
    <id name="Id">
      <generator class="guid.comb" />
    </id>
    <natural-id>
      <property name="EMail" not-null="true" />
    </natural-id>
    <property name="HashedPassword" not-null="true" />
  </class>
</hibernate-mapping>
```

7. Add an `App.config` with the standard NHibernate and log4net configurations.

8. Set the `proxyfactory.factory_class` property to `uNHAddIns.CommonServiceLocatorAdapters.ProxyFactoryFactory, uNHAddIns.CommonServiceLocatorAdapters`.

9. In `Program.cs`, add the following methods:

```
private static void ConfigureServiceLocator()
{
  var kernel = BuildKernel();
  var sl = new NinjectServiceLocator(kernel);
  ServiceLocator.SetLocatorProvider(() => sl);
}

private static IKernel BuildKernel()
{
  var kernel = new StandardKernel();

  kernel.Bind<NHibernate.Proxy.IProxyFactory>()
    .To<NHibernate.ByteCode.Castle.ProxyFactory>()
    .InSingletonScope();

  kernel.Bind<IPasswordHasher>()
    .To<PasswordHasherImpl>()
    .InSingletonScope();

  kernel.Bind<HashAlgorithm>()
    .To<MD5CryptoServiceProvider>()
    .InSingletonScope();

  return kernel;
}
```

10. In `Program.cs`, add the following code to the `Main` method:

```
ConfigureServiceLocator();
NHibernate.Cfg.Environment.BytecodeProvider =
  new BytecodeProvider();
var cfg = new Configuration().Configure();
var sessionFactory = cfg.BuildSessionFactory();
```

How it works...

An NHibernate bytecode provider is responsible for building several factories, including the **reflection optimizer**, which NHibernate uses to instantiate entity classes. The particular reflection optimizer included with this bytecode provider uses Microsoft's common service locator to instantiate our entity classes. This allows us to use dependency injection to inject services into our entities. It also disables NHibernate's checks for a default constructor. Because we are using dependency injection, we'll need constructor parameters.

A typical bytecode provider also provides a factory for creating proxies. Because the common service locator isn't a proxy framework, we need to get this functionality from somewhere else. To fill this requirement, the `ProxyFactoryFactory` included with this bytecode provider fetches an `IProxyFactory` instance from the service locator. We register the castle dynamic proxy factory as the implementation for the `IProxyFactory` service.

Additionally, we must register implementations for the services required for our entities, and all of their dependencies. In this case, we register `PasswordHasher` for `IPasswordHasher`, and register .NET's implementation of MD5 as our hash algorithm.

There's more...

uNHAddIns also includes inversion of control bytecode providers specifically for Ninject, castle windsor, and spring IoC, though any of these may also be used through the common service locator.

Bland passwords need salt

As we learned in the *Creating an encrypted string type* recipe, a hashing algorithm is used to generate a hash value from the data. The hash value can't be reverse-engineered to calculate the original data, but a hash of the same data, with the same key, will always result in the same hash value. Also, any change in the original data results in a wildly different hash value. Finally, there is a near zero chance of two different strings of data resulting in the same hash value.

If your database is compromised, the passwords are hashed. It's a one-way algorithm, so it's safe, right? Wrong. This is not as secure as you may think. Let's say 14 of your accounts have the same password hash value. You don't know what their password is, but you know it's the same across all 14 accounts. Two of those accounts have *Twilight*-related e-mail addresses: sparklyVampire32@yahoo.com and JealousBella1974@gmail.com. Could you guess the password in 42 attempts or less? Easily. That's three chances for each of the 14 accounts. Congratulations. You now know the password for e-mail accounts, Facebook, Twitter, and countless other websites for nearly all of those 14 people. Only two of them used a password that was easy to guess, but they led to the downfall of the others.

When hashing data for storage in the database, you should always salt the data. Append some non-secret data to the secret data before hashing. In this recipe, we prepend the e-mail address to the password. The e-mail is the salt. Now, those 14 accounts will each have a different hash value. A hacker won't know which passwords are the same, which makes it much more difficult. When a user attempts to log in, prepend the e-mail and calculate the hash value in exactly the same way. If the hashes match, log them in. In a real application, you'll most likely want to clean up the e-mail address and convert it to lowercase. The slightest difference will change the hash value.

See also

▶ *Creating an encrypted string type*

▶ *Creating an audit-event listener*

Creating an audit-event listener

Auditing is another common security-related task. An audit log is an append-only record of changes in a system that allows you to trace a particular action back to its source. In this recipe, we will show you how you can easily create an audit log to track changes to your entities.

How to do it...

1. Create a new console application project named `AuditEventListener`.

2. Add a reference to our `Eg.Core` model from *Chapter 2, Models and Mappings*.

3. Install the `NHibernate` and `log4net` packages using the NuGet Package Manager Console by executing the following commands:

```
Install-Package NHibernate

Install-Package log4net
```

4. Add an `App.config` with a standard NHibernate and log4net configuration.

5. Just before the end of the `sessionfactory` element, add the following three event elements:

```
<event type="pre-insert">
  <listener class="AuditEventListener.EventListener,
          AuditEventListener" />
</event>
<event type="pre-update">
  <listener class="AuditEventListener.EventListener,
          AuditEventListener" />
</event>
<event type="pre-delete">
```

```
      <listener class="AuditEventListener.EventListener,
              AuditEventListener" />
</event>
```

6. Add the following `IAuditLogger` interface:

```csharp
public interface IAuditLogger
{

    void Insert(Entity entity);
    void Update(Entity entity);
    Void Delete(Entity entity);

}
```

7. Add the following `AuditLogger` class:

```csharp
public class AuditLogger : IAuditLogger
{

    private readonly ILog log =
        LogManager.GetLogger(typeof(AuditLogger));

    public void Insert(Entity entity)
    {
        log.DebugFormat("{0} #{1} inserted.",
            entity.GetType(), entity.Id);
    }

    public void Update(Entity entity)
    {
        log.DebugFormat("{0} #{1} updated.",
            entity.GetType(), entity.Id);
    }

    public void Delete(Entity entity)
    {
        log.DebugFormat("{0} #{1} deleted.",
            entity.GetType(), entity.Id);
    }

}
```

8. Add the following event listener class:

```
public class EventListener :
  IPreInsertEventListener,
  IPreUpdateEventListener,
  IPreDeleteEventListener
{

  private readonly IAuditLogger _logger;

  public EventListener()
    : this(new AuditLogger())
  { }

  public EventListener(IAuditLogger logger)
  {
    _logger = logger;
  }

  public bool OnPreInsert(PreInsertEvent e)
  {
    _logger.Insert(e.Entity as Entity);
    return false;
  }

  public bool OnPreUpdate(PreUpdateEvent e)
  {
    _logger.Update(e.Entity as Entity);
    return false;
  }

  public bool OnPreDelete(PreDeleteEvent e)
  {
    _logger.Delete(e.Entity as Entity);
    return false;
  }

}
```

9. In `Program.cs`, configure NHibernate and log4net, and build a session factory just as we did in *Chapter 1, The Configuration and Schema* and *Chapter 3, Sessions and Transactions*.

10. Finally, in `Main`, add code to save a new entity, update it, and then delete it.

11. Build and run your application.

How it works...

NHibernate uses an event model to allow applications to hook into the NHibernate pipeline and change behavior. In this case, we simply write a message to the log4net log whenever an entity is inserted, updated, or deleted. The `pre-insert`, `pre-update`, and `pre-delete` event listeners are called just before each change. We set these events with the `event` element in our NHibernate configuration. They can also be set programmatically through the `Configuration` object.

Log4net includes appenders capable of writing to different types of permanent storage, such as files and databases. We can use active context properties to record additional information such as the user who caused the change. More information about these advanced log4net configurations is available in the log4net manual at `http://logging.apache.org/log4net`.

There's more...

NHibernate provides the following events:

- auto-flush
- merge
- create
- create-onflush
- delete
- dirty-check
- evict
- flush
- flush-entity
- load
- load-collection
- lock
- refresh
- replicate
- save
- save-update
- pre-update

- ▶ update
- ▶ pre-load
- ▶ pre-delete
- ▶ pre-insert
- ▶ post-load
- ▶ post-insert
- ▶ post-update
- ▶ post-delete
- ▶ post-commit update
- ▶ post-commit insert
- ▶ post-commit delete
- ▶ pre-collection recreate
- ▶ pre-collection remove
- ▶ pre-collection delete
- ▶ post-collection recreate
- ▶ post-collection remove
- ▶ post-collection update

See also

- ▶ *Creation and change stamping of entities*
- ▶ *Generating trigger-based auditing*
- ▶ *Using NHibernate Envers*

Creation and change stamping of entities

Although it does not track the full history of an entity, another option for auditing is to record information about the entity's creation and the most recent change directly in the entity. In this recipe, we will show you how to use NHibernate's events to record creation and change data on your entities.

How to do it...

1. Create a new class library project named `Changestamp`.

2. Install the `NHibernate` package using the NuGet Package Manager Console by executing the following command:

   ```
   Install-Package NHibernate
   ```

3. Create an interface named `IStampedEntity` with the following code:

   ```
   public interface IStampedEntity
   {

       string CreatedBy { get; set; }
       DateTime CreatedTS { get; set; }
       string ChangedBy { get; set; }
       DateTime ChangedTS { get; set; }

   }
   ```

4. Create an interface named `IStamper` with the following code:

   ```
   public interface IStamper
   {

       void Insert(IStampedEntity entity, object[] state,
         IEntityPersister persister);
       void Update(IStampedEntity entity, object[] oldState,
         object[] state, IEntityPersister persister);

   }
   ```

5. Create a new `EventListener` class as follows:

   ```
   public class EventListener :
     IPreInsertEventListener,
     IPreUpdateEventListener
   {

       private readonly IStamper _stamper;

       public EventListener()
         : this(new Stamper())
       { }

       public EventListener(IStamper stamper)
       {
   ```

```
      _stamper = stamper;
    }

    public bool OnPreInsert(PreInsertEvent e)
    {
      _stamper.Insert(e.Entity as IStampedEntity,
        e.State, e.Persister);
      return false;
    }

    public bool OnPreUpdate(PreUpdateEvent e)
    {
      _stamper.Update(e.Entity as IStampedEntity,
        e.OldState, e.State, e.Persister);
      return false;
    }


}
```

6. Create a base `Entity` class with the following code:

```
public abstract class Entity : IStampedEntity
{

    public virtual Guid Id { get; protected set; }

    public virtual string CreatedBy { get; set; }
    public virtual DateTime CreatedTS { get; set; }
    public virtual string ChangedBy { get; set; }
    public virtual DateTime ChangedTS { get; set; }

}
```

7. Create a `Product` class with the following code:

```
public class Product : Entity
{

    public virtual string Name { get; set; }
    public virtual string Description { get; set; }
    public virtual Decimal UnitPrice { get; set; }

}
```

8. Create a mapping with the following XML:

```xml
<?xml version="1.0" encoding="utf-8" ?>
<hibernate-mapping xmlns="urn:nhibernate-mapping-2.2"
    assembly="Changestamp"
    namespace="Changestamp">
  <class name="Product">
    <id name="Id">
      <generator class="guid.comb" />
    </id>
    <discriminator column="ProductType" />
    <natural-id>
      <property name="Name" not-null="true" />
    </natural-id>
    <property name="Description" />
    <property name="UnitPrice" not-null="true" />
    <property name="CreatedBy" />
    <property name="CreatedTS" />
    <property name="ChangedBy" />
    <property name="ChangedTS" />
  </class>
</hibernate-mapping>
```

9. Create an implementation of IStamper with the following code:

```csharp
public class Stamper : IStamper
{

  private const string CREATED_BY = "CreatedBy";
  private const string CREATED_TS = "CreatedTS";
  private const string CHANGED_BY = "ChangedBy";
  private const string CHANGED_TS = "ChangedTS";

  public void Insert(IStampedEntity entity, object[] state,
    IEntityPersister persister)
  {
    if (entity == null)
      return;
    SetCreate(entity, state, persister);
    SetChange(entity, state, persister);
  }

  public void Update(IStampedEntity entity, object[] oldState,
    object[] state, IEntityPersister persister)
  {
```

```
  if (entity == null)
    return;
  SetChange(entity, state, persister);
}

private void SetCreate(IStampedEntity entity,
  object[] state,
  IEntityPersister persister)
{
  entity.CreatedBy = GetUserName();
  SetState(persister, state, CREATED_BY, entity.CreatedBy);
  entity.CreatedTS = DateTime.Now;
  SetState(persister, state, CREATED_TS, entity.CreatedTS);
}

private void SetChange(IStampedEntity entity,
  object[] state, IEntityPersister persister)
{
  entity.ChangedBy = GetUserName();
  SetState(persister, state, CHANGED_BY,
    entity.ChangedBy);
  entity.ChangedTS = DateTime.Now;
  SetState(persister, state, CHANGED_TS,
    entity.ChangedTS);
}


private void SetState(IEntityPersister persister,
  object[] state, string propertyName, object value)
{
  var index = GetIndex(persister, propertyName);
  if (index == -1)
    return;
  state[index] = value;
}

private int GetIndex(IEntityPersister persister,
  string propertyName)
{
  return Array.IndexOf(persister.PropertyNames,
    propertyName);
}

private string GetUserName()
```

```
        {
            return WindowsIdentity.GetCurrent().Name;
        }

    }
```

10. Set the `pre-insert` and `pre-update` event listeners in the `App.config`, just as we did in the previous recipe.

How it works...

In this recipe, we've added four additional properties to our standard entity. Our `pre-insert` and `pre-update` event listener is responsible for setting the values of these properties. The task of setting these properties is handed over to our `IStamper` implementation. The pre-entity listeners happen late in the process of updating the database. NHibernate has already read our entity's property values into the object array `state`. This object array provides the actual values written to the database. However, failing to keep the object in sync with the state array can lead to a number of strange and unexpected behaviors later, so we must update both the state array and the object properties.

When an object is inserted, we set the create and change properties to the current user and date/time. When an object is updated, we update these change properties with the current user and date or time.

The `GetUserName` method of `Stamper` uses `WindowsIdentity.GetCurrent()`. This may not return a meaningful user identity, but rather the identity of some service account. The correct implementation of the `GetUserName` method depends on your application's architecture.

See also

▸ *Creating an audit-event listener*

▸ *Generating trigger-based auditing*

▸ *Implementing a soft-delete pattern*

Generating trigger-based auditing

Another approach to auditing involves tracking each change to an entity in a separate audit table. In this recipe, we will show you how to use NHibernate to generate audit triggers for your entity tables.

Getting ready

Download `uNHAddIns.dll` from the unofficial NHibernate AddIns project at `http://code.google.com/p/unhaddins/`. Save the file to your solution's `Lib` folder.

How to do it...

1. Create a new console application project with all standard NHibernate references, the standard NHibernate and log4net configuration, and the `Eg.Core` model from *Chapter 1, The Configuration and Schema*.

2. Add a reference to `uNHAddIns.dll`.

3. Set the `dialect` to `uNHAddIns.Audit.TriggerGenerator.ExtendedMsSql2008Dialect, uNHAddIns`.

4. Add the following code to the `Main` method of `Program.cs`:

```
var cfg = new Configuration().Configure();

var namingStrategy = new NamingStrategy();
var auditColumnSource = new AuditColumnSource();
new TriggerAuditing(cfg, namingStrategy,
    auditColumnSource).Configure();

var sessionFaculty = cfg.BuildSessionFactory();

var se = new NHibernate.Tool.hbm2ddl.SchemaExport(cfg);
se.Execute(true, true, false);
```

5. Build and run your application.

How it works...

NHibernate has three distinct levels of mapping. First, NHibernate simply deserializes the mapping documents into their equivalent .NET objects. Second, NHibernate transforms these mapping objects into a second, more detailed set of classes named mapping metadata. Finally, NHibernate transforms these detailed classes into the final persisters. We have an opportunity to manipulate this second-level mapping up to the point where we build the session factory.

The uNHAddIns trigger generator code reads the structure of each table from the mapping metadata and constructs a matching audit table and set of triggers.

We can use the standard `NamingStrategy` or provide our own. When naming audit tables, the default naming strategy simply appends `Audit` to the name of the data table. For trigger names, it appends `_onInsert`, `_onUpdate`, or `_onDelete` to the data table name.

An implementation of `IAuditColumnSource` should return a list of `AuditColumns` to be added to each audit table. For example, to record the current date and time when an entity is changed, we would use this `AuditColumn`:

```
new AuditColumn()
{
  Name = "AuditTimestamp",
  Value = new SimpleValue()
  {
    TypeName = NHibernateUtil.DateTime.Name
  },
  IsNullable = false,
  IncludeInPrimaryKey = true,
  ValueFunction = delegate(TriggerActions action)
  {
    return "getdate()";
  }
};
```

The default implementation returns three audit columns: `AuditUser`, `AuditTimestamp`, and `AuditOperation`. This is sufficient to answer what changed, who changed it, and when. Unfortunately, SQL does not have a handy function to answer why. The trigger generator also defines an `IExtendedDialect` interface, which adds some additional trigger-related SQL dialect functions to the standard dialects. A Microsoft SQL Server 2008 and SQLite implementation are both included. This recipe uses the `ExtendedMsSql2008Dialect`.

The `TriggerAuditing Configure()` method adds the appropriate objects to our second-level mapping to be included in our database schema output from `hbm2ddl`.

The objects added to our mapping all implement `IAuxiliaryDatabaseObject`. This interface is used by `hbm2ddl` to include `drop` and `create` SQL statements for database objects outside the scope of NHibernate, such as triggers and non-entity tables. As we will see in the next recipe, these can also be defined using XML mappings.

Because we get the current username from SQL's `system_user` to get meaningful audit logs using this method, you must use one SQL or Windows account per user when logging into the SQL server. This effectively disables connection pooling, because most connections use different credentials.

In the next recipe, we will show you how you can use SQL's `CONTEXT_INFO` as your username source, avoiding the account maintenance overhead and relieving the stress on the connection pool.

See also

 ▸ *Creating an audit-event listener*

 ▸ *Setting MS SQL's Context_Info*

Implementing a soft-delete pattern

Sometimes you do not want to delete the information from the database, but instead to mark it as deleted. This technique is called soft-delete. In this recipe, we will show you how to implement a soft-delete pattern with NHibernate.

How to do it...

1. Create a new class library project named `SoftDeleteExample`.

2. Install the `NHibernate` package using the NuGet Package Manager Console by executing the following command:

   `Install-Package NHibernate`

3. Add the `ISoftDeletable` interface using the following code:

   ```
   public interface ISoftDeletable
   {
     bool IsDeleted { get; }
     DateTime? DeletedAt { get; }
   }
   ```

4. Add an `App.config` with a standard NHibernate configuration.

5. Just before the end of the `sessionfactory` element, add the following three event elements:

   ```
   <event type="delete">
     <listener class=" SoftDeleteExample.SoftDeleteEventListener,
             SoftDeleteExample" />
   </event>
   ```

6. Add the following `EventListener`:

   ```
   public class SoftDeleteEventListener :
     DefaultDeleteEventListener
   {
     protected override void DeleteEntity(
       IEventSource session,
       object entity,
       EntityEntry entityEntry,
   ```

```
      bool isCascadeDeleteEnabled,
      IEntityPersister persister,
      ISet<object> transientEntities)
  {
    var deletable = entity as ISoftDeletable;
    if (deletable != null)
    {
      deletable.IsDeleted = true;
      deletable.DeletedAt = DateTime.UtcNow;

      CascadeBeforeDelete(
        session,
        persister,
        deletable,
        entityEntry,
        transientEntities);

      CascadeAfterDelete(
        session,
        persister,
        deletable,
        transientEntities);
    }
    else
    {
      base.DeleteEntity(
        session,
        entity,
        entityEntry,
        isCascadeDeleteEnabled,
        persister,
        transientEntities);
    }
  }
}
```

7. Add the `Order` and `OrderLine` classes using the following code:

```
public class Order : ISoftDeletable
{
  public Order()
  {
```

```
    OrderLines = new HashSet<OrderLine>();
  }

  Guid Id { get; set; }

  public virtual DateTime OrderDate { get; set; }
  public virtual ISet<OrderLine> OrderLines { get; set; }

  public virtual bool IsDeleted { get; set; }
  public virtual DateTime? DeletedAt { get; set; }
}

public class OrderLine : ISoftDeletable
{
  Guid Id { get; set; }

  public virtual string ProductName { get; set; }
  public virtual int Amount { get; set; }
  public virtual bool IsDeleted { get; set; }
  public virtual DateTime? DeletedAt { get; set; }
}
```

8. Add a mapping document with the following XML. Don't forget to set **Build Action** to **Embedded Resource**:

```xml
<?xml version="1.0" encoding="utf-8"?>
<hibernate-mapping xmlns="urn:nhibernate-mapping-2.2"
                   assembly="SoftDeleteExample"
                   namespace="SoftDeleteExample">
  <class name="Order" table="`Order`" where="IsDeleted = 0">
    <id name="Id">
      <generator class="guid.comb" />
    </id>
    <property name="OrderDate" not-null="true" />
    <property name="IsDeleted" not-null="true"/>
    <property name="DeletedAt" />
    <set name="OrderLines" cascade="all-delete-orphan"
where="IsDeleted = 0">
      <key column="OrderId"/>
      <one-to-many class="OrderLine"/>
    </set>
  </class>
  <class name="OrderLine" where="IsDeleted = 0">
    <id name="Id">
      <generator class="guid.comb" />
    </id>
```

```
            <property name="ProductName" not-null="true" />
            <property name="Amount" not-null="true" />
            <property name="IsDeleted" not-null="true"/>
            <property name="DeletedAt" />
        </class>
    </hibernate-mapping>
```

How it works...

The delete event listener works similarly to the event listeners in the *Creation and change stamping of entities* recipe. The code in the overriden `DeleteEntity` method first checks whether the entity implements the `ISoftDeletable` interface. If not, the call is just forwarded to the base class for the default execution (that is, the entity will be physically deleted from the system). However, if the entity implements the interface, we set its `IsDeleted` property to `true` and `DeletedAt` to the current UTC time, and call the `CascadeBeforeDelete` and `CascadeAfterDelete` methods of the base class.

We also use the `where` condition on the `class` and `set` definitions, to restrict loading of the deleted entities.

There's more...

Instead of using the `where` conditions, you can use the filters feature, which is more sophisticated and allows more control over the loading of the entities. You can enable or disable filters as necessary, for example to allow loading deleted entities, if needed.

See also

 ▶ *Creating an audit-event listener*
 ▶ *Creation and change stamping of entities*
 ▶ *Generating trigger-based auditing*

Setting Microsoft SQL's Context_Info

In this recipe, we will show you how to use Microsoft SQL Server's `Context_Info` to provide the current username to your audit triggers.

Getting ready

- ▸ Complete the previous recipe, *Generating trigger-based auditing*

- ▸ Download `Ninject.dll` and `CommonServiceLocator.NinjectAdapter.dll`
  from the Ninject project at `http://ninject.org`

- ▸ Download `Microsoft.Practices.ServiceLocation.dll` from the Microsoft
  patterns and practices team available at `http://commonservicelocator.codeplex.com/`

How to do it...

1. Add a reference to `Ninject.dll`, `CommonServiceLocator.NinjectAdapter.dll` and `Microsoft.Practices.ServiceLocation.dll`.

2. Add the following `IAuditColumnSource` implementation:

```
public class CtxAuditColumnSource : IAuditColumnSource
{


  public IEnumerable<AuditColumn>
    GetAuditColumns(Table dataTable)
  {
    var userStamp = new AuditColumn()
    {
      Name = "AuditUser",
      Value = new SimpleValue()
      {
        TypeName = NHibernateUtil.String.Name
      },
      Length = 127,
      IsNullable = false,
      IncludeInPrimaryKey = true,
      ValueFunction = delegate(TriggerActions action)
      {
        return "dbo.fnGetContextData()";
      }
    };

    var timeStamp = new AuditColumn()
    {
      Name = "AuditTimestamp",
```

```
        Value = new SimpleValue()
        {
          TypeName = NHibernateUtil.DateTime.Name
        },
        IsNullable = false,
        IncludeInPrimaryKey = true,
        ValueFunction = delegate(TriggerActions action)
        {
          return "getdate()";
        }
      };

      var operation = new AuditColumn()
      {
        Name = "AuditOperation",
        Value = new SimpleValue()
        {
          TypeName = NHibernateUtil.AnsiChar.Name
        },
        Length = 1,
        IsNullable = false,
        IncludeInPrimaryKey = false,
        ValueFunction = delegate(TriggerActions action)
        {
          switch (action)
          {
            case TriggerActions.INSERT:
              return "'I'";
            case TriggerActions.UPDATE:
              return "'U'";
            case TriggerActions.DELETE:
              return "'D'";
            default:
              throw new ArgumentOutOfRangeException("action");
          }
        }
      };

      return new AuditColumn[] {
        userStamp, timeStamp, operation
      };

    }

  }
```

3. Add the following `IContextDataProvider` interface:

```
public interface IContextDataProvider
{

  string GetData();
  string GetEmptyData();

}
```

4. Add the following implementation:

```
public class UsernameContextDataProvider :
  IContextDataProvider
{

  public string GetData()
  {
    return WindowsIdentity.GetCurrent().Name;
  }

  public string GetEmptyData()
  {
    return string.Empty;
  }

}
```

5. Add the following `ContextConnectionDriver`:

```
public class ContextInfoConnectionDriver :
  DriverConnectionProvider
{

  private const string COMMAND_TEXT =
    "declare @length tinyint\n" +
    "declare @ctx varbinary(128)\n" +
    "select @length = len(@data)\n" +
    "select @ctx = convert(binary(1), @length) + " +
    "convert(binary(127), @data)\n" +
    "set context_info @ctx";


  public override IDbConnection GetConnection()
  {
    var conn = base.GetConnection();
```

```
      SetContext(conn);
      return conn;
    }

    public override void CloseConnection(IDbConnection conn)
    {
      EraseContext(conn);
      base.CloseConnection(conn);
    }

    private void SetContext(IDbConnection conn)
    {
      var sl = ServiceLocator.Current;
      var dataProvider = sl.GetInstance<IContextDataProvider>();
      var data = dataProvider.GetData();
      SetContext(conn, data);
    }

    private void EraseContext(IDbConnection conn)
    {
      var sl = ServiceLocator.Current;
      var dataProvider = sl.GetInstance<IContextDataProvider>();
      var data = dataProvider.GetEmptyData();
      SetContext(conn, data);
    }

    private void SetContext(IDbConnection conn, string data)
    {
      var cmd = conn.CreateCommand();
      cmd.CommandType = CommandType.Text;
      cmd.CommandText = COMMAND_TEXT;

      var param = cmd.CreateParameter();
      param.ParameterName = "@data";
      param.DbType = DbType.AnsiString;
      param.Size = 127;
      param.Value = data;
      cmd.Parameters.Add(param);

      cmd.ExecuteNonQuery();
    }

}
```

6. Add the following mapping document:

```xml
<?xml version="1.0" encoding="utf-8" ?>
<hibernate-mapping xmlns="urn:nhibernate-mapping-2.2">
  <database-object>
    <create>
      CREATE FUNCTION dbo.fnGetContextData()
      RETURNS varchar(127)
      AS
      BEGIN
        declare @data varchar(127)
        declare @length tinyint
        declare @ctx varbinary(128)
        select @ctx = CONTEXT_INFO()
        select @length = convert(tinyint,
            substring(@ctx, 1, 1))
        select @data = convert(varchar(127),
            substring(@ctx, 2, 1 + @length))
        return @data
      END
    </create>
    <drop>DROP FUNCTION dbo.fnGetContextData</drop>
  </database-object>
</hibernate-mapping>
```

7. In the `Main` method of `Program.cs`, use the following code:

```csharp
var kernel = new StandardKernel();
kernel.Bind<IContextDataProvider>()
  .To<UsernameContextDataProvider>();
var sl = new NinjectServiceLocator(kernel);
ServiceLocator.SetLocatorProvider(() => sl);

var namingStrategy = new NamingStrategy();
var auditColumnSource = new CtxAuditColumnSource();
var cfg = new Configuration().Configure();
new TriggerAuditing(cfg, namingStrategy,
  auditColumnSource).Configure();

var sessionFaculty = cfg.BuildSessionFactory();

var se = new NHibernate.Tool.hbm2ddl.SchemaExport(cfg);
se.Execute(true, true, false);
```

8. Set the NHibernate property `connection.provider` to `<namespace>.ContextInfoConnectionDriver, <assembly>`, to set the namespace and assembly according to the name of your project.

9. Add a mapping element for this assembly so that the `fnGetContextData` mapping document is loaded.

10. Build and run the program.

How it works...

Starting with Microsoft SQL Server 2000, SQL Server provides 128 bytes of context data for each database connection. This data is set using the SQL statement `SET CONTEXT_INFO @ContextData` where `@ContextData` may be a `binary(128)` variable or constant. It can be read using the `CONTEXT_INFO()` SQL function, which returns `binary(128)` data.

In this recipe, we store the current username in the `CONTEXT_INFO`. It's important to note that the `CONTEXT_INFO` is a fixed-length `binary` array, not a variable-length `varbinary`. When placing data into `CONTEXT_INFO`, any leftover bytes may contain trash.

Similar to storing strings in memory, when storing variable-length data in this fixed-length field, we must have some way to determine where the real data ends. The two possible ways to do this are as follows:

▶ Taking the Pascal strings approach, we can use the first byte to determine the length of the data. This limits the amount of data that can be stored to 255 characters. This is fine, because SQL Server only allows half that amount.

▶ Using the C string approach, we place a null terminator (zero byte) at the end of the string. The data can be any length, but we have to search for the null terminator to find the end.

In this recipe, we use the Pascal string approach. The `fnGetContextData` SQL function uses the first byte to determine the correct `substring` parameters to get our username string from the `CONTEXT_INFO()`.

Because the `Context_Info` is tied to the database connection, we need to set it every time we open a database connection. Additionally, because our application will most likely use connection pooling, we should also clear the `Context_Info` when the application releases the connection back to the pool.

NHibernate's `DriverConnectionProvider` is responsible for providing a database connection as needed, and for closing those connections when they're no longer needed. This is the perfect place to set our `Context_Info`. The custom connection provider will set the `Context_Info` after the connection is opened, but before it's passed back to NHibernate. It also clears the `Context_Info` just before calling `conn.Close()` to return the connection to the connection pool.

The `AuditUser` column has been changed from our previous recipe so that our triggers call `fnGetContextData()` instead of using `system_user`.

Finally, we've added `fnGetContextData` as an auxiliary database object with our `database-object` mapping. This mapping provides the drop- and- create scripts used by `hbm2ddl`.

All of this allows us to use the application's current username in our audit logs. We can use any SQL credentials we like, including plain old SQL accounts. Of course, just as with the *Creation and change stamping of entities* recipe, you will likely need to replace `WindowsIdentity.GetCurrent()` with the correct implementation for your application.

See also

▸ *Generating trigger-based auditing*

▸ *Using dynamic connection strings*

▸ *Creation and change stamping of entities*

Using dynamic connection strings

There are cases where an application may need to change connection strings depending on some condition. This can be in the context of a multi-tenant application, or perhaps a database failover scenario. In this recipe, we'll show you how to switch NHibernate connection strings at runtime.

How to do it...

1. Start a new console application project named `DynamicConnectionString`.

2. Add references to `NHibernate.dll`, `log4net.dll`, and the `Eg.Core` model from *Chapter 1, The Configuration and Schema*.

3. Add a reference to `System.Configuration` from the .NET framework.

4. Set up `App.config` with a standard NHibernate and log4net configuration.

5. Add the following `DynamicConnectionProvider` class:

```
public class DynamicConnectionProvider :
  DriverConnectionProvider
{

    private const string ANON_CONN_NAME = "db";
    private const string AUTH_CONN_NAME = "auth_db";

    protected override string ConnectionString
```

```
    {
      get
      {
        var connstrs = ConfigurationManager.ConnectionStrings;
        var connstr = connstrs[ANON_CONN_NAME];
        if (IsAuthenticated())
          connstr = connstrs[AUTH_CONN_NAME];
        return connstr.ConnectionString;
      }
    }

    private bool IsAuthenticated()
    {
      var identity = WindowsIdentity.GetCurrent();
      return identity != null && identity.IsAuthenticated;
    }

  }
```

6. Add the following two connection strings to `App.config`:

```
<add name="db" connectionString=
"Server=.\SQLExpress; Database=NHCookbook;
User Id=AnonymousUser; Password=p455w0rd"/>
<add name="auth_db" connectionString=
"Server=.\SQLExpress; Database=NHCookbook;
Trusted_Connection=SSPI"/>
```

7. Set the NHibernate property `connection.provider` to `DynamicConnectionString.DynamicConnectionProvider, DynamicConnectionString`.

8. Build and run the program.

How it works...

Just like we did in our previous recipe, we are using a custom connection provider. However, this time, we only override the `ConnectionString` property to return different connection strings for anonymous and authenticated users. We set the NHibernate configuration property `connection.provider` to the assembly-qualified name of our custom connection provider, and NHibernate handles the rest.

See also

▶ *Setting Microsoft SQL's Context_Info*

Using custom dialect functions

In this recipe, we will show how you can add mappings for database functions, which are not available by default.

How to do it...

1. Create a new class library project named `CustomDialectExample`.

2. Install the `NHibernate` and `log4net` packages using the NuGet Package Manager Console by executing the following command:

```
Install-Package NHibernate
Install-Package log4net
```

3. Create a new class named `CustomMsSql2012Dialect` using the following code:

```
public class CustomMsSq2012Dialect:
  MsSql2012Dialect
{
  public CustomMsSq2012Dialect()
  {
    RegisterFunction("AddDays",
      new SQLFunctionTemplate(
        NHibernateUtil.DateTime,
        "dateadd(day,?2,?1)"));
    RegisterFunction("AddHours",
      new SQLFunctionTemplate(
        NHibernateUtil.DateTime,
        "dateadd(hour,?2,?1)"));
    RegisterFunction("AddMinutes",
      new SQLFunctionTemplate(
        NHibernateUtil.DateTime,
        "dateadd(minute,?2,?1)"));
    RegisterFunction("AddSeconds",
      new SQLFunctionTemplate(
        NHibernateUtil.DateTime,
        "dateadd(second,?2,?1)"));
    RegisterFunction("AddMilliseconds",
      new SQLFunctionTemplate(
        NHibernateUtil.DateTime,
        "dateadd(millisecond,?2,?1)"));
  }
}
```

4. Use this dialect in your configuration, as described in *Chapter 1, The Configuration and Schema.*

How it works...

The dialect has the `RegisterFunction` method, but it is not public, as all dialects are tightly coupled to the RDBMS they represent. Thus, to register a custom function we create a custom dialect class.

We use the `SQLFunctionTemplate` class to register four of our custom functions. This class implements the `ISQLFunction` interface. This interface is responsible for rendering the function into SQL.

See also

▶ *Configuring NHibernate with hibernate.cfg.xml*

▶ *Configuring NHibernate with .config file*

▶ *Configuring NHibernate with code*

▶ *Configuring NHibernate with Fluent NHibernate*

▶ *Using custom functions in LINQ*

Using custom functions in LINQ

In this recipe, we will show you how to map database functions and stored procedures to LINQ functions.

Getting ready

Complete the previous recipe, *Using custom dialect functions.*

How to do it...

1. Create a new class library project named `CustomLinqGenearatorExample`.

2. Install the `NHibernate` and `log4net` packages using the NuGet Package Manager Console by executing the following command:

```
Install-Package NHibernate
Install-Package log4net
```

3. Create the `SqlFunctions` class using the following code:

```
public static class SqlFunctions
{
  [LinqExtensionMethod]
  public static DateTime AddDays(DateTime dt, int d)
  {
    return dt.AddDays(d);
  }

  [LinqExtensionMethod]
  public static DateTime AddHours(DateTime dt, int h)
  {
    return dt.AddHours(h);
  }

  [LinqExtensionMethod]
  public static DateTime AddMinutes(DateTime dt, int m)
  {
    return dt.AddMinutes(m);
  }

  [LinqExtensionMethod]
  public static DateTime AddSeconds(DateTime dt, int s)
  {
    return dt.AddSeconds(s);
  }

  [LinqExtensionMethod]
  public static DateTime AddMilliseconds(
    DateTime dt,
    int ms)
  {
    return dt.AddMilliseconds(ms);
  }
}
```

How it works...

The LINQ provider will scan all methods inside the `Linq` expression for the `[LinqExtensionMethod]` attribute. For each of these methods, it will call the default LINQ to the HQL generator, simply replacing a call to the method with a call to the corresponding SQL function name. By default, the function name will be the same as the method name, but you can specify it using the constructor argument to the `[LinqExtensionMethod]` attribute.

See also

▶ *Using custom dialect functions*

▶ *Extending the LINQ provider*

Extending the LINQ provider

Sometimes you will need a more sophisticated way to translate method calls to HQL. In this recipe, we will show you how to implement a custom LINQ to HQL generator that is able to do this.

Getting ready

Complete the *Using custom dialect functions* recipe.

How to do it...

1. Create a new class library project named `CustomLinqGenearatorExample`.

2. Install the `NHibernate` and `log4net` packages using the NuGet Package Manager Console by executing the following command:

   ```
   Install-Package NHibernate

   Install-Package log4net
   ```

3. Create the `DateTimeFunctionsGenerator` class using the following code:

   ```
   public class DateTimeFunctionsGenerator
     : BaseHqlGeneratorForMethod
   {
     public DateTimeFunctionsGenerator()
     {
       SupportedMethods = new[]
       {
   ```

```
      ReflectionHelper.GetMethod<DateTime>(
        d => d.AddDays(0)),
      ReflectionHelper.GetMethod<DateTimeOffset>(
        d => d.AddDays(0)),
      ReflectionHelper.GetMethod<DateTime>(
        d => d.AddHours(0)),
      ReflectionHelper.GetMethod<DateTimeOffset>(
        d => d.AddHours(0)),
      ReflectionHelper.GetMethod<DateTime>(
        d => d.AddMinutes(0)),
      ReflectionHelper.GetMethod<DateTimeOffset>(
        d => d.AddMinutes(0)),
      ReflectionHelper.GetMethod<DateTime>(
        d => d.AddSeconds(0)),
      ReflectionHelper.GetMethod<DateTimeOffset>(
        d => d.AddSeconds(0)),
      ReflectionHelper.GetMethod<DateTime>(
        d => d.AddMilliseconds(0)),
      ReflectionHelper.GetMethod<DateTimeOffset>(
        d => d.AddMilliseconds(0)),
    };
  }

  public override HqlTreeNode BuildHql(
    MethodInfo method,
    Expression targetObject,
    ReadOnlyCollection<Expression> arguments,
    HqlTreeBuilder treeBuilder,
    IHqlExpressionVisitor visitor)
  {
    return treeBuilder.MethodCall(
      method.Name,
      visitor.Visit(targetObject).AsExpression(),
      visitor.Visit(arguments[0]).AsExpression());
  }
}
```

4. Create the `CustomLinqtoHqlGeneratorsRegistry` class using the following code:

```
public class CustomLinqtoHqlGeneratorsRegistry
  : DefaultLinqToHqlGeneratorsRegistry
{
  public CustomLinqtoHqlGeneratorsRegistry()
  {
```

```
        this.Merge(new DateTimeFunctionsGenerator());
    }
}
```

5. Register the `CustomLinqtoHqlGeneratorsRegistry` into a configuration using the following code:

```
cfg.SetProperty(
    Environment.LinqToHqlGeneratorsRegistry,
    typeof (CustomLinqtoHqlGeneratorsRegistry).
        AssemblyQualifiedName)
```

How it works...

In the constructor of `DateTimeFunctionsGenerator`, we define the methods that are supported by this HQL generator. In this case, we want to be able to handle `AddDays`, `AddHours`, `AddMinutes`, `AddSeconds`, and `AddMilliseconds` of `DateTime`, and `DateTimeOfset types`. We are using `ReflectionHelper.GetMethod` to extract the methods from the expression tree.

The `BuildHql` method of `DateTimeFunctionsGenerator` is responsible for translating our method call to the HQL expression.

Then we register our custom generator in the HQL generator registry. After that we register our custom registry to the configuration.

See also

▶ *Using custom dialect functions*
▶ *Using custom functions in LINQ*

9
NHibernate Contribution Projects

In this chapter, we will cover the following topics:

- ▶ Property validation with attributes
- ▶ Creating validator classes
- ▶ Setting up full-text searches
- ▶ Auditing data with Envers
- ▶ Using NHibernate Spatial

Introduction

The NHibernate Contribution projects are available at `http://github.com/nhibernate` and provide a number of useful extensions to NHibernate. The recipes in this chapter introduce some of these extremely powerful add-ons.

Property validation with attributes

NHibernate Validator provides data validation for classes. In this recipe, we will show you how to use NHibernate Validator attributes to validate your entities.

Getting ready

Complete the `Eg.Core` model and mappings from *Chapter 2, Models and Mappings*.

How to do it...

1. Create a new class library project named `Eg.AttributeValidation`.

2. Copy the `Eg.Core` model and mappings from *Chapter 2, Models and Mappings* to this new project.

3. Change the namespace and assembly references in the mappings to `Eg.AttributeValidation`.

4. Change the namespaces for the entity classes to `Eg.AttributeValidation`.

5. Install the NHibernate Validator package using NuGet Package Manager Console by running the following command:

```
Install-Package NHibernate.Validator -Project
Eg.AttributeValidation
```

6. Create a new attribute class named `NotNegativeDecimalAttribute` with the following code:

```
[Serializable]
[AttributeUsage(AttributeTargets.Field | AttributeTargets.
Property)]
    public class NotNegativeDecimalAttribute
    : DecimalMinAttribute
{
    public NotNegativeDecimalAttribute()
    : base(0M)
    {
    }
}
```

7. Open `Product.cs` and add the following attributes:

```
public class Product : Entity
{
    [NotNull, Length(Min=1, Max=255)]
    public virtual string Name { get; set; }

    [NotNullNotEmpty]
    public virtual string Description { get; set; }

    [NotNull, NotNegativeDecimal]
    public virtual Decimal UnitPrice { get; set; }
}
```

8. Create a new console project named `Eg.AttributeValidation.Runner`.

9. Install NHibernate, NHibernate Validator, and log4net packages to the `Eg.AttributeValidation.Runner` project using NuGet Package Manager Console by running the following commands:

```
Install-Package NHibernate
```

```
Install-Package NHibernate.Validator
```

```
Install-Package log4net
```

10. Set up an `App.config` with the standard `log4net` and `hibernate-configuration` sections, just as we did in the *Configuring NHibernate with App. config* and *Configuring NHibernate logging* recipes in *Chapter 2, Models and Mappings*.

11. In the `<configSections>` element, add an additional section declaration named `nhv-configuration` with the following xml:

```xml
<section name="nhv-configuration"
type="NHibernate.Validator.Cfg.ConfigurationSectionHandler,
NHibernate.Validator" />
```

12. Add the `<nhv-configuration>` section with the following xml:

```xml
<nhv-configuration xmlns="urn:nhv-configuration-1.0">
    <property name='apply_to_ddl'>true</property>
    <property name='autoregister_listeners'>true</property>
    <property name='default_validator_mode'>
    OverrideExternalWithAttribute</property>
    <mapping assembly='Eg.AttributeValidation'/>
</nhv-configuration>
```

13. Add a new class named `BasicSharedEngineProvider` using the following code:

```csharp
public class BasicSharedEngineProvider :
ISharedEngineProvider
  {
    private readonly ValidatorEngine ve;
    public BasicSharedEngineProvider(ValidatorEngine ve)
    {
      this.ve = ve;
    }
    public ValidatorEngine GetEngine()
    {
        return ve;
    }
    public void UseMe()
    {
        Environment.SharedEngineProvider = this;
    }
  }
```

14. In `Program.cs`, use the following code:

```csharp
class Program
{
  static void Main(string[] args)
  {
    XmlConfigurator.Configure();
    var log = LogManager.GetLogger(typeof(Program));

    SetupNHibernateValidator();

    var cfg = new Configuration().Configure();
    cfg.Initialize();

    var sessionFactory = cfg.BuildSessionFactory();

    var schemaExport = new SchemaExport(cfg);
    schemaExport.Execute(true, true, false);

    var junk = new Product
                {
                  Name = "Spiffy Junk",
                  Description = "Stuff we can't sell.",
                  UnitPrice = -1M
                };

    using (var session = sessionFactory.OpenSession())
    using (var tx = session.BeginTransaction())
    {
    try
      {
        session.Save(junk);
        tx.Commit();
      }
    catch (InvalidStateException validationException)
    {
      var errors =validationException.GetInvalidValues();
      foreach (var error in errors)
        {
        log.ErrorFormat("Error with property {0}: {1}",
          error.PropertyName,
          error.Message);
        }
```

```
        tx.Rollback();
      }
    }
  }

  private static ValidatorEngine GetValidatorEngine()
  {
    var validatorEngine = new ValidatorEngine();
    validatorEngine.Configure();
    return validatorEngine;
  }

  private static void SetupNHibernateValidator()
  {
    var validatorEngine = GetValidatorEngine();
    new BasicSharedEngineProvider(validatorEngine).UseMe();
  }
}
```

15. Build and run your program.

How it works...

NHibernate Validator, or NHV, has a few major components. `ValidatorEngine` is the main class that is used to interact with NHV. Similar to the session factory, applications typically have only one instance. NHV uses an implementation of `ISharedEngineProvider` to find the single instance of the `ValidatorEngine`. NHV can be used independently from NHibernate to validate any class. When integrated with NHibernate, it validates each entity before inserting or updating data. This integration is accomplished through the `ValidatePreInsertEventListener` and `ValidatePreUpdateEventListener` event listeners.

To integrate NHV with NHibernate, we begin by creating a `ValidatorEngine`. The call to `ValidatorEngine.Configure()` loads our NHV configuration from the `App.config`. Next, we create an `ISharedEngineProvider` to return our `ValidatorEngine`. We configure NHV to use the shared engine provider by setting the static property `Environment.SharedEngineProvider`. Finally, after configuring NHibernate, but before creating the session factory, we call `Initialize()`, an NHV extension method, for the NHibernate configuration object.

Our NHV configuration, in `App.config`, contains the following four configuration settings:

- `apply_to_ddl`: When this property is set to `true`, `hbm2ddl` will generate database constraints to enforce many of our validation attributes. For example, the script to create our `UnitPrice` column, shown next, now has a check constraint to enforce our `NotNegativeDecimal` rule:

  ```
  UnitPrice DECIMAL(19,5) not null check(UnitPrice>=0)
  ```

- `autoregister_listeners`: This property determines if the `Initialize` extension method will add the `pre-insert` and `pre-update` event listeners to the NHibernate configuration or not.

- `default_validator_mode`: This property determines the priority of validation rules when using a mix of XML validation definitions, validation classes, or attributes.

- The NHV mapping element behaves similarly to the NHibernate mapping element. It defines an assembly containing our entities decorated with attributes.

In this recipe, we attempt to save a new product with a negative `UnitPrice`. This violates our `NotNegativeDecimal` validation rule. Without NHibernate Validator, our application will silently accept the invalid data, leading to potentially larger problems later. If we had simply added a constraint in the database, our application would attempt to insert the bad data, then throw an unwieldy `SQLException` that gives us no information about which property is invalid and why. With NHibernate Validator, the event listeners validate each entity before data is written to the database. If they find invalid data, they throw an `InvalidStateException` that tells us exactly which properties of the entity are invalid and why.

[When a validation event listener throws an `InvalidStateException`, the session is in an undefined state. Once this happens, the only operation that can be safely performed on the session is `Dispose`.]

You may be wondering why we created a separate `NotNegativeDecimalAttribute` class. Couldn't we have just decorated our `UnitPrice` property with `[DecimalMin(0M)]`? As it turns out, we can't do this. In C#, we can't use `Decimal` parameters in this manner. To work around this limitation, we subclass the `DecimalMinAttribute` and hardcode the zero inside the `NotNegativeDecimalAttribute` class.

In our assemblies, attribute decorations are not stored as **Intermediate Language** (**IL**) instructions, but as metadata. This limits the types we can use as parameters. The C# specification available on `http://msdn.microsoft.com/en-us/library/aa664615` defines the types that can be used as `bool`, `byte`, `char`, `double`, `float`, `int`, `long`, `short`, `string`, `object`, `System.Type`, `enum`, or any one-dimensional array of these types. `Decimal` is not on the list.

If you check your entities for invalid data prior to saving them, you don't run the risk of blowing up the NHibernate session. To validate an object explicitly, your code might look similar to this:

```
var ve = Environment.SharedEngineProvider.GetEngine();
var invalidValues = ve.Validate(someObject);
```

invalidValues is an array of InvalidValue objects describing each failed validation rule. If it's empty, the object is valid. If not, you can easily display the validation messages to the user without risking the session.

NHibernateValidator can be used to validate any class, not just NHibernate entities. You can easily adapt this sort of explicit validation to integrate with ASP.NET MVC's model validation.

See also

▶ *Creating validator classes*

Creating validator classes

In the previous recipe, we saw how to decorate our entity classes with NHibernate Validator. A better practice is to extract your validation rules to separate classes and avoid this dependency. In this recipe, we'll show you how to create validator classes, as well as an alternative method for configuring NHibernate Validator.

Getting ready

Complete the Eg.Core model and mappings from *Chapter 1, The Configuration and Schema*.

How to do it...

1. Create a new class library project named Eg.ClassValidation.
2. Add a reference to the Eg.Core model.
3. Install the NHibernate Validator package using NuGet Package Manager Console by executing the following command:

   ```
   Install-Package NHibernate.Validator
   ```

4. Add the following `ProductValidation` class:

```
public class ProductValidator : ValidationDef<Product>
{

    public ProductValidator()
    {
      Define(p => p.Name)
        .NotNullableAndNotEmpty()
        .And.MaxLength(255);

      Define(p => p.Description)
        .NotNullableAndNotEmpty();

      Define(p => p.UnitPrice)
        .GreaterThanOrEqualTo(0M)
        .WithMessage("Unit price can't be negative.");

    }

}
```

5. Create a new console application named `Eg.ClassValidation.Runner`.

6. Install the NHibernate, NHibernate Validator, and log4net packages to `Eg.ClassValidation.Runner` project using NuGet Package Manager Console by running the following command:

   Install-Package NHibernate

   Install-Package NHibernate.Validator

   Install-Package log4net

7. Set up an `App.config` with the standard `log4net` and `hibernate-configuration` sections, following the *Configuring NHibernate with App.config* and *Configuring NHibernate logging* recipes from *Chapter 1, The Configuration and Schema*.

8. Add a new class named `BasicSharedEngineProvider` using the following code:

```
public class BasicSharedEngineProvider : ISharedEngineProvider
{

    private readonly ValidatorEngine ve;

    public BasicSharedEngineProvider(ValidatorEngine ve)
    {
      this.ve = ve;
```

```
  }

  public ValidatorEngine GetEngine()
  {
    return ve;
  }

  public void UseMe()
  {
    Environment.SharedEngineProvider = this;
  }

}
```

9. In `Program.cs`, use the following code:

```
private static void Main(string[] args)
{
  XmlConfigurator.Configure();
  var log = LogManager.GetLogger(typeof (Program));

  SetupNHibernateValidator();

  var nhibernateConfig = new Configuration().Configure();
  nhibernateConfig.Initialize();
  ISessionFactory sessionFactory = nhibernateConfig.
  BuildSessionFactory();
  var schemaExport = new SchemaExport(nhibernateConfig);
  schemaExport.Execute(false, true, false);
  var junk = new Product
  {
    Name = "Spiffy Junk",
    Description = string.Empty,
    UnitPrice = -1M
  };

  var ve = Environment.SharedEngineProvider.GetEngine();
  var invalidValues = ve.Validate(junk);
  foreach (var invalidValue in invalidValues)
  {
    log.InfoFormat("{0} {1}",
      invalidValue.PropertyName,
```

```
                    invalidValue.Message);
        }

    }

    private static FluentConfiguration GetNhvConfiguration()
    {
        var nhvConfiguration = new FluentConfiguration();
        nhvConfiguration
            .SetDefaultValidatorMode(ValidatorMode.UseExternal)
            .Register(Assembly.Load("Eg.ClassValidation")
                        .ValidationDefinitions())
            .IntegrateWithNHibernate
            .ApplyingDDLConstraints()
            .And.RegisteringListeners();
        return nhvConfiguration;
    }

    private static ValidatorEngine GetValidatorEngine()
    {
        var cfg = GetNhvConfiguration();
        var validatorEngine = new ValidatorEngine();
        validatorEngine.Configure(cfg);
        return validatorEngine;
    }

    private static void SetupNHibernateValidator()
    {
        var validatorEngine = GetValidatorEngine();
        new BasicSharedEngineProvider(validatorEngine).UseMe();
    }
```

10. Build and run your application.

How it works...

In this recipe, we have separated our validation rules into a separate class named
ProductValidation. Just as we did in our previous recipe, we have decided that each
valid Product must have a non-null, non-empty Name, a Description (not more than 255
characters long), and a non-negative UnitPrice.

As we learned in the previous recipe, we use an ISharedEngineProvider to locate our
validation engine.

Unlike the previous recipe, we use the loquacious, or fluent, syntax to configure NHibernate Validator.

We validate our `junk Product`. It fails two validation rules. First, the `Description` can't be empty. Second, the `UnitPrice` can't be negative. As we see in the log4net output, we get the following validation error messages:

```
Description may not be null or empty

UnitPrice can't be negative
```

There's more...

We can also use NHibernate Validator to validate an entire object graph. Let's take our Movie entity as an example. Suppose we want to ensure that the movie entity is valid, as well as all of its ActorRole children. Our validation class would appear as shown:

```
Define(m => m.Director)
  .NotNullableAndNotEmpty()
  .And.MaxLength(255);

Define(m => m.Actors)
  .HasValidElements();
```

The `HasValidElements` runs the ActorRole validation rules on each object in the `Actors` collection.

See also

▶ *Property validation with attributes*

Setting up full-text searches

While many relational databases provide some mechanism for full-text searches, these databases are optimized for **Online Transaction Processing** (**OLTP**) type workloads. Full-text search engines, on the other hand, are designed specifically for text queries, and excel at them. In this recipe, we'll show you how to use NHibernate search and `Lucene.Net` to provide full-text search capabilities to your applications.

Getting ready

Complete the `Eg.Core` model and mappings from *Chapter 1, The Configuration and Schema*.

How to do it...

1. Install the NHibernate Search package the to `Eg.Core` project using NuGet Package Manager Console by running the following command:

   ```
   Install-Package NHibernate.Search
   ```

2. In the `Entity` base class, decorate the `Id` property with the `[DocumentId]` attribute from `NHibernate.Search.Attributes`.

3. Add the following attributes to the `Product` class:

   ```
   [Indexed]
   public class Product : Entity
     {
     [Field]
     public virtual string Name { get; set; }

     [Field]
     public virtual string Description { get; set; }
     public virtual Decimal UnitPrice { get; set; }
   }
   ```

4. Add the following attributes to the `Book` class:

   ```
   [Indexed]
   public class Book : Product
   {
       [Field(Index = Index.UnTokenized)]
       public virtual string ISBN { get; set; }

       [Field]
       public virtual string Author { get; set; }
   }
   ```

5. Create a new console project named `Eg.Search.Runner`.

6. Install the NHibernate search and log4net packages to the `Eg.Search.Runner` project using NuGet Package Manager Console by running the following commands:

   ```
   Install-Package NHibernate.Search
   ```

   ```
   Install-Package log4net
   ```

7. Add an `App.config` file with the standard `log4net` and `hibernate-configuration` sections.

8. Add a new class named `SearchConfiguration` using the following code:

```
public class SearchConfiguration
{

  public ISessionFactory BuildSessionFactory()
  {
    var cfg = new Configuration().Configure();
    SetSearchProps(cfg);
    AddSearchListeners(cfg);
    var sessionFactory = cfg.BuildSessionFactory();
    return sessionFactory;
  }

  private void SetSearchProps(Configuration cfg)
  {
     cfg.SetProperty(
     "hibernate.search.default.directory_provider",
      typeof(FSDirectoryProvider)
      .AssemblyQualifiedName);

       cfg.SetProperty(
       "hibernate.search.default.indexBase","~/Index");
  }

  private void AddSearchListeners(Configuration cfg)
  {
    cfg.SetListener(ListenerType.PostUpdate,
      new FullTextIndexEventListener());
    cfg.SetListener(ListenerType.PostInsert,
      new FullTextIndexEventListener());
    cfg.SetListener(ListenerType.PostDelete,
      new FullTextIndexEventListener());
    cfg.SetListener(ListenerType.PostCollectionRecreate,
      new FullTextIndexCollectionEventListener());
    cfg.SetListener(ListenerType.PostCollectionRemove,
      new FullTextIndexCollectionEventListener());
    cfg.SetListener(ListenerType.PostCollectionUpdate,
      new FullTextIndexCollectionEventListener());
  }
}
```

9. In `Program.cs`, use the following code:

```
class Program
  {
    static void Main(string[] args)
     {
       XmlConfigurator.Configure();
       var log = LogManager.GetLogger(typeof(Program));
       var cfg = new SearchConfiguration();
       var sessionFactory = cfg.BuildSessionFactory();
       var theBook = new Book()
         {
            Name = @"Gödel, Escher, Bach: An Eternal Golden Braid",
            Author = "Douglas Hofstadter",
            Description = @"This groundbreaking Pulitzer
              Prize-winning book
            sets the standard for interdisciplinary writing,
              exploring the
            patterns and symbols in the thinking of mathematician
              Kurt Godel,
            artist M.C. Escher, and composer Johann Sebastian
              Bach.",
            ISBN = "978-0465026562",
            UnitPrice = 22.95M
         };
       var theOtherBook = new Book()
         {
            Name = "Technical Writing",
            Author = "Joe Professor",
            Description = "College text",
            ISBN = "123-1231231234",
            UnitPrice = 143.73M
         };
       var thePoster = new Product()
         {
            Name = "Ascending and Descending",
            Description = "Poster of famous Escher print",
            UnitPrice = 7.95M
         };
       using (var session = sessionFactory.OpenSession())
       using (var tx = session.BeginTransaction())
         {
            session.Delete("from Product");
            tx.Commit();
         }
```

```csharp
      using (var session = sessionFactory.OpenSession())
      using (var tx = session.BeginTransaction())
       {
         session.Save(theBook);
         session.Save(theOtherBook);
         session.Save(thePoster);
         tx.Commit();
       }
   var products = GetEscherProducts(sessionFactory);
      OutputProducts(products, log);
      var books = GetEscherBooks(sessionFactory);
      OutputProducts(books.Cast<Product>(), log);
  }
  private static void OutputProducts(
  IEnumerable<Product> products,
  ILog log)
   {
      foreach (var product in products)
       {
         log.InfoFormat(
         "Found {0} with price {1:C}",
         product.Name,
         product.UnitPrice);
       }
   }
  private static IEnumerable<Product>
  GetEscherProducts(
  ISessionFactory sessionFactory)
   {
      IEnumerable<Product> results;
      using (var session = sessionFactory.OpenSession())
      using (var search = Search.CreateFullTextSession(
      session))
      using (var tx = session.BeginTransaction())
    {
      var queryString = "Description:Escher";
      var query = search
      .CreateFullTextQuery<Product>(queryString);
      results = query.List<Product>();
      tx.Commit();
    }
   return results;
   }
```

```
private static IEnumerable<Book> GetEscherBooks(
ISessionFactory sessionFactory)
  {
   IEnumerable<Book> results;
   using (var session = sessionFactory.OpenSession())
   using (var search = Search.CreateFullTextSession(session))
   using (var tx = session.BeginTransaction())
   {
    var queryString = "Description:Escher";
    var query = search
    .CreateFullTextQuery<Book>(queryString);
    results = query.List<Book>();
    tx.Commit();
   }
   return results;
  }
 }
```

10. Build and run your application

How it works...

In this recipe, we've offloaded our full-text queries to a Lucene index in the bin/Debug/ Index folder.

First, let us quickly discuss some Lucene terminologies. The Lucene database is referred to as an Index. Each record in the Index is referred to as a document. In the case of NHibernate Search, each document in the Index has a corresponding entity in the relational database. Each document has fields and each field comprises a name and value. By default, fields are tokenized or broken up into terms. A term can best be described as a single, significant, and lowercase word from some string of words. For example, the string Bag of Cats can be tokenized into the terms bag and cat. Additionally, Lucene maintains a map of terms in a field, details of which documents contain a given term, and the frequency of that term in the document. This makes keyword searches extremely fast.

Entity classes with the Indexed attribute will be included as documents in the Lucene index. The remaining attributes are used to determine which properties from these entities should be included in the document, and how that data will be stored. Automatically, the _hibernate_class field stores the entity type. Each searchable entity must have a field or property decorated with the DocumentId attribute. This is stored in the Id field, and is used to maintain the relationship between entities and documents. In our case, the Id property on Entity will be used.

To be useful, we should include additional data in our documents using the `Field` attribute. For keyword searches, we've included the tokenized name and description of every product, and the author of every book. We've also included the ISBN of every book, but have chosen not to tokenize it because a partial ISBN match is useless.

The `SearchConfiguration` class is responsible for building an NHibernate configuration, adding the necessary NHibernate Search settings to the configuration, and building an NHibernate session factory.

The `Search.CreateFullTextSession` method wraps the standard NHibernate session and returns `IFullTextSearchSession`. These sessions behave as normal NHibernate sessions, but provide additional methods for creating full-text search queries against the Lucene index. The `CreateFullTextQuery` method of the session takes a Lucene query in string or query object form and returns a familiar NHibernate `IQuery` interface, the same interface used for HQL and SQL queries. When we call `List` or `UniqueResult`, the query is executed against our Lucene index. For example, the query in our `GetEscherProduct` query will search Lucene for documents with a `Description` containing the term escher. This query returns two results: the GEB book and the M. C. Escher poster. The IDs of all of those search results are gathered up and used to build a SQL database query similar to the next query.

```
SELECT  this_.Id          as Id0_0_,
        this_.Name        as Name0_0_,
        this_.Description as Descript4_0_0_,
        this_.UnitPrice   as UnitPrice0_0_,
        this_.Director    as Director0_0_,
        this_.Author      as Author0_0_,
        this_.ISBN        as ISBN0_0_,
        this_.ProductType as ProductT2_0_0_
FROM    Product this_
WHERE   (this_.Id in ('5933e3ba-3092-4db7-8d19-9daf014b8ce4' /* @p0
*/,'05058886-8436-4a1d-8412-9db1010561b5' /* @p1 */))
```

It is amazingly fast because this database query is performed on the primary key. The Lucene query is fast because the index was specially designed for that purpose. This has the potential for huge performance and functionality gains over the weak full-text search capabilities in most relational databases.

There's more...

This is just the most basic example of what we can do with NHibernate Search. We can also choose to store the original value of a field in the document. This is useful when we want to display Lucene query results without querying the SQL database. Additionally, Lucene has many more features, such as search-term highlighting and spell-checking. Although Lucene is a very capable document database, remember that it is not relational. There is no support for relationships or references between documents stored in a Lucene index.

Auditing data with Envers

A common business requirement in application development is auditing changes to stored entities. Which entities were added, modified, or deleted? Who made the change? Which properties were modified?

In this recipe, we'll use NHibernate Envers, which provides exactly that kind of auditing functionality.

Getting ready

Complete the Eg.Core model from *Chapter 2, Models and Mappings*.

How to do it...

1. Create a new project named Eg.Envers.
2. Copy the Eg.Core model and mappings from *Chapter 2, Models and Mappings* to this new project.
3. Change the namespace and assembly references in the mappings to Eg.Envers.
4. Install NHibernate Envers using NuGet Package Manager Console, by executing the following command:

   ```
   Install-Package NHibernate.Envers
   ```

5. On the Product class, add the following attributes:

   ```
   public class Product : Entity
   {
     public virtual string Name { get; set; }
     public virtual string Description { get; set; }

     [Audited]
     public virtual Decimal UnitPrice { get; set; }
   }
   ```

6. Create a new console application named `Eg.Envers.Runner`.

7. Install the NHibernate, NHibernate Envers, and log4net packages to the `Eg.Envers.Runner` project using NuGet Package Manager Console, by running the following commands:

```
Install-Package NHibernate
Install-Package NHibernate.Envers
Install-Package log4net
```

8. Set up an `App.config` with the standard `log4net` and `hibernate-configuration` sections, just as we did in the *Configuring NHibernate with App.config* and *Configuring NHibernate logging* recipes in *Chapter 1, The Configuration and Schema*.

9. In `Program.cs`, use the following code:

```
class Program
{
    static void Main()
    {
        XmlConfigurator.Configure();

        var cfg = new Configuration().Configure();

        cfg.IntegrateWithEnvers(
        new AttributeConfiguration());

        var sessionFactory = cfg.BuildSessionFactory();

        var schemaExport = new SchemaExport(cfg);
        schemaExport.Execute(true, true, false);

        using (var session = sessionFactory.OpenSession())
        using (var tx = session.BeginTransaction())
        {
            session.Delete("from Product");
            tx.Commit();
        }

        Guid productId;

        using (var session = sessionFactory.OpenSession())
        using (var tx = session.BeginTransaction())
        {
```

```
            productId = (Guid) session.Save(new Product
            {
                Name = "A product",
                Description = "Some product we sell",
                UnitPrice = 143.73M
            });
            tx.Commit();
        }

        using (var session = sessionFactory.OpenSession())
        using (var tx = session.BeginTransaction())
        {
            var product = session.Get<Product>(productId);
            product.UnitPrice = 900M;
            tx.Commit();
        }

        using (var session = sessionFactory.OpenSession())
        using (session.BeginTransaction())
        {
            var reader = AuditReaderFactory.Get(session);
            var oldProduct =
            reader.Find<Product>(productId, 1);
            Console.WriteLine(
            "Product price at revision 1 is " +
                oldProduct.UnitPrice);
        }
    }
}
```

10. Build and run your program.

11. You should see `Product price at revision 1 is 143,73000`.

How it works...

NHibernate Envers implements event listeners to intercept changes to entities. The changes are recorded in tables that Envers creates for each audited entity. These tables can be used to retrieve and query historical data without much effort.

Similar to source control systems, Envers has the concept of revision. One transaction is one revision (unless the transaction did not modify any audited entities). As revisions are global and have a revision number, you can query for various entities of that revision, retrieving a (partial) view of the database at that revision. You can find a revision number having a date, and the other way round, you can get the date at which a revision was committed.

In this recipe, we configured Envers using the attribute configuration. First, we mark the properties that we want to audit with the [Audit] attribute. Then we tell NHibernate that we want to integrate with Envers. If we want to audit all properties in an entity, you can mark the whole class with the [Audit] attribute, and if you need to exclude some properties from being audited you can exclude them by marking them with the [Exclude] attribute.

At the cfg.IntegrateWithEnvers(new AttributeConfiguration());line, Envers analyzes all mapped entities and creates additional metadata for auditing. It also registers the necessary event listeners.

We continue with saving an entity to the database. Later, we get this entity from a database and change the audited property UnitPrice.

At the end, we create an instance of IAuditReader. The IAuditReader interface provides an interface to query the audit data stored in a database. This interface is very rich, and you can perform complex queries in addition to just retrieving old entity states.

There's more...

NHibernate Envers also offers fluent configuration by code. To configure by code, just use the following code:

```
var enversConf = new FluentConfiguration();
enversConf.Audit<Product>()
  .Exclude(x => x.Name)
  .Exclude(x => x.Description);
cfg.IntegrateWithEnvers(enversConf);
```

As you can see, when using FluentConfiguration there is no ability to specify that we want to audit only one property in an Entity, so we need to exclude properties we do not want to audit.

More information about NHibernate Envers is available at https://envers.bitbucket.io.

See also

▶ *Creating an audit-event listener*

Using NHibernate Spatial

NHibernate Spatial brings the spatial capabilities of several relational databases to the NHibernate API. In this recipe, we'll show you how to use NHibernate Spatial with Microsoft SQL Server 2014 to query for a geographic region containing a point.

Getting ready

In SQL Server 2014 Express, create a new, blank database named Spatial.

Download State shapes from the US Census website by following these steps:

1. Inside the solution directory, create a directory named `SpatialData`.

2. Download the Shape file containing all 50 states, D.C., and Puerto Rico from the United States Census website at `https://www.census.gov/geo/maps-data/data/cbf/cbf_counties.html` or from the code download for this book. The file is named `st99_d00_shp.zip`.

3. Extract all three files to the `SpatialData` folder. The files are named `st99_d00.shp`, `st99_d00.dbf`, and `st99_d00.shx`.

Import the data from the Shapefile into the `Spatial` database using the following steps:

1. Inside the solution directory, create a directory named `SpatialTools`.

2. Download the SQL Spatial tools from the SharpGIS website at `http://www.sharpgis.net/page/SQL-Server-2008-Spatial-Tools.aspx`.

3. Extract the files to the `SpatialTools` folder.

4. Run `Shape2SQL.exe` from the `SpatialTools` folder.

5. When prompted, enter your database information as shown in the next screenshot, and click **OK**:

6. Click on the ellipses next to the **Shapefile** textbox to browse for the Shapefile. Select the co99_d00.shp Shapefile we downloaded and extracted in the SpatialData folder.

7. Check the **Set SRID** checkbox, and enter 4269 as the SRID.

8. Change the table name to `StatePart`, as shown in the next screenshot:

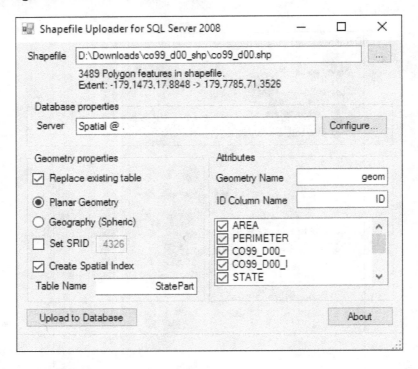

9. Click on **Upload to Database**.

10. When the upload process is complete, close the Shape2SQL tool.

Test your imported data using the following steps:

1. Open the `Spatial` database in Microsoft SQL Server Management Studio 2014.

2. Run the following query:

```
SELECT * FROM StatePart WHERE Name LIKE 'Texas'
```

3. The **Results** tab should contain two rows.

4. The **Spatialresults** tab should display the following image:

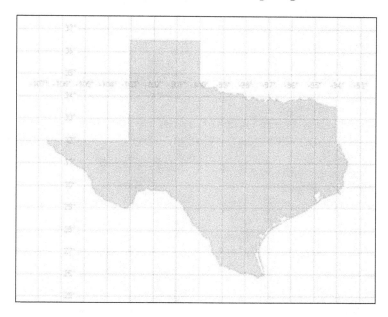

How to do it...

1. Create a new, empty class library project named Eg.Spatial.

2. Install the GeoAPI package using NuGet Package Manager Console by executing the following command:

    ```
    Install-Package GeoAPI
    ```

3. Create a class named StatePart with the following code:

    ```
    public class StatePart
    {

        public virtual int Id { get; protected set; }
        public virtual string Name { get; protected set; }
        public virtual float Area { get; protected set; }
        public virtual float Perimeter { get; protected set; }
        public virtual IGeometry Geometry { get; protected set; }

    }
    ```

4. Create an embedded resource mapping file for `StatePart` with the following XML:

```xml
<?xml version="1.0" encoding="utf-8" ?>
<hibernate-mapping xmlns="urn:nhibernate-mapping-2.2"
  assembly="Eg.Spatial"
  namespace="Eg.Spatial">
 <typedef name="Geometry"
   class="NHibernate.Spatial.Type.GeometryType,
   NHibernate.Spatial">
   <param name="srid">4269</param>
   <param name="subtype">GEOMETRY</param>
 </typedef>
 <class name="StatePart"
   table="StatePart"
   mutable="false"
   schema-action="none">
    <id name="Id" column="ID">
    <generator class="assigned" />
    </id>
   <property name="Name" column="NAME"/>
   <property name="Area" column="AREA"/>
   <property name="Perimeter" column="PERIMETER"/>
   <property name="Geometry" type="Geometry"
    column="geom" />
 </class>
</hibernate-mapping>
```

5. Create a new console project named `Eg.Spatial.Runner`.

6. Add references to the `Eg.Spatial` model.

7. Install the NHibernate, NHibernate Spatial Form Microsoft SQL Server, and log4net packages using NuGet Package Manager console by executing the following commands:

```
Install-Package NHibernate

Install-Package NHibernate.Spatial.MsSql

Install-Package log4net
```

8. Add an `App.config` file with standard `log4net` and `hibernate-configuration` sections as implemented in *Chapter 1, The Configuration and Schema*.

9. Change the connection string to point to the Spatial database, as shown in the following code:

```xml
<connectionStrings>
  <add name="db" connectionString="Server=.\SQLExpress;
  Database=Spatial; Trusted_Connection=SSPI"/>
</connectionStrings>
```

10. Change the NHibernate dialect property to the `MsSql2012GeometryDialect`:

```
<property name="dialect">
  NHibernate.Spatial.Dialect.MsSql2012GeometryDialect,
  NHibernate.Spatial.MsSql
</property>
```

11. Use the following code in the `Main` method of `Program.cs`:

```
static void Main()
{

    XmlConfigurator.Configure();
    var log = LogManager.GetLogger(typeof (Program));

    var cfg = new Configuration().Configure();

    cfg.AddAuxiliaryDatabaseObject(
        new SpatialAuxiliaryDatabaseObject(cfg));

    var sessionFactory = cfg.BuildSessionFactory();

    //Houston, TX
    var houstonTX = new Point(-95.383056, 29.762778);

    using (var session = sessionFactory.OpenSession())
    {
        using (var tx = session.BeginTransaction())
        {
            var query = session.QueryOver<StatePart>()
            .WhereSpatialRestrictionOn(x => x.Geometry)
            .Contains(houstonTX);
          var part = query.SingleOrDefault();
          if (part == null)
          {
            log.InfoFormat("Houston, we have a problem.");
          }
          else
          {
            log.InfoFormat("Houston is in {0}", part.Name);
          }
          tx.Commit();
        }
    }

}
```

12. Build and run the program.

13. Check the log output for the line `Houston is in Texas`.

How it works...

In this recipe, we have simply created a `Point` with the latitude and longitude of Houston, Texas. Then we created an NHibernate criterion query to find the geometries containing that point. The `geom` field in each row of our `StateParts` table has a single polygon representing some distinct landmass. For example, Texas has two rows. The first polygon defines the border of mainland Texas while the other represents Padre Island, the large barrier island that runs along the South Texas shore. When our query returns the `StatePart` entity that contains our point, we output the `Name` field.

To allow for the additional spatial-related SQL keywords and syntax, we use the `MsSql2012GeometryDialect`.

The `Geometry` property on our `StatePart` entity is an `IGeometry`. This is mapped using the user type `GeometryType`. We also provide the **Spatial Reference Identifier** (**SRID**), for our datum, and a subtype as parameters for this user type. Datums and SRIDs are explained later in this recipe.

There's more...

This recipe barely scratches the surface of what is possible with NHibernate Spatial. With just basic spatial data, it's possible to query for any number and combination of criteria, from the availability of valuable natural resources to the standard find the nearest retail location feature on a website.

Geography or geometry?

To rephrase this question differently, should you use a globe or map? Geography corresponds to the round-earth model, much like a globe. It works well for making measurements over great distances, accounting for the curvature of the earth.

Geometry, on the other hand, corresponds with the planar system or flat-earth model, like a map. As with a map, some distortion is tolerated, and this system is best-suited for smaller regions. However, standards for full-featured geometry data types are well established, while standards for geography data types are generally lacking. NHibernate Spatial has full support for geometry, as well as limited support for geography.

What's this SRID?

A datum is a model of the shape of the earth, combined with defined points on the surface used to measure accurate latitude and longitude. It's a sort of calibration where an exact location is defined in the datum as being at a precise latitude and longitude, and then everything else is measured from that point. For example, the North American Datum of 1927 (NAD 27) defines a marker on Meades Ranch in Kansas as 39° 13' 26.71218" N, 98° 32' 31.74604" W. Using NAD 27, every other point in North America was measured from this one point.

Each datum has a corresponding spatial reference identifier or SRID. The census Shapefile we used was built with the North American Datum of 1983, or NAD 83, an update to NAD 27. A query of SQL Server's `sys.spatial_reference_systems` table reveals that the corresponding SRID for NAD 83 is 4269.

Incidentally, most GPS devices use the World Geodetic System of 1984 (WGS 84), which corresponds with SQL Server's default SRID of 4326. NAD 83 and WGS 84 are essentially interchangeable for all but the most accurate applications. Given a set of coordinates, the location measured with NAD 83 will be at most, about one meter away from the location measured with WGS 84. That is, the two systems differ by about one meter at most.

Spatial data types

Spatial data can be broken down into three essential data types. First, a point consists of a simple X and Y coordinate. It has no length or area. A linestring is simply two or more points in sequence, and the shortest possible line from each point to the next, as shown in the following diagrams. It has length, but no area. There are two special cases. A simple linestring is one that doesn't cross itself. A ring is a linestring whose first point is the same as its last.

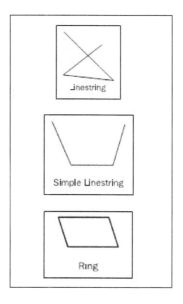

In its most basic form, a polygon is a simple ring. It has length (or rather perimeter), as well as area. As shown in the second diagram, the line string forming the perimeter of the polygon must be simple; it cannot cross over itself to form a bow tie. A polygon may have inner negative areas defined with inner rings. The linestrings forming these rings may touch, but they can never cross each other or the outside ring. This can best be explained with the following diagrams:

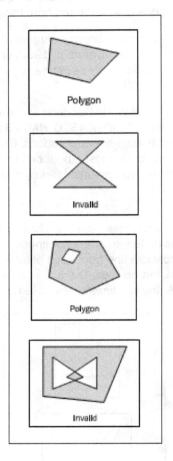

Index

Symbol

<subselect> mapping
using 119-122

A

aggregates
using 193-197
App.config
used, for configuring NHibernate 10, 11
appenders 17
application startup time
reducing 237-240
Aspect Oriented Programming (AOP) 316
ASP.NET
session action filter, creating 135-138
transaction action filter, creating 140-142
attributes
used, for property validation 393-399
audit-event listener
creating 363-367
automatic dirty checking 154

B

base entity class
setting up 63-65
batcher 7
bidirectional one-to-many class relationships
setting up 86-92
bulk data changes
bulk inserts 226
making, with Hibernate Query
Language (HQL) 223-225

C

calculated properties
using 107-110
child collections
criteria 258
eager loading 251-253
limiting functions, rendering 253-255
multiple collections eager loading,
avoiding 257
queried class' properties, eager loading 255
QueryOver 258
class
mapping, with XML 28-33
XML mappings 33
class components
creating 43-46
class hierarchy mappings
creating 36-40
table per class 40, 41
table per concrete class 42
collections
about 53
bags 53, 54
filtering 226-229
lists 54
map 55
sets 54, 55
collections of elements and components
mapping 59-62
common service locator
reference 320
concurrency
handling 66-69
handling, with session.Lock 155-158

none mode 158
read mode 158
upgrade mode 159
UpgradeNoWait mode 159
connection provider 7
context info, Microsoft SQL
setting 378-385
convention mapping, components
model inspector 79
model mapper 79
CriteriaQueries
used, for eager loading 211, 212
using 184-188
C# specification
reference 398
custom dialect functions
using 387, 388
custom functions
using, in LINQ 388-390

D

data
preloading, with SQLite 300-303
data access layer
ICriteria, using 328-331
LINQ specifications, using 336-338
named queries, using 320-327
paged queries, using 332-335
setting up, for transaction
    auto-wrapping 314-316
Data Access Objects (DAO) 313
database
entities, saving to 143-147
generating 19, 20
scripting 21, 22
sharding, for performance 275-281
updating 22, 23
dependency injection
hash value 362, 363
using, with entities 358-362
Detached Queries
reference 222
using 221, 222
dialect 7

dictionaries
using, as entities 160-163
driver 7
dynamic components
using 114-118
dynamic connection strings
using 385, 386

E

eager loading
Criteria, using 211, 212
Hibernate Query Language (HQL),
    using 214-216
LINQ, using 207-209
QueryOver, using 212-214
SQL, using 216-218
encrypted string type
creating 340-347
entities
dictionaries, using as 160-163
different flush modes, using 148
partially dynamic 164
persisting 148
SaveOrUpdate 148
saving, to database 143-47
updating 148
enumerations
mapping 92-94
unnecessary updates 94, 95
Envers
used, for auditing data 410-413
Equals
reference link 66
extra lazy collections
using 233-235
working 236

F

Fluent NHibernate
used, for configuring NHibernate 14, 15
Fluent NHibernate persistence testing
reference 305
using 304, 305

flush modes
always 149
auto 149
commit 148
never 149
using 148
full-text search
setting up 403-409
Futures
using 248-251

G

GetHashCode
reference link 66
Ghostbusters test
using 306-312
Glimpse
reference 291
used, for profiling NHibernate 290

H

hbm2ddl tool (hibernate mapping to data definition language) 20
hibernate.cfg.xml
used, for configuring NHibernate 4-6
Hibernate Query Language (HQL)
about 83
used, for eager loading 214-216
used, for making bulk data changes 223-225
using 197-204

I

ICriteria
using, in data access layer 328-331
ID generator
selecting 35
immutable entities
about 95
using 96
working 98
installation
NHibernate 2, 3
Intermediate Language (IL) 398

J

joins
mapping 104-106

L

lazy properties
using 102-104
LINQ
batching, used as alternative solution 210
custom functions, using 388-390
eager loading multiple collections, avoiding 210
result set, limiting 209
used, for eager loading 207-209
using, to NHibernate 177-183
LINQ provider
extending 390-392
LINQ specifications
composition 338
reference 338
using, in data access layer 336-338
LinqSpecs library
reference 336
log4net
reference 366
loggers 17
logging mechanism, NHibernate
configuring 15-18
logger, used for troubleshooting NHibernate 18
log providers, using 19

M

many-to-many relationship
mapping 56-59
mapping
by code 70-76
by convention 76-81
creating 82-85
Microsoft patterns
reference 359, 379
Model View Presenter (MVP)
about 127
reference 127

Model View View Model (MVVM)
about 127
reference 127
money type
creating 348-352
MultiCriteria
using 241-243
MultiQuery
using 244-247

N

named queries
named SQL queries 220, 221
using, in data access layer 320-327
using 218-220
Native SQL
using 204-207
natural key 34
NH4CookbookHelpers library 174
NHibernate
architecture 6, 7
configuring, with App.config 10-12
configuring, with code 12, 13
configuring, with Fluent NHibernate 14
configuring, with hibernate.cfg.xml 4-6
configuring, with Web.config 10-12
dialects 8
drivers 8
homepage link 2
installing 2, 3
LINQ, using 177-183
logging mechanism, configuring 15-18
profiling, with Glimpse 290, 291
properties 7
reference 229
releases, reference link 2
troubleshooting, with logger 18
using, with transaction scope 164-170
NHibernate AddIns project
reference 316, 359
NHibernate Contribution projects
reference 393
NHibernate Envers
reference 413

NHibernate.Logging
download link 19
NHibernate Profiler
common misuses 288-290
download link 283
using 283-290
NHibernate properties
adonet.batch_size 8
command_timeout 8
connection.connection_string 7
connection.connection_string_name 7
connection.driver_class 7
connection.isolation 7
connection.provider 7
current_session_context_class 8
Dialect 7
format_sql 8
generate_statistics 8
prepare_sql 8
query.substitutions 8
reference link 8
show_sql 7
sql_exception_converter 8
NHibernate repository
reference 319
setting up 316-320
NHibernate Schema Tool
download link 24
using 24-26
NHibernate source code
reference link 2
NHibernate Spatial
data types 421, 422
geography 420
geometry 420
SRID 421
using 414-420
nhusers Google group
reference link 2
NHV configuration, App.config
configuration settings 398
Ninject project
reference 359, 379
NMoneys
reference 353

non-primary keys
relations, mapping to 98-102
NST
command-line options 25
NUnit
download link 292

O

Object Relational Mapper (ORM) 91
one-to-many relationship
collections 53
lazy loading collections 50, 51
lazy loading proxies 52
mapping 46-50
Online Transaction Processing (OLTP) 403
optimistic concurrency 68

P

paged queries
using, in data access layer 332-335
pessimistic concurrency 69
POID generators
Counter 35
Foreign 36
guid 35
guid.comb 35
guid.native 35
hilo 35
Increment 35
Seqhilo 36
uuid.hex 35
uuid.string 35
property validation
attributes, using 393-399

Q

query entities, by ID
about 175, 176
session cache 177
Session.Get 176
Session.Load 176
QueryOver
used, for eager loading 212-214
using 189-192

QueryOver projections
using 193-196

R

read-only entities
query to load entities, setting
as read-only 264, 265
session, setting as read-only 264
specific entity, setting as read-only 265
using 262-264
**Relational Database Management System
(RDBMS) 5**
relations
mapping, to non-primary keys 98-102
result transformers
AliasToBean 232
AliasToBeanConstructor 232
AliasToEntityMap 231
creating 232
DistinctRootEntity 231
PassThrough 232
RootEntity 232
ToList 232
using 229, 231

S

second-level cache
configuring, with code 271-274
entity cache 269
query cache 270
timestamp cache, updating 270
using 265-269
using, rules 270
serializable values
using 110-114
session 6
session action filter
creating, for ASP.NET 135-138
view models, using 140
Web API 139
session.Lock
used, for handling concurrency 155-158
session.Merge
using 149-151

session-per-presenter
setting up 127-135
session-per-web request
companion library, using 124
manual setup 124-126
setting up 124
session.Refresh
using 152-154
soft-delete pattern
implementing 375-378
Spatial Reference Identifier (SRID) 420, 421
SQL
used, for eager loading 216, 217
SQLite
reference 292
used, for preloading data 300-303
SQLite in-memory database
used, for fast testing 292-299
SQL Spatial tools
download link 414
stamping entities
changing 367-372
creating 367-372
stateless sessions
using 259-262
surrogate key 34

T

transaction action filter
creating, for ASP.NET 140-142
transactional write-behind 6
transaction auto-wrapping
data access layer, setting up 314-316
trigger-based auditing
generating 372-374

U

United States Census
website link 414
Unit of Work pattern
reference link 6

V

validator classes
creating 399-403
versioning
handling 66-70

W

Web.config
used, for configuring NHibernate 10-12
well-known instance type
using 353-358

X

XML
used, for mapping class 28-33

www.ingramcontent.com/pod-product-compliance
Lightning Source LLC
Chambersburg PA
CBHW060921060326
40690CB00041B/2855